PRATAP

Praise for *Pratap*

'I remember the Urdu newspaper *Pratap* with great nostalgia. I was very young at the time; the elders would gather in Delhi's Roshanara Bagh every morning and discuss the headlines in great detail. *Pratap* was like a freedom flag in the battle for Independence. It was respected like the conscience of India.'

—**Gulzar**

PRATAP
A Defiant Newspaper

CHANDER MOHAN | JYOTSNA MOHAN

HarperCollins *Publishers* India

First published in India by HarperCollins *Publishers* 2025
4th Floor, Tower A, Building No. 10, DLF Cyber City,
DLF Phase II, Gurugram, Haryana – 122002
www.harpercollins.co.in

2 4 6 8 10 9 7 5 3 1

Copyright © Chander Mohan and Jyotsna Mohan 2025

P-ISBN: 978-93-6569-844-2
E-ISBN: 978-93-6569-699-8

The views and opinions expressed in this book are the authors' own and the facts are as reported by them, and the publishers are not in any way liable for the same.

Chander Mohan and Jyotsna Mohan assert the moral right to be identified as the author of this work.

All rights reserved. No part of this publication may be reproduced, stored in a retrieval system, or transmitted, in any form or by any means, electronic, mechanical, photocopying, recording or otherwise, without the prior permission of the publishers.

Typeset in 11.5/16.3 Minion Pro by
HarperCollins *Publishers* India

Printed and bound at
Thomson Press (India) Ltd

This book is produced from independently certified FSC® paper to ensure responsible forest management.

For

Virendra,
as unwavering in his beliefs as in his love for freedom.

And

Raj Lakshmi,
the quiet strength.

The detailed notes pertaining to this book are available on the HarperCollins *Publishers* India website. Scan this QR code to access the same.

Contents

Preface ix

PART 1

1. Terroristan: Then They Came for Us — 3
2. Scarface: The Betrayal of Silence — 25

PART 2

3. Circa 1919, Lahore: Tryst with Truth — 53
4. The Son Rises: Who Lives If India Dies? — 69
5. The Great Escape: *Khoon Ka Badla Khoon Se* — 81
6. Eye of the Tiger: Saunders and the First Imprisonment — 88
7. Romancing the Future: Making the Deaf Hear — 99
8. India Calling: Home, They Brought Her Warrior Dead — 113
9. The Bomb: Cult or Philosophy? — 124
10. Ground Zero: A House on Bahawalpur Road — 142

PART 3

11 *Sar Par Kafan Lapete:* Shooting the Governor — 159
12 Prison Raj: Where the Mind Is without Fear — 172
13 War and Peace: Graduation in Jail — 183
14 *Chaar Aana:* The Brave and the Cinema — 191
15 The Opposition Within: Mahatma and Revolutionaries — 204
16 A Day of Hangings: An Eyewitness Account — 226
17 Empires Crumble, Ideas Survive — 237
18 Remarriage Rumours: An Aeroplane for Mr Nehru — 247
19 Of 'a Clogged Brain' and 'Conceited Arrogance' — 258

PART 4

20 *Jinney Lahore Nai Vekhya: Azadi* — 279
21 From the Raj to Punjab: Jalandhar — 296

PART 5

22 Truth and Dare: The Midnight Knock — 307
23 Before the Ink Dries: Elegies and Sunsets — 326

Acknowledgements — 345
Notes — 347
Index — 349

Preface

Aisa lagta hai ki har imtihan ke liye zindagi ko hamara pata yaad aaya
(It seems that for every test life remembered our address)

It is not often that the protagonists of a story become the story themselves. This is what happened with Virendra and his family newspaper, *Pratap*. In colonial India and the succeeding years, *Pratap* and Vir Ji, as he is fondly remembered, were pushed and pulled between the two roles, living and sharing a slice of history that we were privileged to know firsthand. As we learnt, history is not only in the books.

Pratap was launched in Lahore just days before the Jallianwala Bagh massacre – the popularity and support it received instantly was unprecedented. It was a newspaper with a spine. Its editorials were hard-hitting and its tone intrepid and unapologetically

Preface

nationalist. Occasionally, old and frayed pages are required to be dusted to encapsulate a journey that ends in our present. In this book, we have attempted just that by revisiting editions of *Pratap* from yesteryears and through them sharing glimpses of significant proceedings, public debates and, at times, existential questions.

Pratap's ringside view of events leading to India's independence is only second to what Virendra witnessed. He followed the family profession of journalism. His journey though had a detour of nineteen years that he dedicated to India's freedom. During this time Virendra was jailed nine times by the British and was a hardened member of the revolutionary club led by Chandrashekhar Azad and Bhagat Singh. This passage of his life was a fascinating mix, one degree of separation from moments that created history, and a gap bridged now and then. Through this book, we hope he no longer remains an unsung hero of India's independence struggle.

What mettle were our freedom fighters made of? They unflinchingly stared at, or down at, death while burying all emotions to unshackle India from the Raj. It is in stark contrast to the faux nationalism and noise that pervades us today. Where have those men and women gone? In seventy-five years, how did the character of bravery change so drastically? Ironically, the term 'shaheed', martyr – a privilege used exclusively for names like Bhagat Singh – is thrown around loosely in present-day India. Will we no longer aspire for leaders of the stature of those who handheld India and its refugees as they together embraced the seminal folds of an unfamiliar destiny?

Virendra's life is not just an eye-witness account of a momentous past but also gives an insider peek into the lives – with their hits

Preface

and misses – and from time to time, the martyrdom, of the young revolutionaries as they inspired a nation. Former Prime Minister Inder Kumar Gujral wrote, 'Very few have recorded the events that they helped in shaping, or what they saw from close quarters. Virendra had one advantage; his association with a leading newspaper, *Pratap*, whose influential editorials couched in an intimate personalized style, were shaping the attitudes of an entire generation.'

Pratap's editors, before Virendra and since, remained equally resilient. The significant occurrences that the book traces touched them and the fearless newspaper they shaped through three generations.

The book also connects the unsaid – heroic acts with revolutionary defiance and, at times, plain impudence. There is a similarity between books and history – both don't age, although tinkering with them is not unusual. By wiping a past off its integral persona, communities and recollections of unimaginable valour or inconceivable loss are allowed to disappear. If not, they are sanitised to reflect collective behaviour and emotion.

This happened in Punjab in the '80s and early '90s when its people didn't know if they would return home for their next meal. Among them were Virendra and his family. A defining moment that the book touches on is the phase of terrorism in Punjab that brought a flourishing state to its knees and cleaved its people of a brotherhood that had together survived the horrors of Partition and much more.

During these decades *Pratap* and the family found themselves prominently targeted. There was disbelief. From Lahore to Jalandhar, the journey of 136 kilometres may have begun with a single step, but there were footsteps in independent India which still brought dread and terror. Perhaps, writing this finally allows for the closure of a period where freedom was won but peace was still being held hostage to senseless violence.

Over many lost years, our Hindi newspaper *Vir Pratap* – started after Partition – was a constant target of militants, and family members had more than a few providential escapes. In those circumstances, it would have been easier to leave. But what generations of family have learned over time and through journeys – individual and shared – is that to give in may be easier, but what doesn't kill you, makes you defiant. It may not necessarily make you profitable! So, something of the old fearless spirit – a legacy – has remained. Filling the footprints that are bequeathed is a timeless tale.

In free India, *Pratap*, through its editorials, and Virendra, through his pen, carried on without faltering, whether it was the hit list of terrorists or facing the Indira Gandhi–imposed Emergency, where his editorials were not submitted for censorship. Virendra was amongst a handful of journalists who rebelled; they did not compromise on their ideals or that of journalism. Similar to the brave men who fought against the colonialists, upright journalists are equally rare.

As a society in transition gathered steam, social and political mores began changing rapidly. Principles became conditional and the middle class correspondingly shallow. Where are those who took to the streets after Nirbhaya's rape? Why has their fire died down for similar atrocities in the present? With the spartan lifestyle of the earlier generations turning extravagant and showy, almost every aspect of life, including the privacy of faith, became public. The newspaper industry was not isolated from the churning. The rigid no-nonsense style of journalism practiced by *Pratap* and *Vir Pratap* had fewer and fewer takers; times changed but we didn't.

> *Kisi ko ghar se nikalte hi mil gaye manzil, koi humari tarah umar bhar safar mein rahe.*
> Some found their destination just as they left home, others like us were in transit all their lives.

And yet, although it had many more ups and downs, this 'safar' has not been without gratification.

The aim of this book is linear; there are stories within the story that we believe are worth sharing. Although as any writer will admit, we too are not without self-doubt. There is a choice of takeaways from this large canvas that we have tried to colour through words, images, and a glint of the mirror.

Pratap was retired, *Vir Pratap* ended its innings just short of a century.

> *Na Sar chipa kar jiye hum, na sar jhuka kar jiye*
> *Sitamgar ki nazaroan se nazare mila kar jiye*
> *Ab agar ek raat kum jiye, to kum he sahi,*
> *Yeh bahut he ki mashalein jala kar jiye*
> We did not live hiding our head, nor did we live bowing our head
> We lived by glaring back at the tyrant.
> Now, if we lived one night less, so be it.
> It is enough that we lived by lighting torches.

Chander Mohan
Jyotsna Mohan

PART 1

1
Terroristan:
Then They Came for Us

24 June 1983: It began as another ordinary day. Schools had closed for the summer and the family was visiting relatives in Delhi. There was a palpable buzz across the country – Kapil's Devils were looking to make history against the West Indies in the Cricket World Cup final the next day, in what had been an unbelievable journey by a band of accidental heroes.

At Pratap Bhavan on the dusty Nehru Garden Road in Jalandhar, it was an easy Friday. This was the hub of two daily publications – the Urdu newspaper *Pratap*, and its Hindi-language sister, *Vir Pratap*.

What happened next not only shattered the morning calm, it left a scar that has never healed.

At 11 a.m., the peon – as was the practice – brought dak from the post office which was a few hundred metres away. As per usual, it was kept on my desk. Among the letters and newspapers, there was a parcel wrapped in white cloth that was addressed to my father, Virendra, the chief editor of both papers. I picked it up and saw that it was sent from a post office in the Amritsar district, but I did not pay much attention to it. Packages like this were not unusual in our office. After going through the rest of the mail, I tried opening the parcel, but it had been hammered shut with so many nails that I gave up. Thinking that it must be the usual propaganda stuff that newspapers were being flooded with in those days, I called a peon to take the parcel and open it, and then bring it back. I then forgot about it. Ten minutes later, there was a loud explosion in the room next to mine. The package had exploded – three employees were grievously injured, two of whom died in the nearby Civil Hospital.[1]

It was the first time a parcel bomb had been used as a weapon in Punjab, as the country learned of a new terror modus operandi.

The powerful blast shook the double-storeyed building; windows were shattered as the explosive disintegrated into debris that went flying across rooms. The next morning's editorial by Virendra, *Pratap*'s owner, spoke of how it was an attack in waiting.

Antt wohi hua jiska khatra tha. Vigat dedh varsh se jo patra mujhe prapt hue hain unse spasth tha kee kuch na kuch toh hoga. Abhi teen din pehle hee mujhe ek patra prapt hua tha

Pratap

... Jin hone yeh kaam kiya hai veh bahut galat fehmi ka shikar ho rahe hain. Yadi veh samajte hain ki is tarah veh Pratap aur Vir Pratap kee zuban band kar denge, yeh gardan kat toh sakti hai jhuk nahi saktee.
What transpired in the end was what we had feared. From the letters I had received over the last year and half, I knew something would happen. Just three days ago I received another letter ... The perpetrators are under a grave misconception if they think that they can shut the voice of *Pratap* and *Vir Pratap* through this act. This neck can be cut, but it will never bend.

Through the haze of shock and panic, the three injured employees were rushed to the closest hospital – all three were below the age of thirty and had families to take care of. Krishan Alang died before they could reach the hospital, while Indresh Kumar was operated on for six hours, but did not survive either. Both victims left behind a young wife and a child.

I distinctly remember that one of the employees, Indresh Kumar, whose stomach had been ripped wide open by the explosion, spoke to me through his blinding pain as we rushed him down the twenty steps of the office saying, 'Sir, I have also made a sacrifice for the country.'

The rest of the day went by in a blur of hospitals, post-mortems, grieving widows and cremations. Meanwhile, a huge crowd gathered outside *Pratap*'s office where an acquaintance overheard a group of men murmur regretfully, 'Oh, taan bach gaye (the *Pratap* editors have escaped).' They were strangers, but this was Punjab in 1983 – on the razor's edge, only to succumb in the coming years as the 'they' and 'us' rhetoric tore the state apart.

A mention here of an old friend Harbrinderjeet Singh Dhillon, popularly known as Harji, who stayed with me throughout the day. We had great differences of opinion; I suspected him of having a sneaking admiration for Jarnail Singh Bhindranwale, an obscure Sikh preacher turned dreaded militant, who was instrumental in starting a process that destroyed peace in Punjab – the folly of appropriation that haunts India – and his extremist policies. Yet, throughout the traumatic day, he was next to me like a pillar. I even urged him to leave, fearing there may be a mob backlash, but he stood his ground. So, all was not lost.

Niraja Mohan, Chander Mohan's wife recounts:[2]

I was visiting my parents in Delhi with my children when a phone call came from Harji. As he was narrating the news of the bomb blast, the phone line went dead, as was often the case with STD calls in those days. I was barely able to hear that my husband was safe. The kids and I rushed back to Jalandhar, where the driver met me and said, 'Sahib bach gaye (Sir has survived).' There was relief, but there was also sorrow that two innocent employees had been killed. It was an incident that shook not just the family but also Punjab's dynamics.

In a vitiated atmosphere, Punjabi-language newspapers published from Jalandhar – a historical ancient city, where a majority of Urdu and Punjabi press settled post-Partition – did not condemn the incident. The owners of Jalandhar newspapers were a friendly bunch; yet not a single representative from a Punjabi daily called to condole the deaths at *Pratap*. Basic civility and the famed Punjabi brotherhood had become a casualty of the attack.

Who sent *Pratap* the parcel bomb? No answers have been forthcoming to date, nor was the family ever given any official response. The matter was closed after a shoddy investigation and all queries were stonewalled. It was concluded officially that the attack was the handiwork of extremists; however, without the clarity of a proper inquiry, it was based on presumption. Terrorism could not be ruled out either, but a lot more was floating around Punjab in those days. There was also an attempt to keep the communal pot boiling. Were we the victims of this conspiracy?

A foreign ambassador to India met the family and said, 'If I was in your place, I would have gone running till I reached a safe place.' And yet, despite two lives being sacrificed, thoughts of abandoning Punjab and the newspaper were furthest from the family's minds. Displaced from Pakistan, there was no question of relocating again within India.

Warnings from the police to shuffle daily travel commutes intensified. The distance between the residence and office was barely a three-minute car ride, and did not give much scope for improvisation. On a fateful evening not taking the police's advice nearly backfired as Virendra was involved in a high-speed chase by an unknown vehicle.

Situated on India's northwestern frontier, Punjab has faced innumerable challenges throughout its history. However, what the state faced in the 1980s was unprecedented – as was the internal challenge put forth before independent India from Punjab. Egged on by Pakistan, a section of the Sikhs turned to extremism to avenge what they alleged were slights to their 'quam' and the supposed neglect of Punjab. The failure to resolve the issue of Chandigarh, which Punjab shares with Haryana as a joint capital, and the river water–sharing complications came in handy. Those who opposed their thinking or believed in the Centre's point of view became the 'other' to be silenced – violently, if need be. One such victim was us.

Nearly a year after the *Pratap* explosion, Jalandhar witnessed another dark day. On 12 May 1984, the editor of *Punjab Kesari*, Ramesh Chander, was killed at a busy roundabout in the centre of town.

> A few minutes earlier, I had passed the roundabout and saw a car with its bonnet open and men dressed in kurta pajamas. Their heads were bent over the car. My gunman said, 'Theek nahin lugde', they don't seem right. Anyway, we passed them and reached home, which was barely a two-minute drive from the roundabout. As I got down at home, we heard the staccato fire of an AK-47.[3]

Instinctively, thoughts went to the suspicious car with its exposed bonnet – apprehensions that were not unfounded. Coming from the opposite side, Ramesh Chander was shot dead sitting upright in his car. He was driving the vehicle with a lone gunman seated alongside, his firearm carelessly discarded on the floor of the car. Rumours circulated that the assailants had two choices, *Pratap*'s editor or *Punjab Kesari*'s editor.

Virendra and family lived to fight another day.

Jalandhar was on fire, but its deputy commissioner had his plans; police in riot gear were ordered to collect outside his bungalow to safeguard the bureaucrat. It was only hours later that the police marched in front of the family's bungalow – metres away from the DC's residence – towards disturbed areas.

Ramesh Chander's murder raised several questions. Less than three years earlier, his father, veteran journalist and chief editor of *Hind Samachar*, Lala Jagat Narain had been assassinated on 9 September 1981, near Ludhiana.[4] His name, the family alleges, was drawn by Jarnail Singh Bhindranwale in a 'lottery'.[5] It was a killing that marked a turning point in the state. After Jagat Narain's murder, it was feared that Ramesh Chander was also a marked man. A month before his murder, he told Chander Mohan, '*Day to day jee rehe hein* (We are living from day to day).' *Punjab Kesari*'s editor feared the worst, yet his security remained lackadaisical – a lone gunman was accompanying Ramesh Chander when he was shot down. The ease with which the journalist was killed was a wake-up call, at long last, for officials were now out of excuses to undermine the severe threat to newspaper editors. And it had taken two assassinations and a bomb explosion for them to take cognisance.

There was more. Ramesh Chander was murdered at a bustling roundabout, Namdev Chowk. The district commissioner and the senior superintendent of police (SSP) both lived in the vicinity. It was an area lined with police checkpoints. How did the assassins flee? Vijay Chopra, the ninety-two-year-old brother of Ramesh Chander and editor-in-chief of the *Hind Samachar* group of newspapers, says, 'He had to go to a prayer meeting and, unknown to him, was being watched. On his way back from the prayer meeting, he reached the roundabout where they killed him and left. The police arrived at the spot later and the killers were arrested eventually. They had hidden in a petrol pump owned by an Akali leader.'⁶

Ramesh Chander's family cried foul but, once again, no heads rolled. In a repeat of the Pratap Bhavan explosion, those who orchestrated the killing stayed in the shadows. The known was intimidating and the unknown was no less daunting, wrapped as it was in a sense of foreboding.

A few days after the explosion in Pratap Bhavan, a man, a Hindu, came to meet me. He brusquely asked, 'Which office should we burn? The office on your left or the office on the right?' On one side was the newspaper *Akali Patrika* and on the other, the Punjabi newspaper *Ajit*. I had not met him before. I replied, 'Burn both. But remember, after that, *Vir Pratap* will also burn and so will *Punjab Kesari*.'

That man was never seen again. Who was he?⁷

In May 1984, a curfew was imposed in Amritsar and there were rumours of villagers marching to the Golden Temple in large numbers. By the beginning of June, Punjab was cut off from the rest of India. Helplessness was mixed with despondency, and there was a sense that the government had abdicated its responsibility. By then, there was nothing normal about the family's life and the threat of being targeted at any moment was stronger than ever.

Niraja recounts:

> I developed breathing problems and an excruciating pain in my jaw which made it difficult for me to even swallow. All my medical tests were clear, and the doctor said that the root cause was stress. We were living in terror; there was lawlessness and panic. One night, we were woken up by the sound of shots being fired; the next morning we were told it was near Lal Rattan, Jalandhar's most popular cinema. Another time, we heard firing from a nearby market where a judge had been shot dead. This was life in those days.

Outside the walls of her red-brick house, the disconnect between Hindus and Sikhs was reaching alarming proportions. The Sikh community, by and large, blamed the central government, but there was almost no criticism of Akali leadership and its surrender to extremists. Three prominent Sikhs, Chief Minister Darbara Singh, Home Minister Zail Singh and senior Congress leader Buta Singh were not only pulling in different directions, they were also creating difficulties for each other. With no resolution in sight, frightened citizens were forced to fend for themselves.

The family home was in a tranquil part of town – it overlooked official bungalows, and the road outside rarely had any traffic after dusk. In the last week of May, that serenity was broken by the movement of army trucks. Soon, instructions came to switch off all electricity points and there was a blackout in the area. Dinners were eaten on the porch in complete darkness, with the constant movement of trucks in the background. A few mornings later, the news broke. Jarnail Singh Bhindranwale – just the name was enough to cause visible panic – had been killed in an army operation at the Golden Temple.

Four months later, at the beginning of October, Virendra travelled to Delhi to meet Prime Minister Indira Gandhi. He was accompanied by his younger son, Chander, and daughter-in-law, Niraja. As they entered the office of India's Prime Minister, she stood up smiling from her chair. She was acquainted with Virendra but looked at the other two and asked warmly, '*Yeh kaun hain* (Who are they)?' Once introductions were over, the PM and Virendra got down to discussing Punjab, Operation Blue Star and its consequences. Indira Gandhi perused the documents shared by Virendra and kept them with her. He then warned her, '*Aap target hein* (You are a target).' She replied, '*Hoon nahin par banayi ja rahi hoon* (I am being made a target).'

Days later, Indira Gandhi was dead – assassinated by her own Sikh security guards whom she had refused to change saying, 'I cannot distrust any community.'[8] The PM was cognisant of the danger to her life after the army stormed the Golden Temple.

How the troubles in Punjab began is well documented. On Baisakhi, 13 April 1978, a clash between Sikhs and the Nirankari sect left at least sixteen people dead,[9] mostly Sikhs, in what was a watershed moment in Punjab's tilt towards extremism. When the state finally came up for air, a decade had passed and thousands had been killed, predominantly Sikhs.

The impact of those turbulent years cannot be measured only in statistics; a huge wall of mistrust between the two chief communities of Punjab – Sikhs and Hindus – took years to bridge. Operation Blue Star left a gaping wound in the Sikh psyche. Soon after her guards killed Prime Minister Indira Gandhi at home, anti-Sikh riots erupted in the country with thousands of Sikhs killed in Delhi alone.

The long, uneasy road back to peace was debilitating – no land deserves an encore of a period so dark. The all-subsuming nature of the communal genie is such that once out of the bottle, it flirts with danger till obsession takes over. A priest, Jarnail Singh Bhindranwale, was plucked out of obscurity by the Congress leadership to destabilize the moderate Akalis. As former Research and Analysis Wing (R&AW) officer G.B.S. Sandhu writes in his book, *The Khalistan Conspiracy*, he received information that 'as advised by Sanjay Gandhi, the Prime Minister had taken a decision to win the next general elections by using services of Bhindranwale to create a serious Hindu–Sikh divide and plant the fear of Khalistan in the minds of the majority community.'[10]

This brand of cynical and low politics was to cost the country dearly. Mark Tully and Satish Jacob also write in their book, *Amritsar: Mrs Gandhi's Last Battle*, 'By surrendering justice to petty political gains, the government itself created the ogre who was to dominate the last years of Mrs Gandhi and to shadow her until her death.'[11] The political conspiracy left a trail of blood, terror and death in its wake. Operation Blue Star became inevitable in the end as there were umpteen opportunities to put the genie back in the bottle, but they were missed – wilfully or otherwise.

Bhindranwale could have been neutralized much before he became a threat. Instead, he and his militia were given a free rein, and, when the government came to its senses, it needed an iron fist to dig itself out of the hole it found itself in. The repercussions echoed in the state for more than a decade. In September 1981, at the time of Jagat Narain's killing, the self-styled preacher was in Chando Kalan in Haryana's Hisar district. He was named in an FIR filed by the police after the murder, and yet was allowed to travel 300 kilometres to his headquarters in Chowk Mehta. Any checkpoint in Haryana or Punjab could have detained Bhindranwale, but there were instructions from Home Minister Zail Singh's office to allow him to pass through. Despite being a cabinet minister, Zail Singh had his score to settle with Chief Minister Darbara Singh – a side story that contributed to Punjab's mayhem.

It was an open secret in Punjab that the Akal Takht was being reinforced through the smuggling of arms in kar seva trucks, but the dangerous activity was allowed unhindered. A litany of complaints was sent to the government in Delhi, yet no action was taken; the central and state government both must share the blame for this criminal negligence – deliberate or otherwise.

The Akal Takht was so heavily fortified that an unprepared army faced fierce resistance when it stormed the premises. As is known, the consequences were disastrous. By then, was there an alternative to control the terror originating from the shrine's premises? 'Did they have to be taken out? There was no doubt. That they had to be taken out by force? There was no doubt there also,' says Ajai Sahni, executive director, Institute of Conflict Management, adding:[12]

Within Sikh traditions, there is no defence of Bhindranwale at the Golden Temple. In centuries of warfare, no one has ever taken refuge in the sacred place; it is against all tenets of the religion and its history. When the monopoly of a state is damaged by an armed group, a state is to respond. If you take over a holy place and weaponize it, then you are the desecrator – not the state. They turned it into a place where there was also torture and murder. Can you justify mass murder only because the Centre isn't listening? Strategically and tactically, as [Operation] Black Thunder showed, yes, there was an alternative, but not when it came to using the force.

Sarbdeep Singh Virk was deputy inspector general of police, Central Reserve Police Force (CRPF), and stationed at Amritsar when he was fired at in a gali behind the Golden Temple – events that eventually led to Operation Black Thunder. A bullet had pierced his face, and he gave orders from the hospital's emergency ward to keep the holy shrine intact but to bring down the morchas organized within its vicinity. This was not the first time Virk saw violence inside the premises of the Harminder Sahib.[13]

It was in 1985–86, during a rally of the All-India Sikh Students Federation, when swords came out and one person died within the Golden Temple. I went in giving strict orders to my men to remove their shoes, wash their hands and not to shoot. I brought out 300 people but only those involved in the killing were held back. The chief minister was unhappy, saying I had entered without his permission, and I told him that there had been a murder; how could I not go in? At any religious place, if a criminal activity is taking place, then law will take its course. Why adopt a policy not just by the Punjab government but also the Centre of declaring that the police will never enter the Golden Temple? Normally yes, they shouldn't, but if there is a crime there is no option but to enter and investigate.

Another aspect of this sordid saga is the Sikh leadership's silence over the securing of its holiest place and the attacks on Hindus. If they had prevented Bhindranwale from entering the shrine, Punjab's history may have been written differently. Sikhs – an overwhelming majority of them at the time – found villains elsewhere. The Hindu leadership was blamed for declaring Hindi as their mother tongue – perhaps the leadership did go overboard with this move, but did it justify a hate campaign against them, including murder threats?

Vijay Chopra says of his father's assassination:[14]

Three newspapers – *Pratap*, *Punjab Kesari* and *Milap* – all wrote blistering editorials against Bhindranwale and the terror he had unleashed. But because Lala Ji's daily programme was published in the newspaper, he became an easy target. There was also a blast at the *Pratap* office. All these newspapers wanted to retain a 'Maha Punjab' and were seen as interfering with the demand for a 'Punjabi Subha'. That is why terrorists went after *Pratap* and *Punjab Kesari*.

As Chopra mentioned earlier, there was an additional reason Hindus in Punjab resisted the state's division – a demand for a 'Punjabi Subha' – on the so-called language basis. They were afraid it would lead to a communal divide with ground ceded to radicals. Unfortunately, their fears played out. What earlier Prime Ministers, Jawaharlal Nehru and Lal Bahadur Shastri, refused to concede was agreed upon by Indira Gandhi in 1966, leaving the door ajar for extremism to nudge in. The demand, couched in linguistic terms, had, as its final goal, a Sikh-majority state. Indira Gandhi assumed splitting the region into Punjab, Haryana and Himachal Pradesh would bring stability to the western frontier. Subsequent events proved how wrong she was.

Some Punjabi newspapers too spearheaded a malicious campaign and Hindu leaders became pointed targets for terrorists who capitalized on the media's deep divide. 'Terrorists also used newspapers to eulogise their leaders. When a militant was killed, obituary advertisements with photographs of the "martyred" militants would be inserted in the media with an appeal to people to attend their bhog ceremonies,' writes Ramesh Inder Singh in his book, *Turmoil in Punjab*.[15]

Equally disturbing was the Sikh leadership's lack of response to the terrorizing of Punjabi Hindus. The reaction of intellectuals, journalists, writers, businessmen and other influential sections of society was no different. In Parkash Singh Badal's words, the relationship between Hindus and Sikhs in Punjab was one of 'skin and nail'.[16] Bhindranwale and his cohorts stomped on those words.

The owners of *Pratap* and *Punjab Kesari* were from two prominent Hindu families of Punjab, and, if both had thrown in the towel and quit, there was every possibility of a large-scale exodus of Hindus from the state. Equally defiant were communists like the *Naya Zamana* newspaper under Jagjit Singh Anand and Satyapal Dang, who stood their ground without surrendering to the carnage. Most others chose to remain quiet.

Surprisingly, there have been no questions raised about this conspiracy of silence. Akali leaders Sant Harchand Singh Longowal, Gurcharan Singh Tohra and Parkash Singh Badal were not supporters of Bhindranwale's cult of violence; yet, they did not dare speak up against him publicly. Taking their cue were some Sikhs, who started to believe that Khalistan was achievable and could indeed become a reality. 'There were forces which you did not see, wheels within wheels. The greater forces that remained behind the scenes played a big role,' says Virk. 'I came on the scene seven weeks after Operation Blue Star when I was deputed from Maharashtra. I soon realized that this was not the Punjab that I had left fifteen years earlier. It was not just the men who were spitting fire, it was when you observed the women, you realized there was a change.'[17]

Alienation, even at a personal level, was ideological, houses were 'numbered' and 'lots' were taken out on who would reside there once the resident families fled. 'The years after Operation Blue Star were not comfortable; Hindu houses were marked and people would openly say that this Hindu house will become mine and you can take the other one. In those days, our wives and daughters were not safe,' recounts Rajiv Talib, whose father was assassinated in Chandigarh.[18]

In Punjab, friends were deserting friends. Ramesh Chander's daughter-in-law, Kiran Chopra, says:[19]

> There was fear and pain because those who had lived like brothers all this while had also started becoming distant. Until then, many families in Punjab had both a Hindu and a Sikh member, but attitudes were changing. Now, once again, we are together. In those days, however, *bahut gadbad hui thi* (a lot went wrong).

Punjab was in free fall. In the 1980s, to spark communal strife, severed heads of cows were thrown in front of a temple for which the Dal Khalsa claimed responsibility.[20] There were other incidents of desecration of temples and gurudwaras, with random shootings in bazaars becoming routine. Despite staring into the barrel of a gun, shopkeepers lifted their shutters day after day. After all, they needed to put food on the table.

By then, Punjab had also become a pariah state – it was safer to watch terror from a distance. People only travelled within the state or out of it if they absolutely had to – the fortunate made it back home to their next meal. Passengers were segregated on communal lines, and when Hindus were taken out of buses and trains and shot, a question was forming: Is this another form of Partition? The year 1983, when the *Pratap* explosion occurred, ended with a particularly brutal wave that flowed into the following years with equal potency, if not more.

On 5 October 1983, a bus was hijacked and six men travelling from Dhilwan to Jalandhar were shot dead. On the same day, two men on a train were shot dead.[21]

On 18 November 1983, four Hindu passengers on a Punjab Roadways bus were ruthlessly killed when nine armed men turned on them.[22]

On 12 September 1984, eight passengers were killed in Batala.[23]

On 25 July 1986, fifteen Hindus were singled out inside a bus and killed, after all the Sikh passengers were asked to leave, by four men on a deserted road in Muktsar in the early hours of the morning.[24]

On 30 November 1986, in a bloody attack, four terrorists ordered all Hindu passengers to get off a bus in Hoshiarpur and then rained gunfire on them as they were disembarking. Officially, the death toll was twenty-four, including three women, but unofficially, reports claimed that fifty people were killed. Assassins escaped on scooters.[25]

On 6 July 1987, thirty-eight passengers were massacred in Patiala district after a gunman took control of the wheels of a Haryana Roadways bus and drove it for 8 kilometres before stopping at Lalru – just inside Punjab's border. Passengers were lined up outside in the darkness while four armed men fired at them from all sides; women and children were among those killed. The only Sikh on the bus was its driver, who was spared. A note left on the bus by the Khalistan Commando Force said a hundred Hindus would be killed for every Sikh. Twenty-four hours later, terrorists struck again.[26]

On 7 July 1987, thirty-two Hindus were killed after a jeep overtook and prevented a bus from moving near Fatehabad in Haryana. In a pattern witnessed a night earlier, five men then drove the bus for a few kilometres, robbing all valuables from the passengers before firing on them. An injured young man drove the bus filled with bodies to the police. The killers, while escaping, fired on another bus, killing four more people.[27]

Night buses in Punjab were suspended and schools became irregular – a generation was growing up in a curfew-induced normalcy. In the Doordarshan era, newspaper editors were the only ones with information. Their phones would ring early in the morning with questions on whether a curfew relaxation in the day was enough to send children to school.

A red-letter day was marked on 15 June 1991. Two trains near Ludhiana were stopped by terrorists, who first pulled the emergency handle, separated the Hindus from the Sikhs and then proceeded to open indiscriminate fire inside the trains. More than 100 people were killed that night – many of them women and children.[28]

Violence by now played on a loop. Not a word of condemnation came from the so-called Sikh leadership, who kept their political game in sight and flirted with extremists. The pusillanimity of the Akali triumvirate – Longowal, Tohra and Badal – contributed to Punjab's tragedy.

Teachers, lawyers, shopkeepers – ordinary and prominent citizens alike – were indiscriminately shot and killed. Nor were the victims only limited to dread-inducing interior areas like Tarn Taran. Professor V.N. Tewari, a Rajya Sabha MP, scholar and father of politician Manish Tewari, was assassinated in his own living room by three men, who entered saying they were his students. Like the *Pratap* explosion, there has been no closure in this killing either.[29]

Decades have passed, but for the families of victims, the loss lingers on just as sharply as the brutal actions that led to it.

In December 1990 and in the capital, Chandigarh, a family was in celebratory mode – the daughter of the house was to be married in four days. The bride's father, Rajendra Kumar Talib, was station director of All India Radio and was a well-known name in the city. He was popularly referred to as 'Talib Sahib'. His son, Rajiv, recounts:[30]

> It was 9.48 a.m., and my father had just come out from a bath and told his bodyguard, 'Let's go out and sit in the sun.' I had just sat down, when I saw two suited Sikhs – one of them was wearing a three-piece suit – come inside the gate. We were careful not to allow my father in front of any strangers as he was on the hit list, but it was as if he had sensed something, and he asked me to get chairs for the men. Just as I reached the door, I heard gunshots. They fired thrice, one straight to his head which took him away. The bodyguard, who was a Sikh, was without his revolver that day and he lay on the ground to save his own life. But I remember him shouting that if he had his revolver, he would have taken them on. They had a plan to kill only my father and fired three shots and escaped on a two-wheeler.

The next day, Babbar Khalsa took responsibility for the shooting, saying Talib had paid the price for not following the 'code of conduct'.

A week earlier, terrorists had released an edict. They were to be referred to as militants or khadkoos (fighters), especially by the media. Terms like 'terrorists' or 'extremists' were forbidden, and, as director of the Chandigarh radio station, Talib was gunned down for not obeying this directive.[31] *India Today* reported at the time:[32]

> Most papers in the region quickly fell in line. So did the radio and television stations in Jalandhar and Amritsar. But the Chandigarh station continued to use 'terrorist' for which it paid the price. Now, even the Centre has permitted the radio and television stations in the region to use 'militant' in English and khadkoo in Hindi and Punjabi.

There were other instances of the government's surrender. Among the list of decrees announced by the terrorists was a ban on the Hindi language and the use of only Punjabi in the state. 'The government too buckled under the threats,' writes bureaucrat Ramesh Inder Singh.[33] The worst instance, he says, was of Governor Virendra Verma, who made the unilateral decision of temporarily discontinuing not just government press releases in Hindi but also suspended advertisements in Hindi newspapers. Eventually, a new policy was adopted, says Singh, in which '50 percent advertisements were to be given to the Punjabi papers, 26 percent to the English papers, and 14 percent and 10 percent respectively to Hindi and Urdu papers'.[34]

The motive was blatant – to intimidate the minority community into leaving Punjab. Families were defeated, and yet they held on, braving the gun and the uncertainty of where the next bullet would be fired from. Boys were dressed up as girls in skirts by family elders; the only code of conduct for survival was instinct. 'Those days, when we travelled from Jalandhar to Delhi, I would make my son wear a frock so that he looked like a girl.

My husband, Ashwini, would wear a turban, and one minister even told us to get plastic surgery and change our faces. Things were that serious,' Kiran Chopra remembers.[35]

Jagat Narain's driver, Somnath, who survived the editor's assassination, drove his body to the steps of a hospital before vanishing. He lived his last years in fear, dressed as a Sikh with a turban and a beard. This coping mechanism was not unusual. Julio Ribeiro, who preceded K.P.S. Gill as director general of police (DGP), Punjab, in 1986, says he had ten guards at any given time – while nine were Jats, the tenth was a Hindu dressed as a Sikh.[36]

The Punjabi Hindu community has often struggled to emerge from the shadow of a robust Sikh society that outsiders mistakenly consider as the only 'Punjabis'. From freedom fighters to the first chief justice of India, Mehr Chand Mahajan, to Prime Minister Inder Kumar Gujral to senior army officers, journalists, industrialists, athletes and diplomats to Bollywood, the roll call of Hindu Punjabis is long. DAV institutions and Kanya Maha Vidyalaya – the latter a Heritage Autonomous Institution where Bhagat Singh took shelter – have also written Punjab's past with indelible ink.

These accomplishments, however, pale in comparison when one considers how the community chose not to abandon its homeland in the darkest days of militancy and stayed back in Punjab, despite provocations, threats and the abject fear of being singled out and their houses marked.

2
Scarface: The Betrayal of Silence

Looking back at Punjab's dark period, a sense of wonder can be felt. How did those of us who lived in the state, and were targeted for our religion and work, survive? Was it sheer luck, providence, government security or the feeling that perhaps some of us were not important enough to be eliminated? Was it bravery or were we simply being foolhardy? It must have been the latter, considering we were targets of a parcel bomb blast, repeated assassination attempts and blunt police warnings that began with the words, 'As you are aware, your name figures in the hit list of extremists...' The SSP of Jalandhar's advice to us was that 'no one should know your programme in advance' and to keep him informed about our 'contemplated journeys and jaunts'. Going on a jaunt was the last thing on the family's mind in those days!

A chilling warning came on 15 May 1985. 'You should avoid going out, especially during the next two weeks,' the police instructions read. That there was a specific time limit was disconcerting, as was the fifteen-page 'Personal Security Guidelines' handed over, with a detailed list of dos and don'ts.

This phase in our lives was bleak and it was not unusual for the family members to feel like they were being shadowed. It was not merely overactive imagination or a vague sense of foreboding – more so when it came to the editor-in-chief Virendra's life. An intruder tried to scale the house's back wall once and was promptly challenged by a sentry posted on the terrace who minced no words in warning him that he would be shot. On another afternoon, Virendra's car was involved in a long and high-speed chase before he managed to safely enter the gates of the house. One night, after dinner, a man attempted to break in through a window in the children's room. He had managed to squeeze half of his body in before he realized he was cornered.

It was not just the men; women and children too needed to watch their steps as all vehicles registered in the family's name were on the terrorists' radar. Police alerts on shuffling daily schedules were as routine as eating breakfast – everyone was only ticking things off their checklist. Then, a threat came that made time stand still; it was about the children's safety.

All three of us were immediately withdrawn from school and strictly instructed to not go beyond the driveway – our every step monitored closely both by family and security men. I managed to sneak my bicycle out of the gate and had barely sat on its seat when a panicking CRPF personnel came running, roaring at me to get inside at once![37]

For several weeks, the three of us stayed home. It was, however, not a permanent solution. We were sent back to school and chaperoned by a police escort, even though campus was just down the road. It was decided that when the time was right, we would be sent out of Punjab.

By then, the family had twenty-four-hour security. The Centre, and later the Punjab government, took care of it. After losing Jagat Narain and Ramesh Chander, the authorities had decided that they couldn't risk the lives of any other newspaper owner or their family members. During terrorism's most challenging years, residential protection was divided between the CRPF, Border Security Force (BSF) and Indo-Tibetan Border Police (ITBP), along with the Gujarat State Reserve Police.

Niraja remembers those days fraught with worry:

> The situation was so tense that my health continued to be impacted. We could not step out; the children also had security cover and curfew was so frequent that we stopped thinking about how unusual it was. The threat to life was at its peak, and that period was one of terror and tension. There was no sense of security, despite guards surrounding us.'

Like chronicles of Partition, where personal suffering and loss of community did not find a prominent mention – at least in the initial years – news on terrorism in Punjab too centred on politics. Families and their stories remained out of the spotlight. This stream of commentary from conflict zones is overlooked; yet, individual narratives could not be more powerful.

In December 1988, a letter from the SSP of Jalandhar notified the family that para-military forces were being withdrawn and sent out of the state, and 'in their place Armed Home Guard personnel are being deployed at your residence'. In his conclusion, the SSP wrote, 'Had I been left with any other option, I would not have deployed Home Guards for your protection.' Understandably, the letter's contents were not encouraging.[38]

A battery of personal gunmen and escort vehicles – including one with a Light Machine Gun (LMG) stationed on it – were part of Prataps' security detail. The gunmen belonged to Punjab Police and were all extremely dedicated – down to the last constable. They were cognisant that if any family member was targeted, there was a probability of a bullet hitting them as well. Vinod, a gunman, acknowledged this fact: 'If there is a bomb, my gun will not be able to do anything.' They were remarkable men; despite the ever-present danger, not one refused to do his duty.

By now, threats were a daily occurrence, and yet, a bodyguard confided to the family that protecting them 'saves us from doing dirty things in the thana'. Men in uniform also found the time for some macabre humour among themselves – 'Have you told sahib which sewing machine is to be given?' They were referring to a government scheme for the rehabilitation of widows of slain police personnel!

On a difficult day, their loyalty to us was unquestionable and the Punjab Police stood by the family like a bulwark. The only refusal to protect us came from a Sikh constable who did not move from his chair, saying he was not prepared to do a Lala's duty. He was an exception; there was no religious slant from the others who protected the family day and night. One afternoon, a Nihang Sikh suddenly came up Pratap Bhavan's steps while Chander Mohan was in his office. With quick reflexes, a gunman immediately came in between the two. The Nihang had come to share some news, but the security staff were not taking any chances.

The escort Gypsy and its AK-47–toting men, who would not allow the family to take any step at all without immediately surrounding them with men, over time, became a sore spot. Ironically, anonymity, which was crucial to staying under the radar, disappeared. It was embarrassing to walk down Shimla's Mall Road – a city that became the family's refuge – followed by men with rifles. As terrorism deepened its roots in Punjab, the quality of escort vehicles correspondingly deteriorated and the Maruti Gypsy often broke down. The replacements sent were worse, despite the SSP's warnings, 'Punjab is passing through very difficult circumstances … You should be careful about your security.'

Complaints were made but were stonewalled by red tape. A letter from the SSP Jalandhar to the deputy inspector general of police (DIG), security, Chandigarh read, 'Chander Mohan is a threatened person, hence a suitable replacement for the escort may be found.'[39] No suitable substitute came. It was hugely disconcerting to sit in a car, while men tasked with protection were busy pushing their jeep. In frustration, a letter was dispatched by the family to the local SSP requesting the vehicle's withdrawal.

For weeks, there was silence, and when a response did come, it was filled with bureaucratic legalese. 'I cannot withdraw because I did not give it to you. It was given by Chandigarh. Only Chandigarh can withdraw it.' He was worried about the consequences of something untoward happening once security was pulled back. After an exhausting battle, the broken-down escort vehicle was finally pulled back.

'When the time came to reap the whirlwind, the leaders of the faith simply abdicated responsibility and handed over the holiest of Sikh shrines to murderers and rapists.' With these piercing words, former DGP of Punjab K.P.S. Gill defines the Sikh leadership's role during the turbulent terrorism-filled years in Punjab. Gill, in his book *Punjab: The Knights of Falsehood*, goes on to say that 'their silence alone, in the face of this onslaught [of Bhindranwale], would be sufficient to condemn them. Their complicity is unforgivable.'[40] 'Complicity' is a tricky word – perhaps, it is too strong to express the part the Sikh leadership, especially the Akalis, played when terror reigned. It must be conceded, though, that Gill had access to internal information, which could have helped him glean insights.

The Akali leadership was taken aback by Bhindranwale's sudden rise after the 1978 attack on Nirankaris that left thirteen Sikhs and three Nirankaris dead.[41] His surging fame among a section of the Sikh population, especially its youth, was equally concerning for them. Terrified and concerned about their safety and their families, veterans of Sikh politics capitulated – showing no spine to oppose Bhindranwale – and disassociated themselves from his violence. Parkash Singh Badal and Gurcharan Singh Tohra were forced to go with the extremist narratives and urged Sikh youth to become marjeevedas (warriors willing to die). At the same time, Badal sent his son, Sukhbir, and nephew, Manpreet, abroad to study.[42]

'Many Sikhs, particularly the unemployed university graduates, and the farmers, did feel that they had genuine economic grievances against the rest of India. The Akali Dal mixed those economic grievances with religious ones and so created a dangerous brand of fundamentalism that the party's leaders eventually could not control … Bhindranwale fanned the flames of the uprising in Punjab with that foreboding, but it was the Akali Dal which started the fire.'[43]

It is impossible to pinpoint a single family member of a Sikh leader who participated in Bhindranwale's movement; yet, none openly condemned him. As bloodshed by the self-styled preacher's murderous gangs exploded in Punjab, Sant Longowal – whom Virendra once met at the Golden Temple – addressed a diwan within Manji Sahib's holy premises where he announced, 'The entire Sikh community supports Bhindranwale.' Longowal was in disreputable company – along with Bhindranwale, he was designated the morchas' 'dictator'. This gave him immunity from courting arrest and, emboldened, Longowal declared that Bhindranwale 'was their stick to beat the government.'[44]

This would support Gill's thesis of complicity – although some benefit of doubt can be given to the Akali leaders. They were helpless, outplayed in a game of chess rolled out by Home Minister Zail Singh, who was unyielding in his vice-like grip on

Punjab's politics. Faced with an existential crisis, along with fears for their safety, the trinity of Badal, Longowal and Tohra threw the dice and their lot with Bhindranwale. In private, Longowal was less circumspect – he called Bhindranwale and his armed followers 'Chambal ki Ghatti'[45] publicly; however, not a word was said. Ironically, Longowal was killed less than a month after signing the Rajiv–Longowal Punjab Accord by an assassin's bullet in August 1985.

The legacy of the three 'wise' men remains the fostering of a belief of victimhood in their community which has led to tragic repercussions. They played on the complexities of belonging and nurtured the post-Partition narrative of 'Hindus got Hindustan, Muslims have Pakistan; where is the land for the Sikhs?' This was supplemented by the periodic flogging of the '*Panth khatre mein hai* (The Panth is in danger)' refrain – an exhortation that is still ignited in diverse forms today. Nothing was further from the truth. The Sikh chiefs were cognisant of this fact, but in politics, even ideology bows before relevance. In order to control their community, their public persona insisted that 'Panth khatre mein hai' whenever there was a willing audience.

The struggle to keep the youth rooted in tradition can be seen even today in the deras that have mushroomed across Punjab – some considered as old as the Sikh religion itself. A 2006–07 study estimated the number to be at a whopping 9,000,[46] a reflection of their reach and influence. While six prominent ones – like Sacha Sauda run by the controversial Gurmeet Singh or the Radha Soami sect – may have larger followings, some of the smaller, nondescript deras also pose a huge challenge. With a discredited Akali leadership currently out of favour with the masses – over corruption allegations and the inability to stamp down on drugs – these deras offer spiritual solace to misguided, jobless youth. The cry of the Panth once resonated in the countryside, and at least for now, through its use and misuse, the Panth itself has forsaken the Akalis. For the first time in twenty years, late Akali patriarch, Parkash Singh Badal, could not save his traditional seat before he passed. The five-time chief minister lost from Lambi in the 2022 elections.[47]

Necessity is also the mother of expediency and, when the time was right, the narratives smoothly shifted to New Delhi doing injustice to Sikhs and neglecting Punjab. Grievances were manufactured, and one of India's most prosperous and vibrant communities was misled by their leaders into believing they were being discriminated against. It was a feeling Bhindranwale exploited with bloody consequences.

His transgression into the Golden Temple and clashes around the premises of the holy shrine, including the killings that took place before Operation Blue Star, were all forgiven – for he was fighting 'on behalf of his people'. Mark Tully and Satish Jacob concurred with this view: 'Everyone knew that Bhindranwale and his followers had been smuggling arms into the complex for many months. Two years earlier, Darbara Singh, the Chief Minister of Punjab, had said in public that he knew arms were also being manufactured in the Golden Temple.'[48]

What turned a significant section of Sikhs into supporters of Bhindranwale's cult? As violence singed the homes of their Punjabi brethren, they looked the other way. Families of victims wondered whether the interpretation of the basic tenet of 'sarbat da bhala' – welfare of all – was flexible. A rare Sikh voice was Congress

Member of Parliament Amarjit Kaur, who publicly acknowledged the community's error in overlooking Bhindranwale's atrocities – not least from within the premises of the Golden Temple. Who invited Bhindranwale into the Golden Temple, she questions, in an excerpt from *Akali Dal: The Enemy Within*.[49]

> When Bhindranwale shifted into the Akal Takht, Sikhs should have openly criticized his move. Sikhs should have also told the SGPC president and the other Akali leaders who had encouraged all this to bring Bhindranwale out of the Akal Takht. They should have strongly objected to the role of the Akalis.

Kaur also questioned the overwhelming silence of the community when Hindus were pulled out from buses and 'shot like dogs on the street', adding:[50]

> Actually the blow to the Sikh community has been quite profound. We are a very proud community. We thought we were the cat's whiskers, the saviour of all. But now it was seen that we did not have the guts to face the situation. We, the Sikhs, should have been the ones to throw Bhindranwale out of the premises of the Golden Temple. We are now finding it difficult to admit our failure. Our so-called dynamism and bravery have disappeared.

Anyone who lived through this period in Punjab knows that the support for Bhindranwale was pervasive. Some thought Khalistan was around the corner, little realizing that terrorists have no loyalty to anyone. A Sikh acquaintance who argued in defence of Khalistan at a dinner one night was shot the next day.

What was it about Punjab that made it cave? Why didn't terrorism raise its bloody head in, say, Bihar or Odisha? Punjab may be a border state, but is that reason alone enough for the thousands of deaths? The answer could again be in the words of K.P.S. Gill, 'The heart of darkness is located in the long and continuous manipulation of the Sikh psyche through the institutions and symbols of religion.'[51]

The groundwork laid out to destabilize and divide Punjab was not in the immediate past – it was prepared by the Akali leadership in the preceding four decades. Blame is not theirs alone; this narrative also suited Sikh leaders of the Congress. Since 1966, no Hindu was made Punjab's chief minister, and the situation today is no different. Political parties of heft in the state would rather not be on the community's wrong side.

If Punjab's plunge into darkness saw its villains emerge, it also gave rise to state actors who played admirable roles in dousing the flames. Some courageous acts, regrettably, remain anonymous and unrecognized. Of those who risked their lives, two individuals stand out. Beant Singh and K.P.S. Gill made an unusual pair, but, together, they brought Punjab back from the edge, allowing the state to begin breathing again. Beant Singh's term as chief minister and K.P.S. Gill's second term as DGP, Punjab, began almost simultaneously, and when they bowed out, terrorism had been contained.

The two men had contrasting personalities – one was an earthy politician who had risen up the political ranks, while the other was an imposing police officer whose confidence at times crossed the proverbial Lakshman Rekha. When Beant Singh took over as chief minister in February 1992, he knew it was, to put it mildly, a crown of thorns. The sentiment of separatism, like the state's famed mustard fields, covered every inch of Punjab's villages, and killings in cities were targeted and precise. Singh's only option was to go to the public to restore its battered and badly shaken confidence. It was a precarious move that would leave him exposed. He chose it. Beant Singh was fearless; some would even say reckless. At his daughter's house in Jalandhar Cantonment, he had a detailed conversation with Chander Mohan on the risks involved – but he was clear about where his duty lay.

The contrast between Singh and Akali leaders was striking. Hidden behind guarded walls, the latter raised demands, knowing the Centre would not concede. Beant Singh, though a politician, was different – a humble man, who sacrificed his life to stem the tide of bloodshed. When *Pratap*'s editor, Virendra, passed away on the last day of 1993, Singh first came to pay his condolences at home. He then followed the family to the cremation ground, where he sat on a wooden bench in full view. He refused all entreaties to take cover; it was simply not in his nature.

In August 1995, the chief minister was assassinated in a bomb blast at the entrance of Chandigarh's Civil Secretariat. Seventeen others died in that attack. Journalist Naveen S. Garewal, *Tribune*'s reporter at the time, was at the assassination site and recalls finding something sticky under the sole of his shoes as he was running to file a report. Decades later, he still has not been able to shrug away the memory of a victim's finger stuck to his shoes. The Secretariat had turned into a straggling body bag that day.

Beant Singh was a shaheed, a martyr – a term used loosely today. It is, however, not his portrait but that of his suicide bomber, Dilawar Singh – a Babbar Khalsa terrorist – which was installed at the Golden Temple's Central Sikh Museum in a ceremony organized by the Shiromani Gurdwara Parbandhak Committee (SGPC), the apex body of the Sikhs.⁵²

With his tall height, impressive moustache, piercing eyes and booming voice, Kanwar Pal Singh Gill was an imposing personality. He was also an unusual police officer – Gill was an intellectual, partial to Urdu poetry. Julio Ribeiro was his boss before Gill stepped into his shoes in 1988 and he remembers the police officer as 'the best I have ever worked with for operations'.⁵³ In his column in *Tribune*, Ribeiro has nevertheless given more than a hint of the dissimilar working styles of the two officers, 'KPS would not have liked being described in the same breath as me. He felt that I was not meant to be a cop, and definitely not in Punjab.'⁵⁴

In state records, they are both pillars who took charge when Punjab had hit rock bottom. Gill galvanized a dejected Punjab Police, transforming it into a force that could take credit for being one that fought and defeated terrorism – although it took a massive toll on the force itself.

By targeting them and their families, Bhindranwale had been able to demoralize Punjab Police to such an extent that a turnaround was nothing short of miraculous. The force's low morale was for all to see when, in 1981, at Daheru, all police officers engaged in an encounter fled, abandoning their weapons.

An incident that sent distress signals beyond the state was the killing of Punjab's third highest-ranking police officer, DIG A.S. Atwal, on 23 April 1983. He was shot in broad daylight on the steps of Golden Temple's main entrance as he came out after offering prayers. Atwal's body lay there for hours as no one dared to come near it. While the lone gunman went back inside the Golden Temple, Atwal's driver and security guards sped away in his official car, even as celebratory shots rang out from within the temple. Was any further evidence needed that the sacred place was fortified and desecrated?

Operation Blue Star did not bring Punjab under control – conversely, the state was pushed further down the abyss. The army action was a huge blow to the Sikh psyche. And there was no let-up in the attacks on forces that had surrendered in all but name. As dusk fell, the police barricaded itself, refusing all calls to move out. Helpless villagers were left to their fate.

Remembers Julio Ribeiro of Punjab in 1986:[55]

The very first night that I came to Punjab, I was told there had been a strike. I said let's go, but I was told by the staff that no one goes out at night. I told them this must change; the police were surprised to see their DGP out at night. Within hours, there was an attack on a jagran. So, in a way, it was a baptism by fire. We caught the terrorists because they didn't expect us to be there and that was our first success. Even the police stations would close at night.

> When I went there, I said this can't be done. Open them up and they must remain open.

Ribeiro himself faced an assassination attempt at the Jalandhar Officers Mess, when two men drove up in an official-looking jeep with 'police' scribbled across it in Gurmukhi. They calmly walked into the compound, dressed as a police officer and an inspector.

> I suddenly heard what sounded like crackers and I knew ... I thought to myself that goodness, they have come for us. I fell to the ground, my reflexes were good, and I took shelter, but my wife got a bullet wound through her leg. Luckily, it was a clean wound. The terrorists thought they had killed me and ran away.[56]

Out of the four men guarding the compound wall, three were shot dead.

As bullets rained across towns, small and sprawling, K.P.S. Gill stepped in. It was May 1988 and, by the time summer transitioned to the harsh winter, a disheartened and lifeless force had been transformed, with a thirst for revenge against those who had targeted their own. How did one man succeed where others had failed? Gill led from the front, but rarely are the nuances of a picture captured by the lens of hindsight. As DGP of Punjab, his dynamic leadership began reflecting in the working of the force and he inspired a batch of young officers who would swear by him – some of whom went on to lead the force.

To put it mildly, some of his methods were non-conformist. There were complaints of fake encounters and human rights violations – the allegations were a mixed bag, both exaggerated and genuine. Ajai Sahni points out:[57]

> The record of human rights excesses is far more than anything that happened. KPS as the DGP had himself created a department for litigation, but the very people who had been protected by the forces changed along with the 'defeated rump', as KPS called them. Numbers were being invented depending on who was being spoken to, but it was done effectively. In terms of counterterrorism and for its future, this needs a serious look because even today, the same tactics are being used successfully and without challenge.

Along with Gill, other police officers paid the price for their 'unconventional' methods – at least a handful of whom continue to be pursued in present-day Punjab. Was it possible to bring the state back from the brink through 'conventional' means? Do the rules of a democratic system apply to terrorists who mock the laws of the land daily? Gill and his force believed in an eye for an eye – a questionable approach in a democracy; yet, on the ground, all alternatives, except an equally ruthless response, had run out. Intimidated, the judiciary found terrorism to be the great leveller. Judges, including those who lived across the road from the family bungalow, recused themselves from hearing cases involving extremists. Some judges skipped going to court altogether, while others paid with their lives.

Ribeiro's neighbours were high court judges, who he says validated the approach of the police force.[58]

When you deal with the underworld in Mumbai, they bribe everybody – from the politician to the policeman. Terrorists do not bribe; they just put a bullet through you. In the first month of my being in Punjab, I was told that all the rules I want put in place ... they will not work. It is our lives versus theirs.

Ribeiro's police team was not easy to convince.[59]

You say we should go out at night, but they know who we are and we don't know who they are. They will put a bullet through us. Allow us to go in plain clothes. I saw merit [in that argument], so we had to change our stand. We cannot use this [tactic] in normal times.

Ribeiro asks the one question that has been missing in most accounts on Punjab terrorism:[60]

What about the human rights of the poor people who had nothing to do with anything? Those who were travelling by bus and were just pulled out and killed, or those who are shot while listening to a jagran? Killing is not legal, but what about the moral part of it? Don't you have to reply to innocent people being killed for terror? Otherwise, what protection do they have?

On his part, Gill was clear about what had gone wrong in the state. It helped. On a visit home – an official affair to assess security every few nights after his daily rounds were completed – he put it succinctly: 'I am a Jat and I know how to deal with Jats.' The rest is unprintable! Excesses by separatists in Punjab's hinterland were gradually changing the peasantry's mindset and the police officer had one mantra. For a turnaround, his focus was on the optics. He had to show that his side was winning. He stuck to this strategy and in the see-saw with extremists, Gill soon got the upper hand.[61, 62]

There was another motivation for Gill. As a devout Sikh, he felt that his religion needed to be rescued from those who, in its name, were indulging in killing, loot and rape. He writes in *Punjab: The Knights of Falsehood*:

> The virulent campaign for 'Khalistan' was fought in the name of specifically my religion. The Sikhs have been involved in warfare almost throughout their history, but no campaign has ever brought odium and disgrace upon them and their faith as this despicable movement did ... most unforgivable atrocities were committed.[63]

Gill uses 'my religion' to express his deep regret, and a similar feeling of dejection began to take over Sikh masses as they turned against the mayhem unleashed. Terrorism was uprooted from Punjab's soil; it is hoped never to return. 'The absence of the explicit political protection which Bhindranwale enjoyed,' says Ajai Sahni, is the difference between darkness and a safe Punjab. Without that patronage, he insists Punjab would not have plunged into darkness.

Fanning the dead embers of 'Khalistan' in today's times is a toss-up between a misplaced national media and steroid-induced social media. Peaceful Punjab is hardly sensational but those burned know the risk of playing with the fire of casual and petty politics in the state. Their singular message is to not let the noise hijack the ground reality.

Some elements within Sikh diasporas in the USA, Australia and the UK periodically flog the K-word, but there is no comparison with Canada which plays the dirtiest. Sikhs are a sizeable vote bank in the country and politicians –the Prime Minister downwards – have ignored their separatist activities, the deadliest of which took place in June 1985. Air India Boeing 'Kanishka' flying from Toronto to Mumbai exploded over the Atlantic Ocean killing all 329 passengers and twenty-two crew members.[64] The revenge attack for Operation Blue Star was planned by Sikh separatists in Canada and executed by the terrorist organization Babbar Khalsa, which planted a bomb in a checked-in suitcase.

Canadian intelligence agencies reportedly had suspicions of the terror plot and had received several warnings of the brewing conspiracy. All three accused were Canadian citizens and, in the country's worst-ever terror attack, only Inderjit Singh Reyat, who made the bomb, was convicted – but decades later. He is no longer in jail; the main accused, Ripudaman Singh Malik, who was acquitted, was shot dead in 2022 outside his family business in Surrey, British Columbia.[65]

As for K.P.S. Gill, he had to pay a price for his gumption. The radical Sikh opinion in Punjab detested him and it did not help that Gill was adept at trespassing norms as he brooked no interference with his 'unconventional' methods. He rode roughshod on many niceties of governance and accepted no intrusion in his work –

in some cases, he was a law unto himself. His personal life too became controversial because of which he flittered away his post-retirement dues. His professional legacy, though, sustains – he was a man without whom Punjab would have remained on the boil for a long time to come. And this is reason enough for him to find a special mention in the annals of policing. For now, he remains the one and only policeman to truly merit the moniker of 'Super Cop'.

The press in Punjab paid a heavy price during the militancy era. Editors, drivers, agents and newspaper hawkers – no one in the distribution network was spared. Many were gunned down in broad daylight. Barring journalists, who could be counted on one hand with fingers to spare, New Delhi never saw the full might of Punjab's terror in the 1980s and 1990s. It was not merely kilometres that separated the two. Organizations like the Editors Guild of India did not show much solidarity; their representatives flew in and out of Chandigarh but stayed away from ground zero – towns like Tarn Taran, which were referred to as Khalistan's capital.

In 1992, a group of journalists from Delhi were brought to the state capital to show the nation that terrorism had been weeded out of Punjab, with just some wild growths here and there left to be snipped. They were flown into the only five-star hotel in Chandigarh. Barring a couple of journalists, others in the delegation did not even leave the hotel, filing stories that were served to them on a platter. 'People were being para dropped from

Delhi and fed with information,'[66] remembers Naveen S. Garewal, the veteran Punjab journalist.

Jalandhar did not fare any better. Members of the Editors Guild visited the city just once and left after a perfunctory meeting at the tightly guarded Circuit House, mumbling something about being busy. Their frightened faces spoke volumes of a story missed. As champions of freedom of the press, it is easy to question a government and prove oneself fearless as long as there are rules, courts and public opinion. It is far tougher to face a situation where there is no certainty, except the fact that the next bullet is coming – one just doesn't know from where and when.

Being a journalist on the ground in those unpredictable times was to stare at death daily. Garewal's office was in Amritsar's Dharma Market, which was adjacent to the Golden Temple.

> Every time there was a blast people would run away and we would run towards it. The terrorists would tie explosives to dead bodies, so that when the police reached the area there would be another explosion. In those days, we had no bulletproof jackets and we would be fully exposed as we took notes in our diary. In front of me, once, there was a ferocious machine-gun firing on the legs of an SSP. He bled to death.[67]

This was not the most brutal killing he witnessed. 'I saw a bullet put through the heart of a one-month-old baby,' he remembers. Grewal reported on the increased frequency of busloads of people coming to Amritsar from remote areas, as villagers filled any gap they could find on the roof of buses. There was an exodus to the cities in the hope that they were safer there, but in Punjab, safe spaces had run out.

Also reporting from Amritsar was *Pratap*'s correspondent, Narinder Sharma. Leaving for work each day[68] felt like it was his last, he says. Sharma was fortunate to survive three bullets.

> That day, we had gone for an interview with terrorists behind Khalsa College on Ram Tirath Road. I was shot near the Agriculture Department – one bullet went through my ear, the second through the neck, and the third bullet went through my right hand, which still does not have complete mobility. They attacked us saying we were giving another group more coverage. My colleague, Comrade Balbir Singh Saggu, was killed on the spot. I made myself fall down and they thought that I had also died. They kicked me just to make sure and then left.[69]

Sharma met Bhindranwale several times in the Golden Temple. 'Till Bhindranwale was alive, we went there and met him and Sant Longowal daily. Longowal would tell us that Bhindranwale is a "daku" and when we went to Bhindranwale, he would say, "*Gandhi ke paas ho aye*?" (Have you met Gandhi – a reference to Longowal) Those days, nothing moved without his order.' And those instructions were implemented by a section of a pliant press. Regrettably, the contribution of the police, and journalists, who were at the forefront in Punjab's fight against terrorism has, by and large, been forgotten.

Among others who remained defiant and paid a price were two organizations: The communists and the RSS, both of whom lost several workers. On 25 June 1989, terrorists gunned down twenty-seven swayamsevaks at an RSS shakha.[70] The communists, who had – and still have – active pockets in the villages, were forced to confront the might of the bullet. They were fully activated and paid the price for it. Their cadre in the countryside was defenceless but brave, as it fought an ideological war against separatism. Communist mouthpiece, *Naya Zamana*, led by the venerable editor Jagjit Singh Anand daringly continued its campaign throughout the period.

Jatinder Pannu, the current editor of the paper, who received his own fair share of warnings from separatists, recounts:[71]

> The parcel bomb at the *Pratap* office was one of the first big explosions when terrorism started in Punjab. The twelve–thirteen years of terror we faced was our misfortune; before that Punjab was ahead in all parameters and after that, we lagged behind everyone. No one left their homes before sunrise and everyone was home before sunset. People picked up guns to fight for the government or to fight against the government, but those who died had no idea whose fight it was or for whom and for what. They were innocent. We need to pray to live in peace; we don't need politics from inside the country or outside.'

Among the defiant communists was a family that personified collective valour at the height of terrorism. In 1993, four members of the Sandhu family were conferred with the Shaurya Chakra, a rare recognition in the country. Comrade Balwinder Singh, his wife, Jagdish Kaur, brother Ranjit Singh and his wife, Balraj

Kaur, weathered sixteen attacks in a matter of eleven months in the militancy hotbed of Tarn Taran. Since they were on the hit list, the government supplied them with weapons, which is how, on 30 September 1990, the family survived. In a fierce assault, 200 terrorists surrounded their house in an attack that went on for five hours. Balwinder was killed in 2020 by two unidentified gunmen on a motorcycle.[72]

'There was no weapon that the terrorists didn't use that day against us – from rocket launchers to LMG, they had everything,' recounts Jagdish Kaur. That fateful day, despite informing the police, she claims that no one came to the family's rescue. 'Those who ambushed us were well prepared and, without any help, we fought on our own. We had rifles and we constantly had to fill them with magazines. *Majboori ke halaat the* (Those were desperate and compelling times).'[73]

Jagdish's son was just a year old when this attack took place. As a homemaker, completely clueless about using weapons, Jagdish trained at her house under the guidance of a relative. 'Even during my wedding, there were security people in our baraat. It was a fight for ideology and we were communists who followed the Gurus. As a Sikh, we do not believe in injustice against anyone and because of that there were forty-two attacks on our house.'[74]

In these circumstances, when normal life had been torn asunder, when it was not unusual to be woken up in the middle of the night by the sound of ominous firing in a lane behind the house, for silence to signal the calm before the storm, only those whose defiance had a dose of foolhardiness to it could choose to keep walking on a path that promised only thorns. An old employee of *Pratap* echoed what the family felt: 'We were uprooted from Pakistan; we refuse to be exiled again.' A thought that was more visible in the older generation that had experienced Partition's horrors.

Throughout the week, *Pratap*'s editor, Virendra, left the office shortly before lunch at 1 p.m. and, instead of heading home in his Fiat car, he first visited the local Rainak Bazaar to buy fruits from a corner shop. The shop never changed and his routine never altered, even though the family tried to dissuade him several times as his name featured prominently on the hit list. He refused – courage under fire was not new to him.

Finally, exasperated with the persistent pleas of the family, he retorted, '*Mein bomb banaye hoye hain* (I have made bombs myself).'

From here begins another story, going back in time to when a young man assembled bombs and lived such a daring life that even terrorists on his trail in Punjab could not faze him.

PART 2

3
Circa 1919, Lahore: Tryst with Truth

'*Aao, Mahabharat ke mere Krishan* (My Krishan of Mahabharata, come)' is how Madan Mohan Malviya, freedom fighter and president of the Indian National Congress, greeted *Pratap*'s founder Mahashay Krishan whenever Malviya visited Lahore. Mahashay, though, was less Krishna and more Arjun – with a tendency to plunge headlong into battle. No reluctant prince, the pen was his sword. And the ultimate compliment, at least he took it as one, he received came from Abul Kalam Azad, independent India's first education minister: '*Yeh kumbukth kalam se nahin teshe se likhta hai* (This damn fellow writes not with a pen but with a chisel).'

That pen was put to paper on 30 March 1919, the day Krishan – his name was prefixed with the honorific 'Mahashay' – launched

Pratap in Lahore as an evening newspaper. The timing was not a coincidence – pages of history were being painstakingly written, and information was being furiously disseminated to quench thirsty ears and eyes.

There was a significant churn from the early years of the twentieth century leading to events that exploded in 1919. The Indian National Congress, under Mohandas Karamchand Gandhi, had energized the nation, and its sessions in Banaras and Calcutta were resounding successes. The Muslim League[75] had come into being and, in cohesion, the two political entities mounted a challenge to the British Raj. Feeling uneasy in Bengal, the British shifted the capital to Delhi under the pretext of centralizing power, but the winds changed direction and trailed them there. In December 1912, as he was making a ceremonial entry into the city on an elephant, a home-made bomb was thrown at Viceroy Charles Hardinge in Delhi's Chandni Chowk. He managed to escape, but not before his flesh was sprayed with shrapnel.[76] The mastermind was a revolutionary from Bengal, whose story is as much the stuff of legend as his bravery.[77]

India's struggle for freedom is laced with tales – some heralded, others forgotten – of men and women who were still in the spring of their lives but courted danger like veterans. One law student at Punjab University volunteered to shoot the Governor while receiving her graduation degree at the annual convocation. Such was her belief in the cause that she not only helped revolutionaries financially but was prepared to train and shoot as well. The decision to assign a man to the task didn't go down well with her and she angrily confronted Virendra, one of the architects of the plot, 'Do you think only men can be brave, and not women? You have a poor opinion about women.'[78] That plot unfolds later in the book.

History in its haste to ink the achievements of the known needs occasional prompting when it comes to the feats of those who chipped away quietly in the background. They were equally passionate, daring and non-compromising with their ideals and their chosen path. There was no glancing back at life.

These individuals epitomized the revolutionary camp and they had collectively sensed a weakness in the British Raj. The Ghadar Party – a coalition of expatriate Punjabis, Hindus, Muslims and Sikhs active in America – capitalized on this by sending youth to galvanize Punjab. Its aim was singular: To be free of the British through an armed struggle. Lahore and Kapurthala became focal areas, and, in the next couple of years, contact was established with underground movements in both Punjab and Bengal. Notably, this was a phase when mass revolts and protests had not yet gained momentum and the Ghadar Party's uprising was inspired by the 1857 war of independence. Their outcomes were similar; both rebellions failed. In the first Lahore Conspiracy trial – not the same as the Lahore Conspiracy Case whose most famous undertrial was Bhagat Singh – in 1915, forty-two revolutionaries were hanged and more than a hundred freedom fighters found themselves sentenced to the notorious Cellular Jail in the Andamans, known at the time as 'Kala Pani'.[79]

Amongst those executed was Kartar Singh Sarabha,[80] whose popularity far exceeded his age. Sarabha joined the party when he was fifteen and was executed four years later, while still a teenager. In deference to his tender age, the judge asked him to appeal. 'Why should I?' he responded. 'Folklore has it that Bhagat Singh was deeply inspired by Sarabha and kept a photo of the young man in his pocket.

A year after the teenager's execution, Lokmanya Bal Gangadhar Tilak announced, 'Swaraj is my birthright, and I shall have it.'[81] This earned him the ire of the rulers who called him, 'The father of the Indian unrest'. Under his and Annie Besant's leadership, the 'Home Rule' agitation was in full swing, while, on the other hand, revolutionaries stepped up their activities, and, after Bengal and Maharashtra, Punjab took over the mantle as the revolutionary hotspot of the country.

The British remained unruffled. Instead of returning the favour for 1.5 million[82] Indian soldiers who fought for the British Empire during World War I, the infamous Rowlatt Act was imposed in March 1919.[83] Civil liberties were curtailed and several Indians, including Virendra, learned that arrest and jail did not need a trial anymore. This was also Mahatma Gandhi's coming-of-age moment.

No longer content to watch from the sidelines, Mahashay Krishan struck. He presented *Pratap*, an Urdu newspaper that was to transform and dominate vernacular journalism for decades.

By the late 1800s and first two decades of the twentieth century, several periodicals and newspapers came out in undivided India. They had a distinct nationalist tenor and stood out in their role of political awakening. In Punjab, if a report was not published in the Urdu press, it was not credible enough from an Indian nationalistic perspective. With Persian having transitioned to Urdu for administration during the Raj, the language itself was a composite cultural bridge of a people oppressed.

As Mahatma Gandhi extolled the press to express their opinion freely, Urdu journalists and editors did not disappoint him. The landscape of the Urdu press was divided between Hindu and Muslim owners when *Pratap* was born. Despite public perception – and more so now for vested reasons – Urdu as a language of Muslims alone has been a grandstanding fallacy.

Our passage to freedom is also the journey of Urdu literature, where poets, journalists and revolutionaries mobilized their angst into powerful words. Urdu became the voice; its poetic activism burying the romantic prose as it not only called out atrocities but also invigorated the masses. The batwara was not kind to the language; it flickers, and, despite its cultural generosity, it burns predominantly in Muslim homes in India where Urdu adds to an identity already under question.

In pre-independent India, Urdu was a distinctly inclusive language – uniting Hindus, Muslims and Sikhs under its umbrella. Subhas Chandra Bose inscribed 'Ittehad, Itmad, Qurbani' as his army's motto, and from Bengal Renaissance writers to the Arya Samaj, Urdu's influence was far-flung. 'Inquilab Zindabad', 'long live the revolution', coined by poet Hasrat Mohani became the battle cry for freedom, and, as Virendra himself was to witness it, Bhagat Singh, Rajguru and Sukhdev shouted the slogan while being taken to the gallows at Lahore Central Jail. A firsthand account of that evening forms a part of this book.

An American scholar of the Urdu language, C.M. Naim, says:[84]

So much of Urdu prose writing was done by non-Muslims, essentially Hindus. There were Kashmiri Brahmins, Kayasthas, Hindus, Rajputs and those who belonged to the Arya Samaj, who were all integral to the language. The British replaced Persian with Urdu and it was a joke that Hindus, Muslims and Sikhs speak Punjabi when they met, but, in offices, they were all communicating in Urdu. Your great-grandfather and grandfather were writing and speaking Urdu not just from their hearts but also from their minds. The sad fact is that Urdu is no longer a language equally shared, with an equal commitment of emotion and talent by both communities. It is a Muslim enterprise, and that has its consequences, both linguistic and non-linguistic.

It was not just the Urdu press that showed a mirror to the Raj, the pens of revolutionaries were cutting, outspoken and uncaring. Bismil Azimabadi's 1921 ghazal[85] was a brazen ode to men with a singular calling: India's freedom. There was one slogan on everyone's lips after poet Ramprasad Bismil recited it audaciously before his hanging in the Kakori Conspiracy Case.

Sarfaroshi ki tammana ab hamare dil mein hai,
dekhna hai zor kitna bazu-e-qatil mein hai

The desire for sacrifice is in our hearts,
let us see how much strength there is in the arms of our killer

The words continue to have a life of their own.

Professor Mrinal Chatterjee, academic and author, says:[86]

> If you look at phases of Urdu literature, there are three to four distinct phases and we have to look at undivided India to find those phases. There was a romantic phase, and, gradually, a social consciousness came [into being], along with it came the idea of revolt through poetry and literature. The beauty of this language was used for the movement and rebellion was spoken about poetically, remember when Akbar Allahabadi says, 'Jab top mukabil ho toh akhbar nikalo (When facing a gun bring out a newspaper).'

Pakistani scholar and poet Abdul Majeed Salik's biography notes that not long after Lala Lajpat Rai took out the Urdu newspaper *Bande Mataram*, Krishan launched the daily, *Pratap*.[87] '*Zamindar*, *Inqilab* and *Siyasat*, though each other's rivals in many respects, forged a common front against Hindu hierarchy,' says a Pakistani report on the layers of pre-partition Urdu press,[88] while singling out *Pratap*, *Bande Mataram*, *Kesari* and *Milap* as Hindu contemporaries.

Former Prime Minister I.K. Gujral's first acquaintance with Lahore was as a young boy, when his parents took him to witness the historic Congress session of 1929–30. He writes in a foreword for Virendra's autobiography, *Veh Inquilabi Din*, that Lahore was a premier centre of media; radio was still in its infancy and TV unheard of.

> The Urdu press was large and diverse. Most of them were anti-imperialist though their outlooks divided them on Hindu-Muslim lines that determined their affiliations, *Pratap* and *Milap* were supportive of the national surge. My childhood and later years were influenced a great deal by first hearing from my mother and later reading the editorials written by Mahashay Krishan.[89]

Pratap's first lifespan lasted a full twelve days. Its support for the freedom movement led by Mahatma Gandhi made it a pariah in the eyes of the British and, less than two weeks later, on 11 April 1919, censorship laws were imposed on the paper. Its owner was ordered to submit content for pre-censorship, which he refused to do, and the next day *Pratap*'s proprietor was thrown into Lahore prison.

Professor Mrinal Chatterjee says:[90]

> Pratap was a subject of attack by the British administration as well as harassment by the government. Its publications were suspended several times, but it continued to have a profound influence among Urdu-reading Hindus of Punjab and Delhi.'

C.M. Naim writes:[91]

The large cohort of sharanarthi [refugee] journalists, forced in 1947 to abandon lives and careers in Lahore, Sialkot, Rawalpindi, or Sargodha, lost little time in building new lives and careers in Delhi, Amritsar, Ludhiana, and Jalandhar … The famous triad of *Pratap*, *Milap* and *Tej* probably never lost a publication day.

It wasn't quite as simple as that!

In *The Politics of Self-Expression*, Markus Daechsel explores the Urdu middle-class milieu in the mid-twentieth century and comes to a similar conclusion: '… even after the partition Urdu titles previously published from Lahore, but now relocated to India, easily outstripped the Hindi Press of Uttar Pradesh in terms of readership [sic],' with Punjab 'boasting of some of the most advanced Urdu newspapers of the period',[92] including, he says, *Pratap*.

Back in Lahore, it was the first of many jail stints for Krishan – in the coming years both his sons, Virendra and Narendra shared his fate as they too found themselves behind prison bars. The older of the two, Virendra, spent most of his youth in and out of colonial jails, building a formidable reputation that the British weaponized to jail him even when innocent. He was to remember 'by a strange irony, [a] conspiracy to do away with Lord Irwin was hatched in Delhi, but we in Lahore were arrested when we were aroused from our sleep in the Congress camp'.[93]

Two days after *Pratap* was censored by the British government, on 13 April 1919 – the day of Baisakhi – hundreds of innocent men and women were killed at Jallianwala Bagh in Amritsar, Lahore's sister city. Apart from the fact it was a tragedy of colossal proportions, it also put paid to any hopes Krishan had of a quick release. He was tried under a Martial Law Commission but by early July, when he was still in prison a man lent his voice in support.

> In my humble opinion the judgment is a travesty of justice. The case is in some respects worse even than Babu Kalinath Roy's [editor-in-chief of *The Tribune*.] There are no startling headlines as in *The Tribune* case. The accused has been sentenced not on a section of the Indian Penal Code but on a rule temporarily framed as a war measure … the learned Judge dismisses the plea that other respectable papers contained about the same statements that the Pratap did.

M.K. Gandhi closed by requesting, 'We hope that the public and the Press throughout India will support the prayer for justice and that it will not go in vain.'[94]

The fame that *Pratap* acquired in its brief existence of just twelve days stood in good stead for the next twelve months. In Mahashay Krishan's words, 'The first issue came out on the evening of 30th March [sic]. It was sold out in Lahore and not a single copy could be sent out. The issue of 31st March [sic] carried news of the atrocities on the satyagrahis in Delhi. Again, it was sold out.'[95] Krishan was released from Lahore Central jail after four months; however, the newspaper was not allowed to go to print and was censored from even taking out coverage of the Jallianwala Bagh massacre.

Pratap finally resumed publication after almost a year – but its reputation for fearless teshe-like journalism stayed – it was, once again, sold out. Israeli writer Rotem Geva in *Delhi Reborn: Partition and Nation Building in India's Capital* gets the pulse of the editor, 'Krishan was a prolific writer who commented on the burning issues of the time, a kind of firebrand who simply would not bow to anybody.'[96]

Throughout its life, *Pratap* was intrinsically linked to the personality of its founder-editor, Mahashay Krishan. He was a crusader, and a non-compromising one at that. On the political front, the nation and its struggle for freedom claimed his loyalty first. Socially, he devoted all his energy to the Arya Samaj and its creed of reform. It was on these twin pillars that *Pratap*'s reputation was built.

Born Radhakrishan Vohra, he was the only son in a family, comprising three brothers, with no tradition of learning or writing. Pampered and spoiled, Radhakrishan was married off at the age of ten to a girl who was a year older. Once he was exposed to the teachings of the Arya Samaj, he rebelled against Hindu orthodoxy, and chose to walk a path that was severe, puritanical and uncompromising. On this journey, he also fought against the caste system, shedding the family surname of 'Vohra'.

Historian and professor Richa Raj says:[97]

The Arya Samaj, from its very inception fought orthodox Hinduism and [the] caste system and instructed that every member should abandon the caste of their birth while taking the membership of the Arya Samaj. For the census of 1931, it was felt by the Arya Samaj leaders that Arya Samajis should write 'Vedic' for religion and 'Arya' for caste, as opposed to writing 'Hindu' and the name of the caste in which they were born, respectively. This issue has been in discussion since 1927. The census officials did not agree to the proposal that 'Arya' be written in place of caste, but they agreed that if any person did not want to write their caste, they would not be forced to do so. Thus, in most of the cases, the columns for caste were left blank in the 1931 census.

Krishan's sons, throughout their lifetime, were known simply as Virendra and Narendra respectively, but it complicated foreign travels – so a generic 'Kumar' was added to their passports.

Mahashay Krishan built for himself a daunting reputation as an uncompromising, unrelenting and – some would say – stubborn champion of the freedom of the press. Others saw him as a fundamentalist, a rigid Hindu journalist, unrelentingly anti-Muslim and regressive. In his family life, at least, Krishan was far ahead of the times.

In 1939, his eldest son, Virendra, married Raj Lakshmi, daughter of Diwan Niranjan Prasad Khosla of Patiala. At the ceremony, the ritual of kanyadaan was not performed. The parents of the bride sent a request: They were against the orthodox tradition. The reply from Lahore was spontaneous – their thoughts were in tandem. It was a replay of a similar scene a decade earlier, at Virendra's older sister Savitri's wedding – the groom's family was informed that the ritual would be shunned.

These events played out nearly a century ago. The pernicious tradition of kanyadaan, where the father of a bride 'donates' her, is not just prevalent but also integral to a marriage ceremony in many parts of contemporary India. This socio-cultural construct stalls any attempts at conversation over an outdated custom with overwhelming patriarchal strains.

Imagine then – circa 1929 or even 1939 – when objecting to this archaic belief needed not just a special mindset, it also required a strong reformist mind to stand up against prevalent social mores. At Virendra's wedding family elders on both sides baulked, with the matriarchs of the two families – one of whom was illiterate, while the other was educated only till Class 10 – voicing their objections openly. The practice of not performing kanyadaan continues in the family – no daughter has been given away nor accepted as daan in marriage.

Incidentally, Raj was twenty-five years of age when she got married – unusually late for an Indian woman living in the pre-Partition era. Child marriage had been outlawed barely ten years earlier, when the Sarda Act was enacted in 1929, but the legal age for women to be married was still very young at fourteen. The reason she got married so late could be that for most of the 1930s, Raj's father was diwan of Bijawar, a princely state in central India, where suitable matches may not have been easy to come by!

It was Partition that broke Raj. A multi-storeyed bungalow, the *Pratap* office in Gawalmandi, prestige – overnight, it was all left behind in Lahore. Also forsaken were memories of college; she had graduated from Lahore's Kinnaird College for Women. Life was rebuilt as a refugee across the border in Jalandhar in a newly divided Punjab. This was a family that once had a

German-made Adler car in which an unsteady Virendra – in part, inexperience, but in equal part, nervous about his co-passenger – drove Jawaharlal Nehru around in Lahore; and now they were celebrating when they bought their first bicycle in Jalandhar. One small win at a time, a story was re-written.

Once India became independent, Krishan turned his pen against the government of the day for what he perceived were shortcomings in their policies. The finest hour of the newspaper, though, remains its unbending crusade against the British Raj.

After *Pratap* resumed publication in February 1920, it had no trouble in re-establishing itself in the hearts of its readers as a champion of the suppressed. The British were not pleased; they considered the paper as one of the chief troublemakers of the time and the next stand-off occurred sooner than anyone had anticipated. Shortly after the paper resumed operations, its security of Rs 3,000 – which was no ordinary sum in those days – was forfeited by the government. This was the beginning of another saga involving the newspaper – punishment of stripping it of its security money and reimposing a fine became routine. *Pratap* did not budge from its stance.

Barely a year later, Krishan was arrested under sections 124A and 153A of the penal code on charges of sedition against the Crown. The 'crime' he committed was to reprint an article written by Mahatma Gandhi in *Young India* for which Gandhi himself had been sentenced to six years of imprisonment. In Krishan's memoir, the incident finds prominence.[98]

The late Sir Ganga Ram was very fond of me. Those days the sentence for sedition was very severe. Sir Ganga Ram therefore met Sir John Maynard, the finance minister, and persuaded him to withdraw the case if I apologised. After that, he rang me up, but I refused to apologise ... Sir Ganga Ram was furious with me, but I stood my ground.

This refusal cost Krishan a two-year imprisonment sentence but, interestingly, barring a fine of Rs 500 that he had to pay, the punishment was never carried through. The government did not want to make a further hero of the editor and his publication, *Pratap*.

The process of imposing and forfeiting a newspaper's security was an old trick of the British government to keep editors in line. The *Tribune*, published from Lahore, on 5 August 1922, stated:[99]

With the announcement of the decision of the Special Bench of the High Court in the Pratap Forfeiture of Security Case, the curtain falls on an extraordinary chapter in the history of a legislative measure. The Press Act was so conceived that it was impossible for even a body of angels to work it without causing grave injustice from time to time, and when worked by a bureaucracy like ours, which owes no responsibility to the people, it was bound to become, as it did become in many cases, even worse in its actual operation. But we venture to think that in the history of the administration or maladministration of this measure in various parts of a country as big as a continent, there had never been a case of such injustice as was perpetrated by the Punjab Government when in the exercise of its powers under this Act, it declared the security of the Pratap to be forfeited. The Punjab Secretariat justified the forfeiture …

The *Tribune* goes on to add:

It was pointed out in these columns and elsewhere that so far as one of the two papers – the Pratap – was concerned, the statement in the official communique that it had published articles to 'arouse hatred and disaffection against the Government' was incorrect; that it had published no article at all, and that, therefore, the very basis of the official action was wrong.

Soon, Krishan's trysts with the British authorities became predictable. After *Pratap* supported Gandhi's Dandi March and Non-Cooperation Movement, it had to forego a security of Rs 2,000 and a fresh sum of more than double the amount was demanded. Neither party caved in. *Pratap* protested against the police atrocities on satyagrahis in Lahore, the punishment was a forfeiture of Rs 5,000 with an additional surety of the same amount.

4

The Son Rises: Who Lives If India Dies?

The crusade for Independence, like any other struggle, had its highs and lows. At times, the movement was paused by its leaders and at other moments, it lay in wait to be revived. By 1915, the revolutionary network was dormant and, barring the odd episode, this state of limbo stretched on until the Kakori train robbery a decade later. Tax money being transferred to the British treasury was looted near Lucknow by revolutionaries, who halted the train carrying it.[100] The incident revived the hunger for freedom, which peaked two years later, when four revolutionaries – Ram Prasad Bismil, Ashfaqullah Khan, Rajendra Singh and Roshan Singh – were executed in the Kakori Conspiracy.

The story of India's independence is incomplete without the tales of deep friendships seen during the time. Trust was as important for revolutionaries as secrecy – without it, men on the run were vulnerable. Khan was a Muslim; Bismil, an Arya Samaj Hindu, who was a teetotaller with an interest in physical fitness – a trait his protégé Chandrashekhar Azad picked up. Their friendship symbolized the coming together of a pre-Partition India where nationalism was not dictated by religious identity. There were many firsts among equals who displayed strength of character – how else can death be embraced so willingly? Poignantly, they died together, leaving behind a mutual love for poetry. Ashfaqullah Khan stepped up to the noose with these parting lines: *Kuch arzoo nahin hai, hai arzoo to yeh hai, rakh de koi zara si khak-e-vatan kafan par* (There are no longings, but if there is any longing left it is that someone should keep a little dust of my homeland on my shroud).

A day after the hangings, a meeting was held in Lahore's Bradlaugh Hall, which was to become the hub of the freedom movement. Rousing tributes were paid to the four martyrs. In the audience that day was a young Virendra.

In April 1927, as spring faded to summer, a sixteen-year-old joined Forman Christian College (FC College) in Lahore. He had recently cleared his matric examinations. Around him were signs of restlessness; the youth was no longer content to be bystanders in the resistance movement. There was, however, no clarity on the road ahead. Parallel strains of thought dominated the political discourse. Spearheading one was Gandhi and his crusade of non-violence. But the country's young were reluctant to wear khaddar and go to jail – independence, they felt, needed a special nudge. For them, the second way of thinking, based on the French Revolution, the Russian Revolution and the American War of Independence made for a much more appealing manual.

Two men – Jawaharlal Nehru and Subhas Chandra Bose – who had given up lives of privilege to join the freedom movement impressed them. Ironically, both were themselves confused, unsure if Gandhi's path was the right one to follow. What they had clarity on was his undisputed leadership, and that of stalwarts like Pandit Motilal Nehru, Lala Lajpat Rai, Pandit Madan Mohan Malviya and Dr Mukhtar Ahmed Ansari who surrounded him. Even within the Nehru family, father and son were not on the same page. It was not long before Jawaharlal Nehru made up his mind and became a staunch follower of Gandhi – the Mahatma was to become no less than a father figure to him. Subhas Chandra Bose's dilemma lasted longer. He had skirmishes with Gandhi; never, though, at the expense of losing his respect for the great man.

When young Virendra joined FC College, three seniors caught his attention and they were to have a lasting impact on his life. Avinash Chander Bali, Durga Das Khanna and Hans Raj Vohra were leaders of the students' movement, the core that attracted and influenced students against colonial rule.

Virendra was unaware that the trio were members of the secret organization, Hindustan Republican Army (HRA), whose leaders were Chandrashekhar Azad and Bhagat Singh. In 1926 – three years before the Assembly bombing – students in Lahore were active in two other groups, Naujawan Bharat Sabha, founded by Bhagat Singh, and Punjab Students' Union. Both groups had the same aim – to intensify anti-British sentiments across college campuses.

Bhagat Singh's inner circle included two other men, Dhanvantari and Bhagwati Charan – Virendra was to meet them and Sukhdev Raj soon. The job of these men was to stake out potential enlisters, those who were courageous enough, sometimes even recklessly so, to willingly become martyrs. The chain of responsibility was clear-cut. Once identified, Durga Das and Vohra swooped in, contacting and recruiting the young men.

Lahore's police had its eyes on the city, but the underground movement stayed a step ahead. Once Bali, Khanna and Vohra were convinced of a target's loyalty, the person was taken under their wing and given revolutionary material to read. This is how they zeroed in on Virendra, son of the famous newspaper editor Mahashay Krishan.

Virendra's initiation into the revolutionary club, though, was outside the campus – it was at Bradlaugh Hall that, for the first time, he heard fiery speeches to protest the Kakori Conspiracy hangings. The teenager was yet to win the confidence of either Khanna or Vohra, and his tender age didn't do him any favours. He was put to the test through literature and Virendra was handed books like *My Fight for Irish Freedom* by Dan Breen, which was exceedingly popular among the rebels. *Mother* by Maxim Gorky and *The Cry for Justice* by Upton Sinclair, which had writings and speeches of renowned revolutionaries, was also given to Virendra.

Secret literature was making its way into the country not just from Russia but also from China. Durga Das Khanna hid the books in a newspaper and handed it over to Virendra who was to write later, 'It increased my appetite for this literature. I not only began reading this literature more and more, but I became a part of the revolutionary movement.' As a committed freedom fighter, Virendra closely saw history in the making. As with his comrades, he was not immune to some personal blows either – the movement's biggest setback was when a mentor became a turncoat. Hans Raj Vohra, the man who recruited idealistic young men into the revolutionary fold, was honey trapped and turned approver in the Lahore Conspiracy Case. His evidence led to Bhagat Singh's hanging.

The family's political activism had rubbed off on Virendra. He was made to work hard before he was embraced into the fold. Once he had a foot in, it was a different story. Virendra not only became a vital cog in the movement, but also forged a bond with Khanna and Bali that remained unbroken through their stints in jails and outside.

Forman Christian College in Lahore was carving out a name for itself as a budding centre of nationalism – its students were at the forefront, supported wholeheartedly by their college staff. Run by an American missionary society, the principal and teachers were unruffled by external events and did not think it necessary to toe the official British line. They not only tolerated patriotism in students within the campus, it was actively encouraged. The attitude of the principal, Dr Lucas, a Canadian who remained resolutely behind his students, frustrated the British, but there was nothing the latter could do about it.

Dr Lucas stood his ground the day the police arrived at his college campus to arrest Virendra. After a public reprimand for entering the grounds without his permission, he asked them to withdraw immediately. The police was instructed to remain outside the college premises where Virendra was handed over to them. Over time, the institution's gate had a permanent police picket and Central Investigation Department (CID) presence.

On the face of it, Lala Lajpat Rai and Bhagat Singh had little in common other than their desire to free India. One was an old-fashioned, mature leader who would be considered 'right-wing' today. The other was a young firebrand who was a self-confessed atheist. Yet, their fates entwined, causing a seismic shift in the country's history.

Lajpat Rai published an Urdu daily, *Bande Mataram,* and he frequently crossed swords with Mahashay Krishan. This was a peculiarity of vernacular journalism in pre-Partition India – those fighting for the same team had no qualms about getting personal with each other. Hindu and Muslim editors who wrote in Urdu topped the list, invariably taking potshots at each other. When differences cropped up between Lajpat Rai and Pandit Motilal Nehru over Assembly elections, Krishan, through personalized editorials, sided with Nehru, which resulted in a sharp exchange between him and Lajpat Rai.

So, it was with some trepidation that Virendra, Krishan's son, went along with Durga Das Khanna, Avinash Bali and Hans Raj Vohra – who had not yet turned approver and was still in the fold – to invite Lajpat Rai to preside over the Punjab Students' Union conference. Lala Ji was sitting in his garden, and, on seeing the four youngsters, he smiled and asked, 'How has young India come today?'

This was the first conference organized by the Punjab Students' Union and Bradlaugh Hall was packed to capacity. Virendra remembers it clearly. 'He roared like a lion. One felt as if the walls were trembling,' he wrote in his autobiography. From that day onwards, the group of four began visiting Lala Lajpat Rai's house frequently. They also started dropping in at the Durga Das Library that Lala Lajpat Rai – whose legion of supporters had begun calling him 'Punjab Kesari' – had started and where he donated all his books, including revolutionary literature. Since CID presence outside FC College was now permanent, the library afforded them a venue where they could plot and plan without having to look over their shoulders.

Their idealistic existence got a rude awakening, however, with the appointment of the Indian Statutory Commission, which comprised members of the British Parliament under Sir John Simon and became infamously known as the 'Simon Commission'. It changed and charged the atmosphere in ways unseen – much has been written about it in history books. It was set up to decide India's future; ironically, without any Indian as its member. The Congress and the Muslim League buried their ideological differences, and joined hands to oppose it. The common man – Hindus, Sikhs, and Muslims – too pushed all disagreements aside to stage protests. This was a deep cut, and Gandhi, Nehru and Jinnah closed ranks to oppose it.

Lala Lajpat Rai and Pandit Motilal Nehru also let go of their past acrimony, and, along with Pandit Madan Mohan Malviya, they forged a common front. All three were members of the National Assembly and were equally competent speakers. Malviya was not only a scholar of Sanskrit and Hindi, his English was eloquent and he held the record of speaking for seven hours in the Assembly! They were fortunate that the speaker was Sardar Patel's elder brother, Vithalbhai Patel, who allowed them to express their mind freely, quite unlike Parliament proceedings in present-day India.

30 October 1928: The date was set for the Simon Commission to visit Lahore. It had been boycotted in every Indian city and town, and greeted with demonstrations. Lajpat Rai took its presence as a personal affront and called a meeting of Congress members. Also invited were workers from the Naujawan Bharat Sabha and Punjab Students' Union. Outlining the urgency of giving the Simon Commission a 'better welcome' than what it had received in other cities, Lajpat Rai, despite being in poor health, declared that he would lead the protest – an announcement that roused the crowd. Preparations for the protest march began in earnest.

It was a landmark day and Virendra remembers the procession itself as being extraordinary. In Lajpat Rai's footsteps walked luminaries like Pandit Madan Mohan Malviya, Dr Gopichand Bhargava, Dr Sheikh Muhammad Alam, Maulana Zafar Ali Khan and Baba Kharak Singh. They were followed by a loud slogan-shouting crowd made up of young men, including Bhagat Singh. That day, Bhagat Singh's long hair was tied in a turban, and he was dressed in a kurta–pajama, layered with a coat on top. As the procession turned towards the railway station, Durga Das introduced young Virendra to Bhagat Singh. 'For a while, we chatted as we walked in the procession. Suddenly he disappeared.'[101] The association between the two was to last till the day Bhagat Singh was hanged.

Meandering through the bazaars of Lahore, the procession finally reached the railway station. The train carrying members of the controversial commission was yet to arrive on the platform, but barbed wire and barriers were already in place to stop protestors from proceeding forward. Mounted police was on full parade and it was then that Virendra recollects Bhagat Singh vanishing. The freedom fighter was busy dodging the CID, which was hot on his trail. Many personnel in the intelligence department had lost their jobs as Singh had made a habit of cleverly scooting away from their sight. In the meantime, Lajpat Rai and other leaders made their way near the barbed wire, and the entire area began to echo with loud cries of 'Simon Commission go back, Simon Commission murdabad.'

As the train arrived, the tempo of sloganeering went up many notches, and the commission members were quickly bundled into cars and taken away to safety. Then, in one of the British Raj's most infamous acts that was a chilling reminder of the Jallianwala Bagh atrocities, the police without any provocation turned on the protestors. The commission members had left the railway station without the procession breaching any barricades and the non-violent demonstration would have dissipated by itself, sooner rather than later.

Instead, the British officers had tasted blood in Amritsar and were hungry for more. Over the barrier, they rained lathis – including on Lala Lajpat Rai, who stood his ground as the protestors scattered in panic. The police violence was overseen by Lahore Superintendent of Police James A. Scott and Bhagat Singh was an eyewitness to this attack.

As turning points go, this one was lethal.

Addressing a gathering after the assault, Rai thundered, 'I declare that the blows struck at me today will be the last nails in the coffin of British rule in India.' They were his famous last words to the public. The police had lathi-charged Lala Lajpat Rai on 30 October 1928 and, nearly three weeks later, on 17 November, he succumbed to his injuries. Rai had suffered physical wounds, but since the attack, he was also mentally disturbed. A man of his stature – Punjab's Kesari – assaulted by an ordinary police officer was not just a personal affront, it was also a nation's dishonour. This troubled him more than his injuries and he became not just weak but also plunged into depression.

When news about the police excesses was first published in newspapers, Rai was feted across the country. Mahatma Gandhi's wire to him read, 'Hearty congratulations'; Motilal Nehru urged countrymen to 'follow Lahore'; and Subhas Chandra Bose too sent a message: 'Bengal congratulates you on the success of the demonstration'. Sardar Patel sent this note: 'Respectful congratulations on exemplary discipline.'

As a front-line leader, Lajpat Rai had been arrested several times, but the nation could not reconcile to police violence against a man of such prominence. Renowned for his oration and writings, excesses against him made headlines abroad and the British Parliament took up the matter. As news of his death broke, crowds began gathering at his kothi, Lajpat Bhavan, on Lahore's Court Road. Gandhi led the nation in paying tribute to the fallen leader, 'Lalaji is dead, long live Lalaji.' Such was his mass appeal that strikes were called across India, and businesses and shops shut down to pay homage to him. It became difficult for the British to come out of their homes and the American press took them to task for the lethal assault on a respectable leader.

As the country grieved, a predicament arose. It was anticipated that the funeral ground wouldn't be able to hold Lajpat Rai's legion of supporters. Thousands had gathered to pay the fallen leader their respects It was finally decided that the leader would be cremated on the banks of the river Ravi. The funeral procession began at forenoon and, at every grief-laden step, more mourners joined. Less than three years later, the bodies of Bhagat Singh, Rajguru and Sukhdev would be given an honourable cremation at the same spot.

It took five hours for the leader's body to be brought to its final resting place and, as the pyre was lit, cries of 'Long live Lala Lajpat Rai' echoed. The pyre burned late into the night and, as mourners began to go home, the place descended into silence. Darkness closed in and no one noticed a group of young men standing still. Staring into the dying embers, at last, one of them spoke up, '*Khoon ka badla khoon se liya jayega* (Blood will be revenged by blood).'

The man was Bhagat Singh.

Emotions were running high. The next day, Basanti Devi, freedom fighter Deshbandhu Chittaranjan Das's wife, issued a statement: 'Does the youth and manhood of the country still exist? I, a woman of the land, demand a clear answer.' Chandrashekhar Azad and Bhagat Singh read it. 'Will you give a reply?' Azad asked the younger revolutionary. 'Certainly,' was the answer. This was the moment an idea became a promise.

On the lookout to recruit fresh blood, Durga Das and Hans Raj Vohra asked students to read Basanti Devi's statement. Virendra was probed and hints were dropped by the two men as they gauged his reaction. The scenario presented to him was the shooting of a police officer in a revenge killing.

Nothing was certain yet, but it was becoming abundantly clear that the British were going to pay a price. Calls for a dhamaka were becoming louder. The revolutionaries wanted the world to sit up and notice that India's youth had hit back at the death of their respected leader. Those who wanted revenge by taking blood were also willing to shed their own.

5

The Great Escape: *Khoon Ka Badla Khoon Se*

Under Chandrashekhar Azad's leadership, a new party was formed whose members had no interest in wearing khaddar or weaving it. In their view, even a hundred years on the path of non-violence was not enough to throw the British out, and they pushed back against Gandhi's doctrine. Youth that enrolled in this party were educated – their knowledge came from literature on Ireland's freedom movement, and the revolutions of France and Russia. After Lala Lajpat Rai's death, for its members, everything was fair, including the use of weapons like bombs and pistols.

Virendra recollects:

On 17 December 1928, one month after the death of Lala Lajpat Rai, I was busy with my exams. Hansraj Vohra [sic] did not come to college that day. Durga Das Khanna came for a short while but returned after taking some books from the library. I came home from college by about 5 p.m. Just then, a man came running to my father with information that some young boys had shot dead an officer in front of DAV College.

Khoon ka badla khoon se [The revenge for blood will be blood] – but who had done it?
Lahore turned into a garrison town, and the police marched in bazaars and streets looking for the perpetrators. A British police officer was shot in front of his office and the killers were able to flee. The impact was seismic, as hoped.
Bhagwan Das Mohar was a close associate of Bhagat Singh – he was also part of a group assembled to assassinate James Scott, the superintendent of police who had ordered the lathi-charge during protests against the Simon Commission that led to Lala Lajpat Rai's death. Mohar was a passionate revolutionary and was earlier incarcerated after shooting an approver who had gone against Bhagat Singh. He leaves behind a graphic account of the events:[102]

> Bhagat Singh proposed that revenge must be taken for the death of Lala Lajpat Rai, which was caused by lathi blows of the police. The person who first came forward was Rajguru and it was decided that the police officer responsible for Lalaji's demise would be shot. Rajguru was adamant that he be allowed to fire at the officer while Bhagat Singh's concern was that in case of an arrest, the person responsible should possess the quality of giving a passionate statement.

As Mohar mentions, the plot was not without some forward-thinking with Bhagat Singh's ideological views stamped on it:

> It was also discussed that in case the accused was to be executed, his behaviour at the time of hanging should be exemplary to impress the public so that there is no impression of the killing being the work of misguided youth. Instead, the act should garner respect for their passion so that more educated youth are encouraged to get involved in revolutionary work.

Rajguru, Bhagat Singh and Chandrashekhar Azad lined up to shoot Scott to avenge Lala Lajpat Rai's death. Another revolutionary, Jai Gopal, who later turned approver, was given the critical task of staking out the victim. Once he identified Scott, he was to give a signal. 'For four days the group marked Scott's office, but he was nowhere to be seen. Azad, a strict disciplinarian, turned down an impatient Rajguru's offer to go inside the building and shoot saying the plan must be followed.'

A backup plot was also put in place:

> It was decided that in case the police came out in Scott's aid, Sukhdev, Vijay Kumar Sinha and some other armed young men should be prepared to fight back. Suddenly, we saw a police officer coming out of the building. Jai Gopal indicated that it was perhaps Scott, but Bhagat Singh wasn't convinced and sent a signal back.

What followed was a misunderstanding of epic proportions – one that transformed the character of India's freedom struggle.

Rajguru thought that Bhagat Singh's gesture was to wait to let the man come forward before shooting him. A restless Rajguru though was not willing to delay and as the British officer put his foot on the pedal of his motorcycle, Rajguru shot him through his head. Bhagat Singh realizing that the deed was done also joined in and shot the man with his automatic pistol.

The act was unprecedented. A British police officer had been shot dead on Lahore's busy Mall Road. Hidden in the sensational news was a case of mistaken identity – instead of Officer Scott, the motley crew had shot and killed his deputy, John Saunders.

As people rushed out of the building in panic, British officer Furnace tried to engage Rajguru who attempted to shoot him, but his revolver got jammed. They both then engaged in a fight in which Rajguru got the better of Furnace, leaving him dead on the street. In the charged atmosphere, Channan Singh, Saunders's munshi, was also killed. Singh had tried to persuade the freedom fighters against the shooting, but Azad warned him by firing at his feet. This did not stop the munshi and, as he continued engaging, he was shot through the chest by Azad. After that, he along with Bhagat Singh and Rajguru were able to make good their escape. They ran through DAV College to the hostel where they had kept their bicycles and then calmly cycled down to Muzang, to the house they were staying in.

That night, the walls of Lahore were covered by posters declaring: 'Saunders is dead. Lala ji's death is avenged.'

The tricky question was where to hide the men. Bhagat Singh was already on the police watch and Rajguru had exposed himself. Danger lurked on every corner, and they needed to leave Lahore. The police was patrolling the streets, the intelligence network was on overdrive, and there were lookouts at both the railway station and the bus stand.

A new chapter began here, written by those who connected the dots of the Independence movement. A woman, Durga Devi – who would later become famous as Durga Bhabhi – came forward. It was with her help that Bhagat Singh escaped from Lahore. Singh's colleague Sukhdev Raj[103] writes, 'Bhagat Singh and I reached the house of Bhagwati Charan, Bhagat Singh by now was unrecognisable. He had shorn his hair and the kurta-pajama of a common villager had been replaced by a smart young man in pants and coat. His turban had been replaced by a hat.'[104] Incidentally, Bhagat Singh never wore a yellow turban as depicted in contemporary pictures; he always tied a white one.

Bhagwati Charan had a significant role to play in Bhagat Singh's evolution as a freedom fighter – the two were inseparable – and, in an environment where suspicion and consequences were two sides of the same coin, theirs was a brotherhood. After Saunders' murder, not only was Bhagat Singh given shelter in Bhagwati's house, but it was also his wife, Durga Devi, who accompanied Singh as he fled Lahore to Calcutta.

During that time, the police were active in what was known as the Meerut case. Lots of literature had been seized and, as Bhagwati Charan was a suspect, it was thought best that Bhagat Singh should leave Lahore and go to Calcutta, where there were other revolutionary friends. We told Durga Bhabhi about our problem. It was not sufficient that Bhagat Singh should change his appearance to leave Lahore, we wanted a lady to accompany him so that it appeared that a family was travelling together. After listening to our story, she not only gave Bhagat Singh money but also agreed to go with him so that he could get away from Lahore till matters calmed down.[105]

On a memorable day, a first-class coupé was booked for the 'couple'. At the Lahore railway station, a handsome, tall young man arrived – he was dressed in a coat and pants, and the outfit was completed by an overcoat to ward off the chill of Lahore's bitter winter. The man wore a hat and, on his lap, he held a small child. He was followed by a well-turned-out lady in a sari and shawl. The entourage was rounded up by a 'servant'. They went straight into the train's first-class compartment and sat there. The 'servant' after making them comfortable went and sat in a third-class compartment – he was Rajguru. Bhagat Singh and Rajguru, with Durga Bhabhi's help, thus fled Lahore. Meanwhile, Azad joined a Krishan kirtan mandali and, while singing bhajans such as '*Devakinandan Radheshyam Jai Raghunandan Jai Radheshyam*', he too exited Lahore.

In Calcutta, Durga Bhabhi handed over the responsibility of the freedom fighter to another young woman, Sushila, who was staying in the house of Sir Chajju Ram and was a tutor to his girls. Bhagat Singh joined the household as her 'nephew'. The Congress session was underway in the city and intelligence men had spread across its every nook. A whiff of danger and the 'nephew' would tumble into bed, unwell, with Sushila scattering medicine bottles around his bedside.

The great escape gave these protagonists a breather. In the takedown of the British Raj, this was, however, not even the intermission. They would return to Lahore to make what Bhagat Singh was to term a 'bigger explosion'. In the interim, under immense pressure, the Lahore police cracked down and began arresting people recklessly. Those who found themselves in jail had one thing in common: They were all young. Among them was Virendra.

6

Eye of the Tiger: Saunders and the First Imprisonment

Bhagat Singh, Rajguru and Chandrashekhar Azad left behind a city that, within hours, resembled a fortress. All the roads going out of Lahore were closed. Caught on the backfoot, an enraged Lahore Police tried making amends – patrolling the streets with a maniacal intensity. Local markets were teeming with men in khaki. Their suspicion – and anger – took them on another track and city colleges were put on a priority watchlist.

Saunders was assassinated at 4 p.m.; three hours later, as darkness descended on the late December evening, eighteen-year-old Virendra strolled out of his home. He had barely taken a few steps when two lorries came to a screeching halt next to him.

Police officers who had been sandwiched together tightly on the worn-out seats quickly disembarked and surrounded the house.

Taken aback, Virendra turned around and ran inside to inform his father – understanding, or so he thought, the reason for the police presence. At FC College, where he was still studying, Virendra was active in students' politics and the raid, he guessed, was a result of those activities. The authorities had something else on their mind, though. Onlookers had also started gathering in front of the house. A short while earlier, an officer had been shot. Now, the police had surrounded a house. To them, the correlation was clear.

Mahashay Krishan heard the commotion and rushed downstairs where Jenkins, a British officer, confronted him, while a posse of police officers stood around impatiently. Virendra came into full view just as Krishan was being questioned about the whereabouts of his son. Seeing him, Jenkins roared at his force to arrest him.

Two police officers held Virendra by his arms and another handcuffed him, leaving father and son speechless. In the chaos, all those in the room tried to get a voice in, staunchly vouching for Virendra's innocence. When Saunders was killed, Virendra was taking a college examination – a fact easily verified. Jenkins, however, was not interested in any explanation. Caught napping, he and his police force wanted the killers or scapegoats.

Virendra was missing for two hours between 3 and 5 p.m., snarled Jenkins, arresting the teenager. The family understood later that an employee, Shivnath Rai, who worked at *Pratap*, was a CID informer and had fed the intelligence some unfounded rumours. Rai's report was damning – it insinuated that Virendra had a hand in Saunders' shooting and, if not the actual shooter, he at the very least had information on the whereabouts of the killers. Virendra was handcuffed as the police searched the house, taking their time to meticulously sweep through the different floors. Two fraught hours had already passed by then.

An arrest was not unusual for the family. Several members had seen the inside of a jail during the Raj. But this was different – no one had been put in handcuffs before this. Boxes were searched and the store was ripped apart. Linen, clothes and provisions were all combed ruthlessly in the hunt for a murder weapon. Another three hours later, the police walked out, taking young Virendra, in shackles, with them.

He recounts:[106]

I would be dishonest if I said I was not scared. I was just 18 years old. It was the month of December, which is bitterly cold in Lahore. Inside the police lorry, two constables sat on either side. In front, sat Jenkins, who was glaring at me. I looked back towards my house, my father stood silently but my mother was wiping her tears. People were still gathered around the house, refusing to disperse even though the police had left with me. This was my first arrest and it was to change the course of my life. The vehicle kept moving around Lahore. I could not ask anyone where I was being taken. After some time, the vehicle came to a halt in front of an office. I was to learn it was the same office from where Saunders had emerged to be shot dead. The place was teeming with police officers. As I was taken out of the van, I observed that there was something coloured on the ground and the area was surrounded by four police officers. It was the same spot where Saunders had fallen after being shot and it probably was his blood.

Inside the building, Virendra's gaze locked on a familiar face – Avinash Bali, who had also been arrested. Shortly afterward, another revolutionary Ehsan Ilahi was escorted inside, and then three more young men were brought in, rounding up the solemn party.

Their handcuffs were taken off and the group was moved to a cold, dank room, where they were made to sit on a bench. In the next room, the fireplace was alight, but its warmth did not reach the young men. Time was passing, slowly. It was 2 a.m. and 'one by one, we were sent to another room, but no one returned'. Finally, it was Virendra's turn.

Six police officers sat stiffly around a table, including, two Indians – Rai Bahadur Bhagwan Das and Sardar Bahadur Sukha Singh. Jenkins, who had personally come to arrest Virendra, stood with his angry gaze fixed on the young man. Bhagwan Das broke the silence and addressed the young man. Quoting from the *Bhagwad Gita*, he lectured Virendra, 'A person should not lie even at the expense of losing their life.' The clock ticked another hour – it was 3 a.m. now and the crackling coal from the angeethis was the only other sound in the room.

After Rai Bahadur, it was Sardar Bahadur Sukha Singh's turn. His tone was threatening – if Virendra did not tell them what they wanted to know, he may not return home alive. His warning did not work, forcing Sukha Singh to become the good cop to his own bad cop. He next attempted reason: 'You are still a bachcha. If you are implicated your entire life will be ruined.' That did not get him the answer he desired either, so the police officer went for the jugular: 'Where did you get the pistol with which you shot Saunders and who all were with you when this happened?'

Despite the fluctuating tones and demeanours, Virendra remained unmoved. He was innocent, taking his college exams, he repeated over and over again. His attendance, he told the investigators, could easily be proved by college authorities. Sukha Singh barked back that they had proof of Virendra's involvement in the shooting. 'You came to the spot after finishing your exam,' he declared. Repeat a lie often enough and it becomes the truth seemed to be Sukha Singh's mantra. Virendra's interrogation was in Urdu until Bhagwan Das interjected sharply in English, 'He will not speak out this way.' It was a signal to Jenkins, who slapped Virendra with force. This was the first of many beatings.

Virendra writes:[107]

I knew of a person who was aware of the details of the murder but did not have information on who had fired the shot that killed Saunders. I was in the know-how that something explosive was going to happen but that is as much as I knew, when and the where was not communicated to me. Both Durga Das Khanna and Hans Raj Vohra had indicated to me that revenge was being planned for Lala Lajpat Rai's murder. The police would have let me go if I had named them. But the revolutionary party had a strict code – we were told to confine ourselves to what was being instructed and unnecessary questions were not welcome. Each one of us was told only as much as was required. Therefore, I also did not try to find out what the plan for the badla was.

The police was obviously desperate to implicate Virendra or another suspect through him, and his lack of a response was not going down well.[108]

> Jenkins would have none of it. He kicked me on the right shin with the spike of his army shoe, as if he were kicking in a football goal. It was done with so much force that I screamed. But he was not done. Now he pulled me up by my hair and asked where I had hidden the pistol that killed Saunders. When I again insisted that I had no knowledge [of the pistol], he slapped me hard again. I slumped down. After the beating, it became difficult for me to even stand up. They must have thought that it was sufficient for the day and ordered for me to be taken away. The person who gave this instruction was, I think, Scott, the man who was the original target but instead Saunders was murdered.

Back in handcuffs, Virendra was taken to a police van, which resumed, at a snail's pace, what had by now become its customary rounds of the city. Finally, it stopped at Police Lines. It was 4 a.m. by then. Virendra was given a gunny mat to sleep on the floor and two filthy blankets to cover himself with. They did not help much – irrespective, he could not have slept even if the winter chill was not seeping into his bones. Virendra's leg was throbbing painfully and he couldn't close his eyes even briefly.

The next morning, at 11 a.m., Jenkins confronted Virendra again. The young man expected another round of thrashing, but the police officer was marginally restrained and merely pulled on Virendra's hair. After a few minutes, the British police officer asked, 'Would you like to go home?'

When Virendra nodded, Jenkins replied, 'We will take you home.'

Handcuffed and back in a police van, Virendra waited, not knowing where he would end up next. After thirty minutes, they stopped in front of Mahashay Krishan's residence, where Jenkins disembarked and strode into the house. Seated inside the lorry and surrounded by police officers, Virendra saw several vehicles parked in front of his house and a mob milling around. The news of his arrest and imprisonment had made it to the newspapers, and friends of his father, from Lahore and beyond, had gathered in support of the family. Virendra was in custody not for an article written or words spoken. He was accused of grave charges – the murder of a serving British officer – which could result in the death penalty. At 41, Nisbet Road, despondency and fear felt like two dancers outdoing each other.

Jenkins entered the house. Without a perfunctory greeting, he went straight to the point. The house was to be searched again. Who could stop him? Virendra was led out of the van, his bruised face and body visible not just to his family but also the throngs of people gathered outside. Krishan kept calm, his expression not flickering, and told his son to do the same. 'All will be well,' he whispered to him.

Jenkins started his search on the ground floor. First was Virendra's room and his almirah was ransacked but other than books and clothes, much to the police's chagrin, nothing incriminating was found. After almost ninety minutes spent in that room, Jenkins and his men moved on. Virendra's disconcerted mother sat on a charpoy on the first floor, surrounded by other women. Not as strong as her husband, she fainted upon seeing her son's condition.

The police, brainwashed by their informer Shivnath Rai, or plain desperate by then, refused to confront the possibility that with no proof in sight, they had got the wrong man. After wasting several hours, Jenkins and his team left. This time, along with Virendra, a domestic help working for the family was also forcibly taken into the van. Once again, after doing the rounds of Lahore, the vehicle stopped outside a police station. Virendra was escorted to a small cell, which was to be his home for the next month. Like the previous night, a mat to sleep on the floor and two foul-smelling blankets were disdainfully thrown his way. A utensil in one corner to answer nature's call was an addition.

The room itself was airless and absolutely no light could filter through. The cell had a heavy steel door, effectively barricading him inside, and the only window opened into another cell – but the grille on it discouraged any camaraderie between prisoners. In any case, there was no one on the other side. There was a small bulb in the cell that Virendra kept switched on through the dark hours. The son of one of Punjab's most prominent editors could never have imagined this night. In his first few hours in the cell, Virendra learned that punishment could take different forms. Sleep was forbidden and he was repeatedly called into Jenkins' office. Keeping him awake through the night was to become a new normal of his incarceration.

Food was brought from a tandoor near the police station. The steel door was opened long enough for his meal and water to be slid through, and then he was once again left in the company of his thoughts and an agonizing uncertainty. For the next thirty days, he was not permitted to even comb his hair, let alone taking a bath. Being allowed to change into fresh clothes a couple of times and a clean blanket sent from home was the extent of Jenkins' generosity. Even as the temperature plunged, nothing changed. Virendra still had only a mat on the icy stone floor to lie on.

From across the window, a twenty-four-hour vigil was kept on him. Through the night, he would be prodded with a stick and repeatedly provoked about Saunders' murder: 'Babu, tell us from where you learned how to fire a pistol? You are an amazing shooter. With the first bullet, you shot sahib dead.' Shifts changed every four hours and the new policeman, refreshed, continued from where the last left, devotedly waking Virendra up to needle him with similar questions and hoping to catch him in an unguarded moment.

As the days merged in solitude, despair took over. Not murdering Saunders, he began to think, may not be enough for his freedom; he was beginning to understand the futility of 'innocent until proven guilty' in the British rulebook. The colonial rulers were baying for blood and Virendra was aware that someone would be hanged for the shooting – and it could even be him.

His thoughts that day were broken by the dominating presence of Jenkins. Before the officer could pull Virendra up by his hair, the prisoner rose quickly from the floor. 'How are you?' asked Jenkins, but it was mere rhetoric since he answered himself, 'Feeling fine.' Virendra stood by not uttering a word. 'Let me take you for a walk,' said the Britisher.

Virendra's handcuffs were taken off and he followed Jenkins to a nearby hall – even for this short walk, armed police officers surrounded him. A few men were already in the hall when they entered and Virendra was asked to stand with them. This was to be an identity parade. Soon, a group of men were escorted in. They could not recognize any of them and, to Jenkins' disappointment, left. His entire case against Virendra depended on witnesses identifying him and it had just fallen apart. After that day, Virendra did not see Jenkins but he remained in lock-up.

The police did not give up, though. One night, he was back in the van which stopped at a police thana near the railway station. On entering, Virendra saw his friend Avinash Bali lying on the ground. Both men were disturbed to see the other's dishevelled state, but, for once, they were left alone. The night passed with them exchanging notes on imprisonment and, the next morning, Virendra was taken back to his cell. Why was he taken there for a night? The question perplexed him. The answer wasn't long in coming. The lock-up's wall had deep holes. On the other side were police officers with their ears glued to the wall, listening in on his and Bali's conversation until dawn. Jenkins' luck didn't turn, for neither had anything to disclose about Saunders' murder.

In his one month in jail, Virendra had no visitors from outside. An application by Dr Gokul Chand Narang, a prominent lawyer, for permission to meet him was declined. His father approached the high court for bail but a deputy inspector general of the police swore on the Bible, testifying to Virendra's involvement. As expected, there was no evidence and, finally, Virendra glimpsed freedom. But it was not cheap. He was released on a bail of Rs 50,000 – a fortune in 1929. Thirty days after his arrest, Virendra returned home. He was unrecognizable – unkempt and unshaven, with scruffy hair. The changes were, however, not just in the physical appearance.

Delighted to have their son back, his parents heaved a sigh of relief. Their suffering had been intense and Virendra's mother feared not seeing her son ever again. His father had lost sleep, but it was not just over his son's arrest. Another thought was needling him. He told one of his friends:[109]

> Virendra may never come back but I am worried about another thing. He is young and arrested for the first time. He will be tortured and may be made to sign on false documents. But it will be worse if he turns approver. We will then have nowhere to hide. We will not be able to face the public. If it is destined that he is to be hanged then he will shine in history.

It did not come to either of the two dismal scenarios that Mahashay Krishan feared. The police could not break the young man's spirit but the naïve, idealistic lad who had been jailed was gone – and in his stead, a hardened revolutionary emerged.

7

Romancing the Future: Making the Deaf Hear

The December of 1928, while Virendra was in jail, Lala Lajpat Rai's death loomed large over the Congress's annual session in Calcutta. The young Turks within the party were on edge and there was a loud chorus demanding a call for complete independence. On the other hand, away from the clamour but equally agitated, revolutionaries like Bhagat Singh and Chandrashekhar Azad who were affiliated only to their own movement chipped away, underground. These two parallel tracks on occasion merged and were branded together as 'extremists.'

Moderates, on the other hand, wanted to go slow and create an environment for self-rule that would eventually force the colonialists to leave. Before long, matters came to a head. Leaders like Gandhi and Motilal Nehru – the latter was presiding over the 1928 session – insisted it was not the right time to ask for absolute sovereignty. Gandhi said he was against making a move where the chances of doubling back were high. The first step was the allocation of Dominion status to India within two years. In this, he failed to read the sentiments of a young brigade led by Jawaharlal Nehru and Subhas Chandra Bose.

Jawaharlal Nehru's opposition brought him into open conflict with his father, whom he called a man of 'strong feelings' and 'strong passions'.

> Having cast his lot with the Moderates, Father took an aggressive line. Most of the Extremists, apart from a few leaders in Bengal and Poona, were young men, and it irritated him to find that these youngsters dared to go their own way. Impatient and intolerant of opposition, and not suffering people whom he considered fools, he gladly pitched into them and hit out whenever he could. I remember I think it was after I left Cambridge, reading an article of his which annoyed me greatly. I wrote him rather an impertinent letter in which I suggested that no doubt the British government was greatly pleased with his political activities. This was just the kind of suggestion which would make him wild, and he was very angry. He almost thought of asking me to return from England immediately.[110]

'Motilal was still inclined to treat his son (who was now 32 years of age) as an impetuous school-boy,'[111] historian Sarvepalli Gopal writes in his book *Jawaharlal Nehru*. He paints a picture of the Nehru patriarch as being patiently indulgent of his son, while keeping a check on Jawaharlal's thoughts in the early years of his son's association with the Congress.

Nehru writes of his own relationship with his father:[112]

> Father had been closely watching my growing drift towards Extremism, my continual criticism of the politics of talk, and my insistent demand for action. What action it should be was not clear, and sometimes Father imagined that I was heading straight for the violent courses ... I was not attracted that way, but the idea that we must not tamely submit to existing conditions and that something must be done began to obsess me more and more.

In Calcutta, the older generation advised caution. It had witnessed past uprisings ruthlessly silenced by the British and didn't want another setback for the demoralized public. Gandhi, though, was treading a fine line and he was aware of it – if Jawaharlal Nehru and Subhas Chandra Bose were not satisfied, there was a possibility of them walking out of the Congress, along with an exodus of the young Turks in the party. The leader was in a bind: Without anything tangible and demonstrative by the party, those not averse to violence could go out of control. As it is, under Chandrashekar Azad's leadership, the revolutionaries' restlessness had made them fearless.

Before doing any damage control for the party, Gandhi had one important task before him. He had to build a bridge between a father and a son. The Congress would then be able to save its self-respect and send a message to the British. Matters were, however, taken out of his hands. The differences between Motilal and Jawaharlal Nehru reached a crisis point, and it all unfolded publicly.

The Nehru patriarch was a much-revered leader, who had taken a vow of austerity and openly burned his furniture, clothes and other foreign possessions.[113] By doing away with any remains of his bourgeois upbringing, including giving up his hugely successful law practice, he was the only notable leader to support – after much introspection – the Gandhi-led non-cooperation resolution.[114]

As Motilal Nehru was explaining the merits of settling for Dominion status at the Congress congregation in Calcutta in December, a loud voice interrupted his speech. 'I challenge,' shouted Jawaharlal. It was not the first time that father and son had locked horns openly – their roles in the nationalist movement, at least initially, were far from complementary. But during the 1928 session, the strain in their relations was palpable to all. In Jawaharlal Nehru's words, there had been differences of opinion earlier, '... But I do not think that at any previous or subsequent occasion the tension had been so great.'[115]

Motilal Nehru looked up from the stage and smiled at his son's impetuosity. He did not argue. Extraneous events soon overtook the gentlemanly arguments of political leaders.

The public was keenly following two developments. In Meerut, young men in custody were on trial for a conspiracy to overthrow the British government.[116] Simultaneously, the government had presented the controversial Public Safety Bill, giving it sweeping powers to arrest without the provision of an appeal. The Congress vehemently opposed it; the party claimed it was timed with the ongoing trial in Meerut and could adversely impact the fate of the accused. The Bill's sinister clause was its retrospective stipulations and the party pressed for its complete withdrawal. If not, it asked for the Bill to be deferred at least till the closure of the Meerut trial. Its demands in the Assembly made no headway – the government was adamant that it was not going to dilute the powers of the Bill. The Assembly eventually rejected the proposal but if the Indian leaders assumed they had won this round and could breathe easy, they were mistaken. The goalpost had been changed and, using his special powers, the Viceroy Lord Irwin gave his approval.[117] The date was set, the new Bill was to be announced in the Assembly on 8 April 1929. This decade was exacting every ounce from the Indians.

Opposition came from an unexpected quarter – at least for the British. Speaker Vithalbhai Patel, Sardar Patel's elder brother, was a formidable politician and he had decided that the unlawful measure would not be announced on his watch. Patel was going to use all his powers to block the Public Safety Bill, and a confrontation between the government and the speaker looked imminent.

While the Congress was engaged in the political back and forth, unknown to its leaders, a revolutionary group Hindustan Socialist Republican Association had already prepared its response. A plan was in place: Bhagat Singh and Batukeshwar Dutt were to lob harmless smoke bombs in the Assembly to coincide with the passing of the Bill. They would also throw in pamphlets to explain their actions.

It was nearing 10 a.m. and Bhagat Singh along with Dutt took their seats in the visitors' gallery. Both were dressed in shorts and Singh wore his now trademark hat – a residue of the Saunders' killing. It was after the killing of Saunders that the revolutionary cut his long hair and shorn his beard to go incognito. The two men looked around keenly – it was of utmost importance that no Indian be hurt when they hurled the bombs.

Their particular concern was for the venerable speaker, Vithalbhai Patel – although that morning, it was Pandit Motilal Nehru who led a line of stalwarts in the Assembly. They all had to be protected. Among those also present was a name the Indians disliked immensely: Sir John Allsebrook Simon of the infamous Simon Commission had made his way to the Assembly. The visitors' gallery was packed, and a heated exchange of words between the government and pillars of the Congress party was to be the highlight of the day.

Instead, there were fireworks – quite literally.

Sir George Schuster stood up to announce on behalf of the government that the Viceroy, using his special powers, had given acceptance to the Bill rejected by the Assembly. This was their cue. Bhagat Singh rose from his seat and threw a smoke bomb at the wall behind Schuster. Batukeshwar Dutt tossed another harmless bomb just after him and, as two explosions reverberated in the hall below, pandemonium broke out. In a panic, people crawled under the benches and escape for the two men looked possible. They were, however, not interested and had other ideas. Rooted to their seats, they shouted, 'Inquilab Zindabad', and 'Down with Imperialism.' This was the moment the slogan 'Inquilab Zindabad' captured the public imagination – it is also famous as

Bhagat Singh's last words. Till now, 'Bharat Mata ki Jai' or 'Vande Mataram' were the collective refrains of a nation subjugated.

As the two men showered pamphlets from the gallery, there was no change in the tempo of the slogan chanting – they were shouting so loudly that they could be heard outside the Assembly. 'A loud explosion is required to make the deaf hear': The writings on the pamphlets were inspired by words of French anarchist Auguste Vaillant,[118] who had thrown a bomb on the French Chamber of Deputies in 1893.[119]

Prominent Indian leaders condemned the action and called it a terrorist act. Singh and Dutt were hardly two reckless pirates sailing in the night – the act with the harmless bombs was as much about the journey as it was about the destination. They had the ears of the 'deaf' dispensation:

> … on behalf of the helpless Indian masses, we want to emphasise the lesson often repeated by history that it is easy to kill individuals, but you cannot kill ideas that crush great empires. Empires crumble but ideas survive. Bourbons and Czars fell while revolutions marched triumphantly ahead. We are sorry to admit that we who attach so great sanctity to human life, who dream of a glorious future when man will be enjoying perfect peace and full liberty, have been forced to shed human blood. But the sacrifice of the individuals at the altar of the great revolution that will bring freedom to all rendering exploitation of man by man impossible, is inevitable. Long Live the Revolution.[120]

The leaflets were signed 'Balraj' – a pseudonym widely believed to be used by Bhagat Singh.

As chaos unfolded around them, the two men didn't move from their seats. Finally, an English officer gathered his courage and moved closer to them; they promptly assured him that he was safe. The duo had done their job and detailed reasons for their actions would be presented in court. Emboldened, the officer then called some constables and the two revolutionaries were arrested.

It was a symbolic bombing, Bhagat Singh and Batukeshwar Dutt's unprecedented act made not just The Hindustan Socialist Republican Association but also revolutionaries, mainstream. The low-intensity explosions reverberated loudly, both at home and abroad. Two young men not only threw bombs in the Central Assembly but also stood their ground, defiantly refusing to escape. Their message might as well have been painted in bright red on the walls of the Assembly: Time for the British Raj was running out. While the venerated leaders were advocating patience and peaceful resistance, the youth had shown that they were willing to shed or take blood in the name of freedom.

The leaders were mistaken in their belief that the revolutionaries' actions were simply mindless violence – there was nothing further from the truth. It was a well-thought-out plan with Bhagat Singh's ideological leanings stamped on the political pamphlets and, as the public got their hands on them, the content became as sensational as the feat itself.

Dutt was in the Parliament Street lock-up in Delhi when a well-dressed man passed him, saying, 'Young man, today you have made history.' The rising sentiment did not convince all – many Congress members openly disapproved of the bomb throwing and Motilal Nehru issued a statement: 'All sensible men must condemn the outrage perpetrated in the Assembly Chamber.' The widespread criticism did not shake the revolutionaries' resolve.

The story of Bhagat Singh was to continue till its tragic denouement.

Indian revolutionaries led a life less ordinary; their deaths were no different. Caught and jailed, or executed, the path was bravely trodden – many like Bhagat Singh walked to the noose smiling. He though was the odd man out; for most revolutionaries, killing Saunders to avenge a nationalist leader's death would have been seen as a life well lived. His comrades wanted Singh to flee the country or, at the very least, live permanently outside Punjab for the intentions of the British were clear – hanging him would be their obvious response. Singh was not delusional; he knew that yet another daring repeat would be his death knell.

He did exactly that. The revolutionary went to the Assembly, threw the smoke bombs and the rest, as they say, is history, worth several books and sequels. Killing or throwing a bomb was not the goal – a revolution created by conspicuous sacrifice was his underlying message and it had to be explained in such a way that ordinary people could understand. This, Bhagat Singh sensed only he could do by fusing individual heroism with group ideology. Thinking equally with his heart and his head, this syncretism is reflected in the intellectual ideas he bequeathed: The day people became revolutionaries, revolution, Bhagat Singh insisted, will knock on the door.

The bombs were thrown on 8 April 1929. On 4 June that year, Bhagat Singh and Dutt were sentenced to life imprisonment. While Dutt had a lawyer, Singh, with the aid of a legal adviser, argued the case himself. The joint statement made in court is a classic document – a timeless testament of remarkable courage, patriotism and intellect. Some sections of the testimony read out by noted lawyer Asif Ali are worth recalling.[121]

> When we were told by some of the police officers who visited us in the jail that Lord Irwin in his address to the joint session of the two Houses described the event as an attack directed against no individual but against an institution itself, we realised the true significance of the incident has been correctly appreciated. We are next to none in our love for humanity. Far from having any malice against any individual we hold human life sacred beyond words. We are neither perpetrators of dastardly outrages and therefore a disgrace to the country as the pseudo-socialist Diwan Chamanlal is reported to have described us, nor are we 'lunatics' as the *Tribune* of Lahore and some others would have us believe.
> We humbly claim to be no more than serious students of the history and conditions of our country in her aspirations. We despise hypocrisy. Our practical protest was against the institution which since its birth has eminently helped to display not only its worthlessness but its far-reaching power of mischief ... Time and again the national demand

has been pressed by the people's representative only to find the wastepaper basket as its final destination. We dropped the bomb on the floor of the Assembly Chamber to register a protest on behalf of those who had no other means left to give expression to their heart-rending agony. Our sole purpose was 'to make the deaf hear' and to give the headless a timely warning ... from under the seeming stillness of the sea of Indian humanity a veritable storm is about to break out. We have only hoisted the dangerous signal to warn those who are speeding along without heeding the grave dangers ahead. We have only marked the end of an era of utopian non-violence of whose futility the rising generation has been convinced beyond doubt. We have used the expression 'utopian non-violence' which requires some explanation. Force when aggressively applied is violence and it is therefore morally unjustifiable. But when it is used in the furtherance of a legitimate cause it has its moral justification ...[122]

The judge asked Bhagat Singh his definition of revolution. His response not only clears all doubts about the intersection of Singh's philosophy, ideology and commitment, but also vindicates the shelf life a martyr enjoys. Importantly, it also scratches the surface to lay bare the essence of a man idly romanticized.[123]

A revolution does not necessarily involve sanguinary strife nor is there any place in it for individual vendetta. It is not the cult of the bomb and the pistol. By revolution, we mean that the present order of things which is based on manifest injustice, must change. Producers or labourers despite being the most necessary element of society are robbed by their exploiters of the fruits of their labour and deprived of their elementary rights ... These terrible inequalities and forced disparity of chances are bound to lead to chaos. This situation cannot last long, and it is obvious that the present order of society is on the brink of a volcano. The whole edifice of this civilization if not saved in time, shall crumble. A radical change therefore is necessary, and it is the duty of those who realise it to reorganise society on a socialistic basis. Unless this is done and the exploitation of man by man and of nations by nations is brought to an end, the sufferings and carnage with which humanity is threatened today cannot be prevented. All talk of ending war and ushering in an era of universal peace is undisguised hypocrisy. We have given a fair and loud warning. Revolution is an inalienable right of mankind. Freedom is an imperishable birthright of all. Labour is the real sustainer of society. The sovereignty of the people is the ultimate destiny of the workers.

The underground network was shrouded in secrecy and it was far from easy for the revolutionary movement to become a popular crusade. Only core members had an insight into the thoughts of these fearless men. Bhagat Singh and Batukeshwar Dutt's statement brought them out of the shadows, and forced the public to think outside the box. By spelling out a future roadmap, where economic and social justice, and freedom from man-made binaries were supreme, they made a country look further than its daily dose of colonialism. As the HRSA elaborated, 'The Revolution will ring the death knell of capitalism and class distinction and privileges ... It will give birth to a new state – a new social order.'[124]

The two revolutionaries became heroes; the youth idolised them and cries of 'Bhagat Singh Zindabad' and 'Batukeshwar Dutt Zindabad' echoed not just in Punjab. The bombing of the Assembly also had an impact at an intellectual level – 'revolution' made it to the lexicon of the public and an understanding of its need crept in. The editor of the Urdu newspaper *Zamindar*, Zafar Ali Khan, recited a poem at a gathering in Lahore:

Shaheedane watan ke khoon-e-nahak ka jo sat nikle, to uske zarra zarra se Bhagat Singh aur Dutt nikle (Bhagat Singh and Dutt will come out from every particle of the truth that comes out of the blood of the killings of the martyrs of the homeland).

The two prisoners were given life imprisonment of twenty years each. Outside the jail walls, their hold on the country finally breached the last bastion – it made the Congress sit up and realize that the die was cast. Leaders of the independence movement understood it was time to push the agitation's pace or they risked losing control not just of events but also popular support.

Dutt was released shortly before Independence. Long years of imprisonment took a heavy toll on his health and, in his later years, he was constantly unwell. Shortly before he passed, he visited Virendra in Jalandhar for a few days with his family. 'A more soft-spoken man I have yet to come across; far from the image of the bomb-throwing, fire-breathing revolutionary that I had in my mind,' Virendra's elder son Lalit Mohan remembers his surprise. 'Shortly after India became free, Dutt was given a truck permit by the Bihar government. A man without qualms could make good money out of this scrap of paper. Dutt could not. So, he died in penury, unable to compromise with a system that he could only view with disgust.'

It is hard to find men like these today when India's freedom struggle is itself losing relevance.

A few weeks before he died, Dutt asked for a meeting and it was with none other than Bhagat Singh's mother, Vidyavati. The elderly lady came and lovingly placed the ailing revolutionary's head in her lap. She remembered what her son had said to her days before he was hanged, 'I will now have to go but, in Dutt, I will leave a part of me with you.'

Dutt breathed his last on 20 July 1965. Vidyavati lost not just another son, but the only remaining connection to her son was forever broken now. Dutt had expressed a desire to be cremated at Hussainiwala on the banks of the river Sutlej, where the bodies of his three comrades, Bhagat Singh, Rajguru and Sukhdev, were hastily consigned to flames by the British thirty-four years ago – after villagers rushed in, the charred remains of the three martyrs were retrieved and given a fitting cremation on the banks of the Ravi. Vidyavati accompanied the body from Delhi – where Dutt had died – and, on the banks of the Sutlej, bordering Pakistan, in a voice choked with emotion, she said, 'You four have got together. Now send for me to join you.'

8
India Calling: Home, They Brought Her Warrior Dead

In *Veh Inquilabi Din,* Virendra writes, 'Between 1928 and 1932, the young men who came forward contributed to the freedom movement with their blood. Some were hanged, the police shot some and some gave up their life through hunger strikes. One such brave man was Jatindra Das.'

From Delhi, Bhagat Singh and Batukeshwar Dutt were moved to Lahore. What they saw at Lahore Central Jail and Central Jail Mianwali pushed their bigger fight for India's independence to the backburner and, eventually, that trajectory coalesced with their mission. The treatment of prisoners was barbaric – they noted how even animals were better off. Not the kind of men who looked the other way when there was injustice meted out to anyone, the two revolutionaries began a prolonged hunger strike. Their demand was not just better conditions for political prisoners, they asked for parity with European detainees.

The two were still on a hunger strike when legal proceedings in the Lahore Conspiracy Case – that led to Bhagat Singh, Rajguru and Sukhdev's execution – commenced on 10 July 1929. As days passed and Bhagat Singh weakened, he was carried on a stretcher to court. Even in his emaciated state, jail authorities put shackles on both his feet.[125] Eventually, he was too weak to come to court and the trial went on in absentia.

The British could be overwhelmingly mulish even when history was repeating itself. Ignoring its past experiences of mass movements, the administration brazenly blustered it out over an ultimatum to improve jail conditions. Three days later, matters came to a head, and all undertrials in the Lahore Conspiracy Case joined Bhagat Singh and Dutt in their hunger strike. Among them was Jatindra Nath Das, a member of the Hindustan Republican Socialist Association (HRSA) and the man assigned to make bombs for Bhagat Singh.[126]

Like pouring oil into burning flames, the movement spread rapidly across the country. Political prisoners united in protest by going on a hunger strike across Indian jails, and Motilal Nehru and his son, Jawaharlal, visited the accused in the Lahore Conspiracy Case in court. The men were being tried even as they abstained from eating and, this time, the Congress readily passed a resolution in their support.

The prisoners' health deteriorated, but they were adamant that theirs was a fast unto death unless political detainees were treated in a more humane manner. Life then had as much meaning as death – and for some freedom fighters, even less.

This time, the Raj finally blinked. It appointed a committee, including two Congress members, to investigate prisoners' grievances and promised to implement its recommendations. After a meeting, the committee requested prisoners to withdraw from their hunger strike. The report was still pending and, if unsatisfied, they could restart the fast. On 2 September 1929, the prisoners broke their fast.

Except, Jatindra Nath Das. The status quo lasted barely two days. The recommendations of the Congress members were not agreed to and, on 4 September, Bhagat Singh and others resumed fasting.

Jatindra Nath Das's health declined dramatically, his vital organs were shutting down one after the other and doctors were blunt in their assessment – he had to give up his hunger strike or he would die. Das refused. Jail authorities tried to force-feed him: 'Seven persons held Jatin down, four for the two legs, one each for the arms, and one to hold the head in position. When Jatin was held flat on the bed, a tube was thrust through his nostrils down through the food pipe. Milk was poured through a funnel.'[127] An eyewitness account by Premdatta Verma, a Lahore Conspiracy Case co-accused further testifies on how, despite his weakening state, Das was no pushover. 'With a sputtering coughing, he diverted the milk and took it out from his mouth.'[128]

Das could not be persuaded and it fell on Bhagat Singh to convince the dying revolutionary to eat – a request that put him in a bind. Sitting silently next to his semi-conscious comrade, the legendary freedom fighter debated whether to ask Das to give up his pledge or stay silent. Both men were similar – not only did life not hold any attraction, sacrifice was also a yearning. Gaining some courage, Bhagat Singh said gently, 'We all must go one day. Instead of dying like this, why not die fighting? If we live, we may be able to achieve something. Dying by hunger strike may not achieve much.'[129] Jatindra Nath Das took lime water on Bhagat Singh's bidding and after that told him sternly not to ask again. Others also tried to reason but, despite his deteriorating health, the revolutionary was unmoved. After that day, no other attempt was made to coerce or persuade him to end his hunger strike.

Virendra and Kiron Das were close friends. The news of his brother's hunger strike brought Kiron Das down to Lahore from Calcutta, where he was allowed to meet with Jatindra Nath Das daily. After that, every evening, Kiron met Virendra, who asked the brother to reason with Jatin Das to not waste his life like this. But the young man from Bengal knew – if there was a choice between a dignified death and a life of ignominy, his brother would choose the former. 'Virendra bhai,' Kiron Das told him, you do not know the mitti Bhagat Singh, Chandrashekhar Azad, my brother and their comrades are made of. Life has no value for them if it cannot be used for the service of the motherland. Otherwise, why would they invite death? Bhagat Singh could easily have led a comfortable life. If my brother valued his life, he would not have started his fast. They all have a supreme aim; they will live and die for the same.'[130] Virendra did not bring up the topic again.

As a non-violent means of civil disobedience, a hunger strike awakens interest organically and, more importantly, sustains public imagination – unlike other forms of protests. It hits at the fundamental core of a human being – this form of dissent, if it is done for the right reason, is potent. At the centre of it is one person and their determination, which paradoxically becomes stronger as their body weakens, as in the case of Jatindra Nath Das.

The concept of fasting as a political tool of protest and resistance no longer holds the same meaning today – its overuse in contemporary India has diluted the character that historical giants used it for. In the history of fasts, Mahatma Gandhi is a front runner, undertaking hunger strikes as many as fifteen times as a weapon against the British Raj. He also used it in support of the 'untouchables' as well as for Hindu–Muslim unity.

Historian Mridula Mukherjee categorizes hunger strikes in pre-Partition India into two camps:[131]

> India and Ireland are the main countries where hunger strike has been used as a weapon over the centuries … One form of protest was employed by revolutionaries like Bhagat Singh, Jatin Das and Chandrashekhar Azad while in jail, to protest their treatment. Then there is the Gandhian tradition [where] he employed fast[s] as a means of expressing his strong feelings on any subject – whether as a protest or a refusal to obey. As Louis Fischer said, 'A fast was a means of reaching out to the mass of people.' It is not a weapon that can be used by all and sundry. Firstly, [they] must [have] a very high moral standing in society so that the threat to that person becomes a threat to society.

The scenario that Mridula Mukherjee mentions was unfolding in Lahore. As the government saw the writing on the wall, Jatindra Nath Das's younger brother Kiron Das was contacted. The Raj did not want to be held responsible for the death. Kiron was to arrange for his brother's bail to secure his release. He was made of the same mettle as his elder brother, and Kiron flatly refused. It was to be an unconditional release, he said, otherwise so be it – a death in prison. An almost comatose Jatindra Das also gestured to his brother against arranging any bail. It was a family of warriors; their father also sent an urgent message from Calcutta. His instructions were no different: Under no condition should his son be released on bail.

Desperate times call for desperate measure. Backed into a corner by the family's refusal, the government propped up two people to stand bail for Jatindra. A furious Kiron warned the Raj – the government would be responsible if his brother died while being released against his and his family's will. In desperation, the authorities tried to force-feed Jatindra Nath Das again, but things went wrong and a body that had resisted nutrition for so long went into shock. Sixty-three days after he went on a hunger strike, on 13 September 1929, Jatindra Nath Das, cradled in Bhagat Singh's lap and surrounded by comrades singing his favourite Rabindranath Tagore and Nazrul Islam songs, breathed his last. He was only twenty-four.

Bhagat Singh broke his fast on 5 October 1929. His hunger strike had lasted 110 days.

Autumn was peeking from behind the mountains when Virendra went on a short break to Shimla. Even in the lap of the hill station, he found no solitude and was shadowed without a break by the police. The arrangement was foolproof, or so the police thought. Whenever Virendra boarded a train at Lahore railway station, a constable followed a few steps behind, dutifully relaying travel plans to the station of destination, where the local police would take over. It was the same story in Shimla – on the flip side, the assigned constable on a rare occasion would come out of the shadow and almost forge if not a friendship, at least a relationship of mutual respect!

Shimla was an important town – it had offices of both the central and Punjab government, and news on Jatindra Nath's condition was being regularly conveyed there. On a September afternoon, Virendra was strolling on the Mall Road with noted journalist Chaman Lal Bhikshu when the friendly police officer came up quietly to Virendra and whispered in his ear that Jatindra Nath Das had passed away. Asked how he knew, the officer replied that the police had been alerted to stop any untoward happenings in the aftermath of the revolutionary's death. A call to the United Press of India office in Lahore confirmed the news. Virendra was also informed that Kiron was preparing to take his martyred brother's body to Calcutta via Delhi. Virendra immediately decided to head for Delhi, but it was easier said than done. He needed police permission to go anywhere that was not routine.

Virendra was in a predicament – he could not betray the police officer who had informed him of the death as the man would lose his job. After mulling it over, the revolutionary notified his shadow that he was leaving by the evening train for Kalka, on the way to Lahore. This piece of information promptly reached where it was meant to. Four hours after the journey started, the train inexplicably stopped three kilometres before the Kalka station. After a few words to Chaman Lal to stay in the train till the station from where the journalist could catch the Kalka Mail for Delhi, Virendra noiselessly got down. With a bag in his hand, he walked along the dark railway track till he reached the Kalka station. Then, he put the second part of his plan into action. Instead of boarding the train to Lahore, Virendra climbed into a compartment of Kalka Mail to Delhi and lay down quietly in an upper berth.

Meanwhile, there was panic on the Lahore train. It was searched thoroughly from one end to the other after the police failed to spot Virendra alighting at Kalka. The search expanded to the Delhi train, which was stationary on another platform, but such was the intensity of the hunt that no one bothered to even glance at the upper berths! Undetected, Virendra reached Delhi.

The Lahore police, on the other hand, were proactive. They had already made the by-now-familiar drive to Mahashay Krishan's residence. The men in khaki wanted to know how the revolutionary had left Shimla but not reached Lahore, and Virendra got an earful from his father when he did get home eventually!

At the Delhi railway station, things were running behind schedule and the Lahore train was delayed by almost six hours. The platform was swarming with familiar men from the CID, and Virendra shuffled unobtrusively into a corner of the waiting room and fell asleep. By the time, the train carrying the body of Jatindra Nath Das arrived, the platform was bursting with mourners.

Delhi had come out to pay homage to the fallen hero and the train station began echoing with slogans of 'Jatindra Nath Das Zindabad'.

As the train came to a whistling stop, a mob rushed towards the compartment where the martyr's body was placed in a wooden coffin. Kiron Das stood at the entrance with folded hands and, in a crowd of thousands, Virendra found it difficult to reach the compartment. Kiron, however, saw him and immediately climbed down from the train. Tearfully, the two friends hugged and the younger Das led Virendra to where the body lay.

Virendra remembers every corner of the compartment covered with flowers – they were tributes paid by emotional citizens on Jatindra Nath Das's last journey home. Seated next to his body were Sardar Kishan Singh, Bhagat Singh's father, Bhagwati Charan's wife, Durga Bhabhi, and Avinash Bali. They were all travelling to Calcutta, as were thousands of emotional men and women on the train. When Virendra said, 'I don't know whether to commiserate with you or to congratulate you on being the brother of a martyr', Kiron immediately replied, 'This is no time for sentimentality. Today, we are immensely proud. If he wanted, my brother could have saved his life, but he invited death. Nothing could shake his resolve.'[132]

After several stops, the next day, the train reached Howrah railway station, where a sea of humanity had come together to receive the martyred son of Bengal. Among them were Jatin and Kiron's aged father and Subhas Chandra Bose, with Netaji leading the procession to the cremation ground. On a separate note, a railway station was also the venue of a meeting between Bose and Virendra, who were previously acquainted in Calcutta through

Kiron Das. Subas Chandra Bose had been at Lahore on the way from Dalhousie and had written to Virendra asking for a meeting at the station where he was to change trains.

In *Netaji: Collected Works*, Bose writes of how young Jatindra Nath Das had been invincible – not faltering for one small second but marching straight towards death and freedom:

> His martyrdom functioned as a profound inspiration to the youths of India and everywhere youth and student organisations began to grow up. Among the many messages that were received on the occasion was one which touched the heart of every Indian. It was a message from the family of Terence McSwiney, the Lord Mayor of Cork, who had died a martyr under similar conditions in Ireland. The message ran thus: 'Family of Terence McSwiney have heard with grief and pride of the death of Jatin Das. Freedom will come.'[133]

The scenes in Calcutta were extraordinary; it was hard to say where the funeral procession ended with reports estimating that 5 lakh people had come out on the streets of the city to pay their tributes to the young man. The outpouring of respect and grief was absolute. Even Deshbandhu Chittaranjan Das – one of Bengal's tallest leaders whose funeral march was led by Gandhi – had not received this level of adulation. The difference was in their final acts. While Deshbandhu Das had died a natural death after a brief illness, Jatindra Nath Das had sacrificed his youth for the country.[134] 'I will not start the hunger strike,' Jatin Das had warned his fellow comrades including Bhagat Singh, 'if others start this and I must follow, then I will agree only on two conditions. Either our demands are met, or I will die for the cause.'

Jatindra Nath Das kept his word.

His death had a salutary impact – political prisoners were treated more humanely after that. Bhagat Singh and Batukeshwar Dutt may have lit the fire, but it was Jatindra Nath Das's sacrifice that forced a reluctant government to cave in. It was also after his death and its widespread reaction that the British decided against handing over the bodies of revolutionaries to their families. This was why the bodies of Bhagat Singh, Rajguru and Sukhdev were secretly smuggled out of jail and cremated.

Sukhdev once told Bhagat Singh, 'Dying for the country is not sufficient, if one has to die one should die in a way that one becomes an example for others to follow.'[135]

Jatindra Nath Das had set the example.

9

The Bomb: Cult or Philosophy?

History repeats itself – gloriously and infamously. For the band of men who wore freedom on their sleeves and their hearts, a *junoon* alone was not enough to promise success. Their lack of training meant failure was always one plan away. In December 1911, six years after the province faced the brunt of the notorious divide-and-rule policy under Viceroy Curzon, British monarch George V announced a reversal of Bengal's partition in the Delhi Durbar. Henceforth, on linguistic lines, East Bengal would assimilate into the Bengal Presidency. There was another significant declaration by the king – the capital of the British Raj was to be moved from Calcutta to Delhi.[136]

Viceroy Lord Hardinge, also Governor-General of India, entered Delhi in December 1912, but the ceremonial parade did not last long. A bomb was thrown at the Viceroy as soon as his procession marched into Chandni Chowk. Hardinge escaped with flesh wounds but his elephant attendant – with a parasol in hand – was killed. The parade was in disarray and in the midst of the stampede that followed, the revolutionaries, Rash Behari Bose, Basant Vishwas and their comrades, from the underground movement in Bengal escaped.

Four revolutionaries, Bal Mukund, Master Amir Chand, Avadh Bihari and Basant Biswas – Biswas was sixteen years old, and had dressed up as a woman and thrown the bomb at the Viceroy[137] – were hanged in 1915 in what was known as the Delhi Conspiracy Case. A reward of Rs 1 lakh was announced for Rash Behari Bose, the plot's mastermind, but he managed to escape. The next morning, Bose turned up in his Dehradun office at the Forest Research Institute as though it was business as usual.

The British continued to tail him for his revolutionary activities, including his links with the Ghadar movement. Knowing that a death sentence awaited him, the revolutionary fled to Japan. Bose did not return to India, making a name for himself in his adopted country, where he laid the groundwork for Subhas Chandra Bose's Indian National Army. His popularity in Japan was fascinating and as far removed from his revolutionary activities as he was from Bengal. Bose introduced Tokyo to an authentic Indian curry, which is still served famously as the Nakamuraya curry.[138]

Whether intentionally or by a coincidence, seventeen years later to the day when an assassination attempt was made on Hardinge, another headline-grabbing bid was made in Delhi. The target was again the Viceroy and a bomb was planted on his train.[139] Pages from the past were dusted out and repeated, and, as was Hardinge's fate, Lord Irwin too escaped. Virendra was arrested on the banks of the river Ravi for this attack.

On 23 December 1929, Virendra was still a college student and had enrolled himself in the Congress Seva Dal in preparation for the party's annual session that was to take place in Lahore. His schedule was gruelling. Preparations went on until late into the night, with work not finishing until 2 a.m. in Lahore's unforgiving winter. On the river's open banks, cold seeped into weary bones and, after a long and exhausting day, Virendra snuggled into his quilt and promptly fell asleep.

Barely four hours later, he was woken up by Mangal Singh and Gopichand Bhargava – the latter would go on to be Punjab's first chief minister in independent India. Shaking the blissfully sleeping Virendra awake, Bhargava jocularly said, 'Get up! Jawaharlal Nehru's procession will be taken out tomorrow. Yours is ready to leave just now.' Then, becoming serious, he told the young man explicitly, 'Please get up. The police have come for you and Kiron Das. You are being arrested and I have asked them to wait for half an hour. Collect your belongings and be ready to leave.'

'But why?' a confused Virendra asked.

'Yesterday, an attempt was made to blow up the Viceroy's train. The police have come to arrest you and Kiron Das in that connection.'

Three months earlier, Kiron's elder brother, Jatindra Nath Das, had shaken the Raj with his long hunger strike in jail.

Fully awake now, Virendra tried to make sense of the events but was unable to make any connections. 'Yesterday I was with you in Lahore. How am I connected to what happened in Delhi?' the young man protested to no avail.

'You are on their list of suspects,' Bhargava told him. 'Police have encircled the whole area; you cannot hide or go anywhere. And we have promised to hand you over. If we fail, not only the police but leaders like Gandhiji will be unhappy.'

News of their arrest spread promptly and, within minutes, a mob collected near the Seva Dal camp. Volunteers insisted on taking Virendra and Kiron in a procession to where the police was waiting at Lajpat Rai Nagar's outer gate. The elders were left with little choice but to concede and, surrounded by hundreds of volunteers singing patriotic songs, they marched towards the periphery. Before being handed over to the police, girls stepped up and put a tilak on their foreheads.

No longer their guest in waiting, after a year, the police was once again ready with their hospitality for Virendra. It was déjà vu – from the half-open window of the police lorry, the young man glimpsed the helpless faces of his father and his sister outside. He had seen that look before. The police van, like on the previous occasion, made rounds of the city stopping finally at Borstal Jail. But that is as far as the parallels went. During his first detention, Virendra was kept in police custody, but this time he was sent straight to jail. First, though, he was taken to the jailer's office where his handcuffs were removed and he was made to sit on a bench. Within minutes, there was a flurry of activity and Virendra looked up to see freedom fighters Ehsaan Ali, Dhanvantari, Sukhdev Raj and Ram Krishan make their way into the same room.

The men taken into custody in Punjab did not know about the Delhi incident – this bombing was planned by Bhagwati Charan and Yashpal, the latter going on to become a litterateur and a novelist of prominence. The story of India's independence is also the tale of ordinary people showing exemplary courage. 'Revolutionaries – men and women – who came to the fore during this period were not romantics out to seek personal glory. Each one of them wrote a chapter of our freedom struggle with his or her blood,' remembers Virendra.[140]

The revolutionary struggle at times went one step forward, two steps back. With the British adamantly against the demands raised by Congress leaders, its protagonists sometimes found themselves back at square one. But, with one key difference: Saunders' killing and the Assembly bombing were now prototypes, however tricky or dangerous, of what could happen when the chips were down. This is how another plot was born.

Chandrashekhar Azad was heavily influenced by Ganesh Chander Vidyarthi, editor of *Pratap*, published from Kanpur (no affiliation with the *Pratap* published in Lahore), who helped the revolutionary with finances and advice. His counsel was to avoid any rash acts – timing, he felt, was everything. Instructions went out to Bhagwati Charan and Yashpal to lay low, anything to the contrary would be a move that could embarrass Nehru and not find any public sympathy.

The duo was not convinced – time was running out and, from where they were standing, it looked as though the Congress was in still waters that did not run deep. Yashpal and Bhagwati's hands were, however, tied and they reluctantly agreed to postpone their plan. They had initially zeroed in on blowing up the viceregal train on 22 October 1929.

The two waited, restlessly. The bombs were ready and, without a safe hideout, concealing the explosives was risky. Azad remained unmoved: His mentor's words were sacred to him. Stonewalled, the two men were helpless. Bhagwati's loyalty to his leader won, but, in the end, it still fell short in front of an impatient comrade. Yashpal told him:

> My conscience does not allow me to wait any longer. Therefore, violating the party's discipline and our leader Chandrashekhar Azad's order, I have decided to go ahead. Maybe I won't return alive, maybe I will be captured and hanged. In both cases, I will receive punishment for what I have done. But if I return alive, I will surrender myself to the party. Whatever punishment they give me will be accepted, even if it is to shoot me.[141]

Hearing this, an emotional Bhagwati hugged his colleague and a two-man army went rogue.

As with their revolutionary peers, the pair were not trained bomb-makers. It was not just the preparation of the explosive, placing it covertly under a railway track needed equal precision. It had to be timed to perfection for maximum impact – a task as challenging as making the explosive itself. For some months, Yashpal experimented with bomb building in Rohtak, where he was supported by another young man, Hansraj 'Wireless'. There is a contradiction in the statements of Yashpal and Wireless on who eventually prepared and exploded the bomb, but there is no doubt that the hero of this daring episode was Yashpal.

Once convinced, there was no looking back for Bhagwati – the plan's mastermind was vocal about being the one to push the button that would cause the explosion. Yashpal refused; in the name of a bigger cause, Bhagwati was to remain anonymous and in the background. After Bhagat Singh's arrest, the other man's leadership was critical for the revolutionary cause.

There was another character in this story. Inderpal, a katib, calligraphist, working in *Pratap*, was asked to find a nondescript accommodation near the railway line. From there he was to monitor train timings from Mathura, with special attention to the Viceroy's train and its police bandobast.

Revolutionaries lived a double life; it was in their toolkit to stay out of the firing line and they were experts in disguises. It was not long before Inderpal, with a chillum in one hand, transformed into a sadhu – playing his role to perfection. No one gave him a second glance. Ten kilometres from Delhi near the railway line, the katib found a broken-down khokha, and it was ideal for reconnaissance and role-playing. His approach was simple – Inderpal kept a pitcher of water at hand, offering it to passers-by while casually getting information on incoming and outgoing trains. Soon, on-duty police officers also began to make their way to 'Babaji' and unknowingly discussed rail timetables with him.

Through all the noise, one day, Inderpal received the news he had patiently been waiting for – the Viceroy was to return to Delhi from his tour on 23 December. A couple of days before Lord Irwin's travel, Yashpal and Inderpal stacked two bombs under the railway track near an old fort that locals believed dated back to the Mahabharata era. A 300-metre-long wire was attached to the bombs with a battery fastened at the other end. A push of a button was all that was needed to explode the bombs.

Dressed in army fatigues, Yashpal joined wire to the battery. The darkness of the night was yet to disperse – it was four in the morning, still cold and frosty, and the silence preceding daybreak was loud. The train was scheduled to cross him in a couple of hours, and the minutes moved by with a stubborn lethargy for a man who was on edge. Yashpal had taken cover behind a shrub, hiding his motorcycle with great care.

The clock struck six. Yashpal describes the events himself:

We planned to explode the bomb under the engine. It would derail along with [the] other coaches. I heard a train approaching from [the] Mathura side but in the December fog, it was difficult to make out anything. I could not see the light of the engine [and] heard the approaching train. Now the button of the battery had to be pushed according to the sound of the engine. Though I was not certain, I pushed the button according to what I thought was the right moment. There was a huge explosion as if there had been a collision between two trains. I thought I would hear the derailment of the coaches, but I was hugely disappointed as the train kept on towards Delhi at its speed. The plan had misfired.[142]

Yashpal's despondency lifted marginally when news of the bombing broke in the papers. *The Statesman*'s headline the next day read, 'Lord Irwin in Bomb Outrage.'[143] The plan had not been successful, but it had not been a total failure either. The bomb had exploded under the special kitchen coach, leaving only its steel frame intact as the rest of the compartment was blown away. Fortunately for Lord and Lady Irwin, their carriage had already passed by when the bomb exploded. At the Delhi railway station, the train was parked unobtrusively, its destroyed portion covered by sheets of tarpaulin to keep news of the damage quiet and its impact limited. It was not a foolproof plan, however. Information leaked, and both the British and the Congress leadership found themselves on the same page, acknowledging that the youth's impatience was a ticking time bomb.

On overdrive, the police made arrests, trying to break into the network responsible. After being beaten mercilessly in custody, Inderpal ostensibly agreed to become an approver – the man, however, was not done with his rebellion. When the case came up before court, he dramatically turned hostile, claiming the police had forced him to make false statements. Unstoppable, he also pointed out several holes in the prosecution's theory, making it untenable. Inderpal was sentenced to life imprisonment, but he heroically ensured that none of those involved were condemned to death.

At the turn of 1930, politics took an interesting bend. Freedom fighters had to battle it out on two fronts: The overt struggle against imperialism became secondary to resistance from within the party. The great divide was out in the open in Lahore, where a Congress resolution was passed congratulating Lord Irwin for escaping the train attack. The motion was supported by Gandhi, but not Subhas Chandra Bose. Losing, but not by much in the voting, Bose – unshackled by official responsibility walked out,[144] leaving the session's president, Jawaharlal Nehru, in an unenviable position.[145]

Opposed, along with Subhas Chandra Bose, to the resolution,[146] Nehru had the illusion of choice as the Congress president, but could he step outside the perimeter of Gandhi's beliefs? He found himself backed into a corner, a dharma sankat that may not have been to his liking, although some historians argue that Nehru was where he wanted to be.

Author Tripurdaman Singh says:[147]

Nehru's admiration for revolutionaries was both qualified and tactical. First, he expressed admiration for figures like Bhagat Singh even as he distanced himself from their methods. Ditto with Bose's INA, whose position he disagreed with but who he nevertheless defended in the Red Fort Trials. This obviously played well to the gallery and was a political tactic more than an expression of belief. Second, it helped that many of the 'revolutionaries' were Nehru's co-travellers on the left of the political spectrum and rhymed with his predilections. He didn't seem to express much regard for any such 'revolutionary' activity from the right.

Nehru, Singh adds, was also conscious of the fact that it was hard to enact revolution in a country as large, diverse and divided as the India of his time.

Gandhi's decisions may have been the sacred line for him, but the give and take of respect filtered down in the Congress. Dr Sheikh Muhammad Alam, a fiery speaker gave vent to the frustration of the party dissidents,[148] 'I have tried to understand Gandhiji. And for all my efforts what I have understood is that I have not been able to understand anything.' The leader heard his speech and smiled but did not say anything. Missing in contemporary politics are both the beauty of such words and debates.

In the war for independence, was the railway network a soft target? Built by the British, during the Raj, it was seen as a defining symbol of colonialization. British troops could mobilize in record time over a mere whiff of revolt in the subcontinent and were comfortable in the belief that the 1857 war for independence would not be repeated. Commerce bloomed, but only for the rulers who used the train's expanding network to exploit resources and raw materials.

What the railways also did was to overtly display British suppression over its subjects. Indians travelling on trains were the children of a lesser god – steered like unruly sheep onto wooden benches as third-class passengers. Their punishment for daring to dream of travel was humiliation. These train compartments were as sordid as jail cells and there were no toilets.

British journalist Christian Wolmar writes of the railways and the Raj:[149]

> There was another source of mounting antagonism: the treatment of third-class passengers who were all Indian. While the Europeans travelled in world-class luxury in

first-class, the masses were crammed into world-class squalor. There was even a lengthy battle for them to have toilets on trains and conditions remained squalid well into the twentieth century. This proved to be a major source of dissent and encouraged nationalistic sentiment. The invention that did most to keep the Indians in check proved to be double-edged, stimulating the nationalistic forces which eventually triumphed.

This hierarchy in train travel triggered in those fighting for independence the compulsion to set wrongs, right.

The third-class compartment became Gandhi's tool of resistance. In his mass engagement programmes, he travelled the length and breadth of the country only in third class. Gandhi deliberately used the same colonial juggernaut that the British were so proud of to mobilize anti-imperialism sentiments. His experiences, the not-so-good, the bad and the ugly, were collated in the book *Third Class in Indian Railways*:[150]

> The rush of passengers could not be stayed. The guards or other railway servants came in only to push in more passengers ... the compartment was not swept during the journey. Passengers waded through the dirt. The closet inside the compartment was not cleaned and there was no water in the tank. Everything about the refreshments was dirty – dirty looking, handed by dirtier hands, kept in dirty vessels, sampled by millions of flies, and weighed in equally unattractive scales.

Gandhi, of course, had a deeper association with the railways – thrown out of a train in apartheid South Africa for travelling first class changed his life's course, an episode informally considered his first instance of civil disobedience. Befittingly, Gandhi's final journey was also on a third-class carriage, his remains were kept in an urn in the Asthi Special and taken to Allahabad for submersion.[151]

Paradoxically, a system that remains the country's pulse and is one of the largest in the world was never intended for the 'natives'. Politician and author Shashi Tharoor calls it 'a gigantic colonial scam'.[152] It was transformative but not kind to the Indians who were also barred from holding a prominent position in the railways. For the freedom fighters, it became another front for dissent.

In November 1907, an attempt was made on a train carrying Andrew Fraser, Lieutenant Governor of Bengal and the man believed to be responsible for Bengal's partitioning. His fate was the same as that of Irwin's – he escaped unscathed. Several plans to assassinate Fraser proved unsuccessful. In one incident, detonators did not impact the railway lines and, on another day, despite an explosion, the target was safe.[153] Revolutionaries in Bengal were relatively better skilled in bomb-making than their counterparts in Punjab, but their competence still didn't match their intent.

One of the most high-profile incidents on a train was the 1925 Kakori Conspiracy, when HRA members led by Ramprasad Bismil engaged in a bold armed robbery. Incidents with a train as the background also had implications that resonated far into the future. It was at Lahore railway station that Lala Lajpat Rai was mercilessly beaten, an assault from which he did not recover. Six years later, in 1934, a railway crossing saved Mahatma Gandhi's life. The five-minute delay during his untouchability tour in Pune ensured that the bomb was hurled mistakenly at another car.[154]

The symbolism of the railway is in its positioning as being integral to protests. From images of it being vandalized in protest to rail roko agitations, the Indian railways stays at the fulcrum of politics, ferrying more than 3 billion people a year.[155] Its most abiding image – a black-and-white one – remains of refugees clinging to every corner of a train as Partition unfolded.

Virendra's arrest coincided with proceedings of the Lahore Conspiracy Case in which Bhagat Singh and Batukeshwar Dutt were accused. Given life imprisonment for throwing bombs in the Assembly, the duo was lodged in Central Jail and their colleagues were in Borstal Jail. Hearing this, Virendra and Kiron Das demanded that as political prisoners, they should be put up with the other accused in the Lahore Conspiracy Case. It was not a call the jail authorities were prepared to take favourably. The two, however, were not willing to give up easily either. They insisted that at least they be put in the same barrack. Their demands backfired and they were instead led to separate cells.

The lock-up was bare – this time, there was not even a charpoy for either to sleep on. The jailer pointed to a mound on the ground; this was where they could rest if sleep came, he told them disinterestedly. A chatai and two rancid blankets were handed over to each. In the corner, a utensil for use at night broke the dreary monotony of nothingness.

Virendra and Das managed to get permission for clothes from home but that was where the positives ended; and with other pressing matters at hand, this was hardly a concern. The freedom fighters took the call that if their solitary confinement did not end in twenty-four hours, they would go on a hunger strike. The threat, however, did not move the authorities and, as the status quo remained unchanged, the prisoners hunkered down to go on a fast. Food sent from their homes were returned untouched.

The government panicked when news of their hunger strike made it to the press the following day. The timing was all wrong. Congress leaders had started congregating in Lahore for the session and the administration did not want to give them another reason to question the British Raj. The decision on solitary confinement was recalled and all the freedom fighters were put together in one barrack.

Life eased up. Days passed in sleeping, reading or just exchanging notes. In the barrack, there was one big change – they were given charpoys to sleep on. The wooden beds with a braided rope frame were, however, chained to one another to prevent inmates from using them to scale the walls and escape. The routine of their humdrum existence was broken one day when they excitedly heard some news. The year, they learned, was going to end with a bang. On 31 December, at midnight, Pandit Jawaharlal Nehru was to not only unfurl the flag of independence, but he would also demand full sovereignty from the British Raj. Energized, the political prisoners jumped out of their stupor and decided to celebrate the momentous occasion. Like Chinese whispers, the plan was passed on from barrack to barrack, cell to cell. At the stroke of midnight when Pandit Nehru unfurled the flag, prisoners would sing patriotic songs and raise slogans.

As the jail clock struck the designated hour, Kiron Das began singing *Vande Mataram* in his melodious voice. The Punjabi crowd followed him loudly – singing a song that Bhagat Singh was to make immortal, *Mera Rang De Basanti Chola*. The prison that day reverberated first with songs and then with slogans of 'Inquilab Zindabad'. This was followed closely by a couplet, another Bhagat Singh favourite:

Sarfaroshi ki tammana ab humare dil mein hai,
dekhna hai zor kitna bazu-e-qatil mein hai.

As the Borstal Jail echoed with enthused singing, fearing an uprising, its staff panicked. Superintendent Kheruddin, a strict officer who spoke the language of authority on all days, barring none, stood with hands folded, pleading for the singing to stop. For once, the hat was on the other head and he was fearful of losing his job. Kheruddin's cajoling had no impact and he reverted to his original tactics of threatening the freedom fighters with solitary confinement. But that ship had sailed and no one paid any heed to him or his words. The night was young and the prisoners came together, passionately joining hands, without breaking the momentum of their singing. It was 3 a.m. when they began their final song:

Bagwan ne yeh anokha sitam ijaad kiya,
aashiyan phoonk ke pani ko bahut yaad kiya.

The gardener has constructed this curious torture,
after burning the nest he remembered the water.

Across Lahore, there were raids to find the culprits of the Delhi Conspiracy, but the police had hit a wall. Those in jail were questioned repeatedly and the British learned nothing from them either. Three weeks after they were arrested, the prisoners were released on bail.

The freedom movement was now moving like a seesaw. The playground was a benign struggle in conflict with regulated violence, and both had their ups and downs. Near Allahabad, Nehru said, 'The youth should think dangerously.' A few days later Subhas Chandra Bose went a step further, 'The youth should not only think dangerously, they should also live dangerously.' Dr Alam completed the impromptu motto, 'The youth should think dangerously, live dangerously and act dangerously.'

Needless to say, none of this was palatable to Gandhi.

The contrasting ideologies with their undercurrents could not remain in the background for long – the clash, when it happened, was in the public for all to see. In an article 'Cult of the Bomb', Gandhi, without mincing words, put forth his views on non-violence. Not to be outdone, Bhagat Singh replied with 'Philosophy of the Bomb', a four-page commentary which was secretly distributed across the country. Virendra got his hands on the manuscripts which he furtively circulated, keeping a few copies for himself. Aware that his reputation was like a magnet for the police and his house could be searched without notice, Virendra removed the back covers of two photos hanging on the walls of his house and hid the incriminating papers there. As if on cue, the next day, the police descended on his residence, raiding his belongings. They found no success in this endeavour.

Dramatic events were unfolding. Gandhi was preparing for his next mass civil disobedience movement, the Salt Satyagraha. Revolutionaries, true to their reputation, were not sitting on the sidelines waiting for the tide to change. A new mission, thrilling and perilous, was about to be set in motion. They were going to free Bhagat Singh and Batukeshwar Dutt from jail.

10

Ground Zero: A House on Bahawalpur Road

Bhagat Singh's court appearances kept the police on edge. Was it just a calm before the storm? Was an escape attempt by Bhagat Singh imminent? They constantly worried about these questions. Proceedings were shifted from the courthouse to a tent outside Lahore Central Jail where the freedom fighter was an inmate – there was safety in proximity. This tent became ground zero. It was easier to enter the eye of a needle than the road leading to the jail. Other prisoners were ferried from Borstal Jail with a heavy escort for the proceedings but none of them – individually or together – lost their zeal for the larger cause. During their meetings, collectively as one under the blue summer sky, they sang '*Sarfaroshi ki tammana*'. Special Prosecutor Pandit Krishan's interventions failed. He only made the notes rise higher.

The role of revolutionaries in India's freedom struggle is idealized – violent acts find a breathless mention in commercial interpretations, while it is the nuances of their defiance that is noteworthy. Singing patriotic songs was as much of a rebellion as speaking up through a hunger strike.

One morning, the accused refused to go to court saying it was pointless; the outcome, they insisted, was known. The Raj shrugged, brought out another ordinance and the case continued in absentia. To give it the optics of credibility, a three-member panel of high court judges – Justice Tape, Justice Abdul Kader and a Britisher, Justice Hilton – was appointed.

Most of the suspects were educated and, while reputed lawyers represented them, they were also their own advocates and, on occasion, put witnesses in the dock. Arguments by Bhagat Singh, Kamal Nath Tiwari, and Vijay Kumar Sinha were sharp and pointed, and their cross-examinations made the public sit up and take note. These were no bomb-making mercenaries but young men who were fighting a battle of ideology for freedom.

No weakness was on display, no inch was given. Awed, Subhas Chandra Bose joined Motilal and Jawaharlal Nehru by visiting the jailed revolutionaries in court, frequently issuing statements in their favour. Encouraged by the wave of support, Azad and Bhagwati saw a potential to leverage the situation – the timing, they felt, was right to free Bhagat Singh and Batukeshwar Dutt from jail. The revolutionaries' objective was twofold: An obvious aim was to save the lives of their comrades, but a secondary intent was also to ride their movement on the back of sensational actions.

There was one underlying apprehension, however. That the revolutionaries were unimpressed by Gandhi's methods was no secret; what changed was a gnawing anxiety that the leader may fail – a scenario no member of the underground wanted. Despite their differences, these young men revered Gandhi. They had also done the maths. In their bold act, the winner would be the Mahatma, for any attempt to sideline the revolutionary camp would, by default, take the British on a path that led to Gandhi.

'*Sar par kafan lapete qatil ko dhoond rahe hain* (With a shroud tied on our heads we are looking for the slayer)': From 1927 to 1931, the revolutionary movement was led by foot soldiers – most of them in their twenties – who casually played with their lives. Their days were numbered and there was no undertaking they would be alive to rejoice in an independent India.

With death lurking, Bhagwati and Azad were restless. The thought of their young comrade headed to the gallows was giving them sleepless nights. By now, Bhagat Singh's cult status had become a double-edged sword – his every word in court was a conversation starter.

The ask was tall. Bombs, pistols and other ammunition were the obvious requirements, but not the only ones. For an escape, a motorcycle or any other vehicle was a must, two houses – one for collecting weapons, and another to hide Bhagat Singh and Dutt – were also a mandatory prerequisite. Another matter pending was the question of involving women. What role could they play in the getaway?

Despite courage almost bordering insouciance, the revolutionaries were also practical. They knew collateral damage was a given – whether it was the police, their revolutionary comrades or the probability of getting killed themselves. Azad and Bhagwati took three others, Yashpal, Dhanvantari and Sukhdev Raj into confidence. Two women revolutionaries, Sushila Didi and Durga Bhabhi also joined the closed circle. Soon, the appearance of a normal household unrolled on Lahore's Bahawalpur Road where a furnished home was taken on rent.

Bhagat Singh and Batukeshwar Dutt, lodged in Central Jail, had demanded a meeting with their comrades lodged in Borstal Jail – a concession that was made. Every Sunday, the duo – under a heavy police escort – was brought to the other jail, where they spent the day. This outing was zeroed in as the perfect escape opportunity. On 1 June 1930, the police escort would be attacked on the main road as it exited Central Jail's gates with the two prisoners.

Under the cover of an exchange of fire between the police and the revolutionaries, Bhagat Singh and Dutt were told to run to a stand-by vehicle and escape. The police were to be attacked on two fronts – from one side, a group led by Bhagwati would throw bombs, while, from the other, under Azad's directions, they were to be shot at.

The wheels were in motion. With three days to go, on 28 May, Bhagwati decided to try out the bombs they had made. The group wanted no last-minute surprises that would make them sitting ducks for the police. Along with two comrades, he took a bomb and set out in the morning to the banks of the river Ravi. At the Bahawalpur Road house, the others got down to finishing their designated tasks – several loose ends were still to be tied. Sushila Didi and Durga Bhabhi were busy with household chores, when

Sukhdev Raj, writhing in pain, arrived suddenly on a tonga. One of his legs was tied with a cloth, but blood was gushing out and the cloth was soaked in red. The news he gave the housemates was not good. As Bhagwati was trying out the bomb, it exploded in his hand, cutting it off. Sukhdev Raj, who was standing nearby, was badly injured but was sent by Bhagwati, lying on the banks of the Ravi, to inform the others of the accident. 'I will not survive as I have shed too much blood. You cannot carry me to the house. So best you leave me and go and alert our comrades,' he told his wounded companion.

Minutes earlier, there was frenetic activity in the house, but now silence descended. After Bhagat Singh's arrest, Azad and Bhagwati were the only remaining leaders of stature and, while the plot was risky, such a setback was unanticipated. In shock and panic, the group tried to string their thoughts together coherently. Was Bhagwati even alive? The words remained unspoken. Yashpal, accompanied by two others, left to bring the freedom fighter home.

Bhagwati was breathing, but barely. Lying on the riverbank, gritting his teeth through the searing pain, he whispered, 'Why has Bhaiya Chandrashekhar not come?' His end was near; he asked the three to leave and not put their lives in danger, murmuring in what were to become his final words, a deep regret for not freeing Bhagat Singh.

Yashpal was torn. Having lost one hand and bleeding profusely from multiple wounds, his leader was weaving in and out of consciousness. Bhagwati Charan could not be left alone, but it was not safe to take him quietly into the city. Asking one of the men to keep guard, Yashpal ran to arrange for transport. Meanwhile, on

Bahawalpur Road, its residents were scrambling. Bhagwati had to be saved, injured Sukhdev required medical aid and the challenge of freeing Bhagat Singh remained. There was another problem: Potentially a big one. It was only a matter of time before the police and its informers got a hint of the developments.

Yashpal retraced the journey to the riverbank – by now, Bhagwati's grasp on life was tenuous. Lifting him without a charpoy or a stretcher was not just impossible but also excruciatingly painful for the dying man. The revolutionaries operated in silos; they had no dossier or fall-back knowledge when events spun out of their control. Yashpal may have wasted precious minutes when he could have saved his leader's life, but no one knew any better.

Once again, he moved away from the scene, this time to try and get a platform for Bhagwati to lie on and, if possible, a doctor. As Yashpal left, Bhagwati Charan breathed his last. Seeing his leader lose his battle with life, the man who was left to watch over him fled in fear. A body covered with blood, lying in the sand on a desolate riverbank – these were the last moments of one of India's bravest.

Darkness was creeping in when Yashpal returned with a couple of men, some medicines, two sheets and a charpoy only to find that Bhagwati had forever gone beyond the reach of the British. They covered his body in sheets, but Yashpal's work was still not over. The body needed to be taken home and then cremated – possibly exposing the identity of the deceased. Once again, he made the now-familiar trek back to Bahawalpur Road to consult his comrades, but, this time, his shoulders were leaden. It was on him to shatter the thin thread of hope the others were still clinging to.

That these were not just intrepid men but also extraordinary women was exhibited by Bhagwati's wife, Durga Bhabhi, who could not shed a tear as anything out of the ordinary may alert the neighbours. The house was the headquarters of the revolutionary movement, arms and ammunition were stored there; its residents had to control their emotions.

The night was long. Those in the house were grieving and yet, could not mourn openly. Just before dawn, Azad, Yashpal and two others left for the riverbank – they intended to cremate Bhagwati before daybreak. As they were leaving, however, both Durga Bhabhi and Sushila Didi insisted on going too. The men debated on taking them on their bicycles, but the fear of being spotted by the police weighed heavily on them. Addressing Durga Bhabhi, Azad said, 'We respect your feelings, but you and Bhagwati Bhai decided to forgo your feelings the day you joined this movement. You have sacrificed so much for this movement, please sacrifice some more by not going there.'[156] Azad's words silenced Durga Bhabhi and, with a heavy heart, the men left. She wanted to take one last look at her husband, but, with all her strength, she relinquished any personal feelings for the larger cause.

Bhagwati Charan's sacrifice has faded from public memory and he remains a faceless name in a commentary that seldom digresses from a core narrative or from established names. Fortunately, regional historians are now bringing a change and filling in the gaps. It is also regrettable that by romanticizing their bravery, the sacrifices of revolutionaries are diluted – a view that resonates with writers Prabal Saran Agarwal and Harsh Vardhan Tripathy.[157]

In popular public perception, the story of the Indian revolutionary movement – largely associated with a few names – is a story of spectacular actions: robberies, assassinations, and bombings, a saga of bravery and self-sacrifice; a tale of heroism and romanticism. This dominant framework of the Indian revolutionary movement – which largely flows from and gets strengthened through movies, chapters in school textbooks, and popular story books – works to detach the ideological-theoretical component of Indian revolutionaries from their 'actions'. In this way, the Indian revolutionaries are robbed of their revolutionary ideology and goals, and converted into harmless icons, with ritualised worship on their birth and death anniversaries. They are considered radical not because of their political programme, but because of their actions.

One curious aspect of the revolutionary struggle was the high incidence of failures in attempts to do in individuals who symbolized oppression.

Durga Devi only injured people close to those targeted. Two attempts on the lives of the Viceroy as recounted in Virendra's book had both failed. My father and his friends tried to shoot the Punjab Governor but only managed to injure him. Bhagat Singh and his comrades were out to get Scott but shot Saunders instead.[158]

Lalit tries to find answers to this puzzle.

Men and women who took to the gun to drive the British out were not violent people at heart. While their zeal for freedom helped overcome any concern for their safety, they could not bring to bear upon the preparation and execution of their plans the kind of cold-blooded ruthlessness that comes naturally to hardened criminals or fanatics.

Historian S. Irfan Habib says revolutionaries in Punjab were operating without any training.[159]

They had rudimentary knowledge and learned bomb-making from Bengalis. Jatin Das was brought from Calcutta; Bengalis were hired for training as they were more skilled in this. Those in Punjab and western UP essentially lacked these skills and failed many times. They were all committed like Azad till the end, but their attempts were not properly organized.

Bhagwati's tragedy was not just in his death. During his lifetime, he was suspected by some of his comrades – including Chandrashekhar Azad – of working for CID. The agency knew the truth, aware that Bhagwati ran the show. So they started a whispered campaign of calumny against him which succeeded too well. Azad's doubts were settled only when Bhagwati and Yashpal tried to bomb the Viceroy's train. Bhagat Singh, on the other hand, never doubted the man's loyalty, who, even in death, found no glory. When Bhagwati passed, he was alone, unwept and un-mourned; for hours, his body lay without even a shroud. That his widow could not say a final goodbye to him was perhaps the deepest cut.

Despite losing her husband, Durga Devi's commitment to India's independence was unwavering. She tried to avenge Bhagat Singh's sentencing in Bombay, an episode she recounts to Lalit Mohan, Virendra's son, 'I went there under an assumed name, Sharada. Our target was Lord Hailey, a former Governor of Punjab. We shot at him but only injured two of his companions. I was arrested later and spent three years in prison.'[160] More on this plot later. Incidentally, her three-year-old son, Sachi, who played no small part when he sat on Bhagat Singh's lap during his escape from Punjab after the killing of Saunders, retired in 1993–94 as a company executive in Kolkata. In independent India, Durga Bhabhi moved to Ghaziabad with her only child.[161]

In their short life together, the couple built a formidable reputation and were amongst the most prominent to take on the colonial rulers. Durga Devi shared many interesting behind-the-scenes snippets with Lalit when he visited her in 1993–94. The underground meetings, she told Lalit, were anything but a secret from the British, 'Your father was asked to look after our publicity. We used to meet regularly at his house. Each of us was followed by two CID men. By counting the number of secret service men outside, you could always tell how many people were meeting inside.'

While he was alive, Bhagwati stayed connected with Virendra, who occasionally accompanied him and Durga Bhabhi for walks in Lahore. Needless to say, much more than the weather was discussed during those strolls!

Bhagwati's sudden death was a body blow for Azad. He was now without the services of both his lieutenants – Bhagwati, and Bhagat Singh. If the latter was to live, the onus lay with him and it was a heavy weight to carry. But first, Azad was needed elsewhere. Durga Bhabhi was existing in a vacuum since her husband's death, neither crying nor uttering a single word. Revolutionary acts were built on layers of individual courage and the stoicism of families. In the end, it was the families that were asked for more. Durga Bhabhi simply sat still with her eyes closed.

Azad locked himself in a room and emerged after an hour with a determined expression. The leader had taken a call to honour the last wishes of their martyred comrade. Bhagat Singh was to be freed and Azad was prepared to go alone. This is when Durga finally broke her silence. 'I will go with you and complete my late husband's mission,' she said softly, adding that if death came along the way, she would consider herself fortunate to be united with her husband. As Azad was trying to reason with her, Sushila Didi intervened – Durga needed to stay back for her four-year-old son who had already lost his father. So, instead, she, Sushila, who had no familial responsibilities, would accompany Azad. Eventually, neither woman was allowed to accompany Azad. The plot – a do-or-die attempt – was considered too perilous for them.

On the first day of the scorching month of June, Azad, Yashpal and another revolutionary, Vaishampayan stationed themselves near the gates of the jail. It was time for Bhagat Singh and Batukeshwar Dutt to come out, and the men clutched their pistols, revolver and bombs tightly. The two who had to be rescued were clued in through the jail grapevine. At their first glance, Vaishampayan, standing on one side of the road, would start playing a flute – a signal that the plot was a go. The getaway vehicle with its engine running was to take the jailed freedom fighters to a hideout that had already been zeroed in. Once they escaped, Azad and the rest would engage with the police, whatever the consequences.

A scratch of his head by Bhagat Singh was the sign that he and Dutt were ready. Strangely, when the time came, the revolutionary along with Dutt quietly went and sat in the jail lorry. Within seconds, they were driven away, leaving Azad and his comrades bewildered. A few days later, Bhagat Singh clarified his intentions – their movement had received a big setback with the death of Bhagwati Charan and he was averse to compromise Azad's life. His freedom, he declared, should not be at the cost of another's life, especially when that other was Chandrashekhar Azad.

This failure, coming so soon after his comrade's death, impacted Azad. At Bahawalpur Road, Durga Bhabhi and Sushila Didi were perplexed to see Azad return alone and, instead of answering them, the distraught leader shut himself in his room again. His disappointment was acute, as was the sense that lately all his plans had failed or failed to take off.

That night, Azad stayed awake, fighting thoughts and frustration, but, by the time the first rays of the sun began to spread their light, he was determined. A final effort would be made to free the pair from jail – a group of twenty young men on hire would launch an all-out attack on the police party that escorted Bhagat Singh to jail. If death was their fate, it was simply par for the course.

As he went over the plan in his head, there was suddenly a big explosion in the house. The bombs that had been prepared for Bhagat Singh's escape were lying in an almirah and one of them had exploded. All other thoughts fled as he ordered everyone in the house to gather their belongings and flee immediately. A police raid was only a matter of hours away, and there was no place to hide Durga Bhabhi and Sushila Didi.

Their neighbour was an engineer. Yashpal quickly ran across and took him into confidence, requesting the man not to inform the police for half an hour. The man agreed and notified the police only once everyone had fled. Fearing more explosions, the police, on its part, was in no hurry to enter the house.

Through all this, Sukhdev Raj's wounds needed urgent medical attention but it was too risky to take him to a hospital. On Chamberlain Road, three houses away from Virendra's home, lived Dr Asa Nand, principal of Dayanand Ayurvedic College. Dhanvantari, a former student of his, shared the developments with him and an empathetic Dr Asa Nand immediately offered to look after Sukhdev Raj. But, as was the case more times than not, there was a hitch. To reach the doctor's house, Virendra's residence, which was at the junction of Chamberlain Road and Nisbet Road, had to be crossed. It was dangerous territory – with Virendra now firmly entrenched in the revolutionary group, the police shadowed him mercilessly. When he was home, they openly sat outside and when he stepped out, two policemen followed him on bicycles. Any movement that was not routine would be flagged at once.

Dhanvantari and Virendra finally found a solution. The latter was to leave his house at noon and not return till five in the evening, allowing enough time for the injured Sukhdev to be brought to the Ayurveda doctor without catching the police's attention. The next day, at the appointed hour, Virendra left for his college, dutifully followed by his police shadows. Dhanvantari quickly sneaked Sukhdev Raj into Dr Asa Nand's house, where he was taken to a room and only the good doctor addressed his injuries.

Virendra and Sukhdev were friends since their days in the Punjab Students Union, and Virendra naturally wanted to meet his injured friend. Dhanvantari forbade it; he was worried that Virendra's visit would make the police suspicious. A way was found. Law enforcement duties ended at ten every night; Virendra, it was decided, would visit his friend after 11 p.m. But there was one final obstacle to clear – his formidable father, Mahashay Krishan, who was feared by all and would hardly let his son sneak out in the middle of the night. This is why, despite being next door, Virendra met his friend only once a week, that too after being assured that the intelligence, the police and his father had called it a night! A consensus was taken to not keep Sukhdev Raj in the house on Chamberlain Road for long; as soon as his health improved, he was sent to Amritsar.

Meanwhile, Azad was a disappointed man – his entire edifice had crumbled in front of his eyes. There were also financial requirements to fund not only the revolutionaries but also his activities. Crowdfunding was becoming dangerous; the net was tightening around him and so, one fine day, he left Lahore. In Delhi, he robbed a store and looted a generous Rs 17,000, which he gave to his comrades to buy more weapons. Azad then made his way back to Uttar Pradesh where the revolutionary group had disintegrated and made it the centre of his activities. He was not to return to Lahore.

PART 3

11

Sar Par Kafan Lapete: Shooting the Governor

'The situation by the end of 1930 had become very dismal,' writes Virendra.[162] Gandhi's Non-Cooperation Movement was lurching ahead slowly, it seemed to be losing steam. The revolutionary movement had also become leaderless; Bhagat Singh was in jail with a death sentence hanging on his head, Bhagwati Charan died unfortunately while making a bomb and Chandrashekhar Azad left Punjab for Uttar Pradesh trying to reorganize the movement there. It was only the Lahore Conspiracy Case that was making headlines. The youth, especially in Punjab, were impressed by the impassioned defence of Bhagat Singh and his comrades. At that time some of us started getting edgy thinking, 'Why are we sitting idle?'

An incident earlier in the year had captured Virendra's imagination. If anything could rival the restlessness in Punjab, it was Bengal. In April, a group led by Surya Sen, a former schoolteacher, made a daring attempt to raid the Chittagong (now in Bangladesh) armoury. They aimed to capture weapons and distribute them amongst other revolutionaries to mobilize an armed unit.[163] The plan was elaborate – they took hostages at a Britishers-only club, rail and communication lines to Calcutta were cut, and the city was isolated from other parts of Bengal.

The armoury was captured and Surya Sen, in scenes unseen before this, hoisted the national flag and proclaimed a provisional government in Chittagong. The euphoria, sadly, was short-lived. The men, fighting under the banner of the Indian Republican Army, did not find any ammunition and fled to the nearby hills, where they were outnumbered by a police force of thousands. In a pitched battle, twelve young men were killed. Sen went into hiding but was betrayed by his associate in whose house he had taken shelter. Human weakness, unfiltered, made episodic appearances when colleagues turned into informers and approvers. Tortured mercilessly, Sen was hanged less than a month later.[164]

His exploits lived on, and none were more impressed than the young revolutionaries of Punjab. Durga Das Khanna and Virendra, met every evening. They were joined by a close friend of Virendra, Ranbir whose family owned the Urdu newspaper, *Milap*. Similar to Virendra, Ranbir too was known by a singular name. The three were convinced that Punjab was ready for a Chittagong sequel. As always, this idea sounded simple on paper. Their group was in disarray, comrades were in jail and outsiders could not be trusted with revolutionary acts. There was no one to guide them, but a revolutionary could never be stopped by such issues! The three decided to take matters into their own youthful hands. They zeroed in on two plans – neither were for the weak-hearted.

A British club in Lahore's regal Lawrence Gardens was the centre of English society in the city. It was also out of bounds for Indians. Taking it as an affront to collective dignity, the three set out to change this status quo. Virendra and his comrades did not believe in doing anything by half measures – they would throw a bomb inside the ballroom when the club's members were swaying to the beats of music.

The call taken, the men got down to the basics. For days, the three clandestinely did a recce of the club, trying to find a weakness in the security system from where the bomb could be thrown inside. Everywhere they looked, there were people, security men and orderlies who could intercept them as early as at the entry. There was also the question of the bomb itself. None of them knew how to make a bomb, nor did any of them have a clue on where they could procure one. As enticing as it was, the club was turning out to be too ambitious and, without wasting any more thought over it, they moved to a backup plan.

The other target was the unpopular Governor of Punjab.

The annual convocation of Lahore's Punjab University was held in the college hall in the last week of December. This year, especially, it would be a day to remember, the three pledged. On the agenda was shooting the Governor. Thinking it through, the men came up with three prerequisites that could make or break their mission: A gunman with a strong, unwavering aim, a pistol and a university admit card. There was another thing they had consensus on – the shooter would be one amongst the three, all of whom were not able, but were more than ready.

In 1930, Virendra and Ranbir were both unmarried, but Durga Das not only had a wife, he was also a father to a one-year-old. Family would have to wait, he announced, throwing his hat into the ring and volunteering to fire at the high-ranking British official. In the defiance of the revolutionaries, suffering families – fathers, mothers and wives – looked at danger every day with admirable strength, even as the shadow of death lengthened on the paths of their beloved men. In this instance, however, Virendra and Ranbir were unrelenting. There was no way they would allow Durga Das to be the shooter. That left the two, both of whom had never used a firearm.

The odds stacked against them were extraordinary. Police officers in Lahore across hierarchies were acquainted with Virendra and Ranbir, putting a question mark on their entry into the university hall. The attempt was risky and it could end in a hanging for all three of them. Perversely, for a revolutionary, there was not a more encouraging thought.

While brainstorming for the plan, a plot, unlike any before, was thrown into the mix. Why not get a woman to shoot the Governor, one of them chimed. The others animatedly agreed that it was an idea whose time had come. Unmatched, it was just what was needed to bring the country out of its lethargy; that it would garner praise for Punjab for putting a woman on the frontline was an added advantage. Sir Geoffrey Fitzhervey de Montmorency was the Governor and although there were many attempts made on the lives of Viceroys, none had been made on the life of a Governor. These three men set out to amend that record.

The search began in earnest for a shooter. By now, more than a few women were actively involved in the freedom movement, but participating in a non-violent movement and shooting a British Governor were two completely different things. The person they found was willing to taste blood. A student of law at the Punjab University, her identity remains anonymous now as, post marriage, she wanted this phase of her life to be buried. For convenience, she was renamed Kamala. In the Raj, it was common for revolutionaries to have a pseudonym. Bhagat Singh wrote under one.

Virendra had briefly heard about Kamala from Kiron Das – the two were acquaintances. As he was leaving for Calcutta, Das asked Virendra to keep in touch with the college student, anticipating her value in the freedom movement. He was not wrong and the moment had come. From the sidelines, Kamala had been watching the actions of the revolutionaries with interest; occasionally stepping inside their boundary to donate money to the cause. On a couple of occasions, unknown to her family, she had smuggled out jewellery, which she gave to the men to sell for cash. Those who had the revolutionaries' back were not just strong men, nor was the support they received merely what was visible. The brave hearts who helped them clandestinely had as much to lose.

Whether it was providence or a quirk of fate, Kamala was among the students who were to receive their degree from the hands of the Governor. At last, events were aligned in their favour. Virendra approached Kamala and asked the question: Was she prepared to hide a revolver in her black graduation gown, unmasking it to fire at the Governor as he presented her with a degree? To his surprise, she readily agreed. Virendra asked again, this time laying out without any frills the only two outcomes – both dark and inevitable. You will either get killed on the spot or hanged later, he bluntly told her. Kamala's response did not waver; she was prepared for anything, said the student. Nonetheless, Virendra gave her a few days to think it over.

The plan was on track and appealed to the three comrades, until it hit them. Kamala was no shooter; she needed to practice a firearm which was impossible to do at home – 'misplacing' her money more than often had already made her family suspicious. She could only train in a jungle for which she would have to leave home without raising any eyebrows. In a way, it would also be a test of how seriously she took the whole affair.

The excitement though began to fizzle out, only to be replaced by troubling thoughts. A young woman leaves home and goes on to gun down the Governor. If caught, the police would treat her brutally. If she succumbed to pressure, the outcome would be no less than catastrophic – their entire plot would unravel.

Again, Virendra headed out to meet her; this time, detailing their misgivings. He writes, 'The same doubts had also arisen in her mind, but she had cleared herself of them saying she definitely wanted to do this heroic act. She then told me that you all misunderstand that only men can be brave, women too can be equally daring.'[165] Kamala finished her defence by pronouncing that she wanted to leave home and devote her life to the revolutionary cause.

Her determination almost convinced them. If she were adamant about leaving home, then Kamala could be trained in firing a revolver and, if she mastered it, the next act would unfold at the university convocation. Durga Das, though, was now troubled by a new concern. The revolutionaries were never short of a predicament and never far from the next one.

Kamala's leaving home, he felt, would not go unnoticed. The police could be informed and she could be nabbed even before the plan was executed. The discovery of the revolver itself would send her to jail for years. His musings may seem far-fetched now, but in their world of hits, misses and junoon, it was all plausible. Durga Das's ruminations did not end here. The three revolutionaries, he announced, would be branded cowards for using a woman for such a dangerous mission – more so if she were to name them. The time had not yet come, after all, for Bhagat Singh's female counterpart to rise.

To say Kamala was disappointed was putting it mildly but, in due course, she came around to their point of view. The young woman still wanted to help; however, the prospect of her marriage was looming large at home. She was soon married to a prominent officer and the chapter of the mysterious Kamala ended there.

After Kamala's exit, the three friends were back in a huddle. It was a visitor who finally solved their dilemma. Chaman Lal, a friend of Ranbir's was visiting Lahore from the city of Mardan (now in Pakistan's Khyber Pakhtunkhwa province.) On learning of the plot, he mentioned that a young man from his hometown was looking for an opportunity to do something for the country. A week later, when Virendra went to meet Ranbir, he was introduced to a stranger. The man was of a short height and later Virendra was informed that Hari Krishan Talwar was prepared to gun down the Governor.[166] Only one hurdle, a substantial one, remained. He needed a pass to enter the university hall and Virendra was entrusted to find one.

He scouted the homes of those friends who were likely to be invited to the convocation and even contacted Kamala. As luck would have it, she handed over her father's pass, thereby fulfilling her promise of help. But the men – once again exhibiting the distance between their passion and experience – ruined the card while enthusiastically trying to erase Kamala's father's name.

Virendra was back to square one. After much snooping around, he found a replacement; the card was lying casually on a table. It belonged to a family friend, Thakur Dutt Sharma's son. The Sharma family was widely regarded for its ayurvedic medicines, Amrit Dhara. When all eyes were elsewhere, Virendra quietly pocketed the card which was in Durga Das's hands in no time. The men had learned from their mistake and, this time, with intense concentration they scrubbed off the name, replacing it with that of Hari Krishan.

The man from Mardan had replaced his old shabby clothes and was dressed in a classy, Western outfit. Ranbir and Durga Das were the only people who knew of his hideout. Virendra had no idea, nor did he ask. Another mantra of the revolutionaries was that they worked on a strict need-to-know basis. Virendra did not know where Hari Krishan was, and the others did not know where Virendra found the invitation card. In the end, it was this practice that saved them; the police remained clueless about the origins of the invitation card.

The convocation was on 23 December and, along with the Governor, Dr Radhakrishnan – later, independent India's second President – was the main speaker. In 1930, he was invited in his capacity as a professor at Oxford University. Years down the line, as the country's first citizen, Dr Radhakrishnan was to recall jocularly that providence had saved him that day '… otherwise who knows who would have been hit by the bullets fired by you fellows.'[167]

Hari Krishan was to report at the venue, fifteen minutes before 11 a.m., the function's official start time. He now knew his way around; the others had shown him the convocation hall and familiarized him with the roads around the university. He had also been given strict instructions – Hari Krishan was to attempt an escape after the attack and, in no manner whatsoever was he to emulate Bhagat Singh and Batukeshwar Dutt's surrender in the Assembly.

Virendra, Durga Das and Ranbir, in the meantime, sanitized their rooms of any incriminating material. If there was one thing they were certain of, it was their arrest. Sleep had not come to any of them the previous night. In the eyes of the police, Virendra was a bigger suspect than Ranbir and Durga Das, whose activities in the Punjab Students' Union were public but not their deep involvement in the revolutionary movement. On the evening of 22 December, the three got together – would they meet again? None of them was certain. Their families were oblivious to their activities, including Durga Das's wife who was pregnant with their second child.

The convocation hall was teeming with both the police and CID. Before guests arrived, a man, not very tall, showed his card and calmly seated himself next to the aisle from where the Governor was to make his way. The revolver had been slipped into a cavity in a book he carried. As the clock struck 10.50, the audience – made up mostly of students and their families – stood up and the procession with Governor Geoffrey Fitzhervey de Montmorency, accompanied by Dr S. Radhakrishnan, entered the hall.

The two men took their seats on the dais and proceedings were soon underway. Among those present in the hall to receive a degree was Kamala; apart from the four men, she was the only other person in the know. That something was going to happen, she was convinced of; what and by whom, she had no clue. As the event went about its business and nothing disturbed its monotony, a feeling of disappointment washed over Kamala and she berated herself for not getting the task – she would not have flinched, she told herself.

It was nearing 1 p.m. when the convocation ended, and soon the parade with Sir Geoffrey and Dr Radhakrishnan began to retrace its steps. Kamala was lamenting at what could have been when she heard a shot fired near the main gate. One shot, then the second and then the third. The hall that, minutes ago, was studious and calm was now thrown into chaos as dignitaries flung themselves under chairs and tables for safety. Kamala recounted to Virendra that among those desperately taking refuge were the titled gentry of Rai Bahadurs and Khan Bahadurs, some of whom cowered behind curtains while others ran outside.

Hari Krishan's bullet had injured the Governor. Head Constable Chanan Singh tried to capture him, but Hari Krishan kept shooting calmly. Singh himself caught a bullet; profusely bleeding, he died that evening. The Governor survived; badly shaken, he was admitted to Edward Victor Hospital – built as an 'elitist' hospital, where he received treatment and was soon discharged.[168] All six bullets over – fired in a way so that no harm came to Dr Radhakrishnan – Hari Krishan was overpowered as he was reloading his revolver. Despite the instructions, he made no attempt to flee, and, by all accounts, was brutally tortured at the Lahore jail and made to lie between ice slabs in peak winter.[169] When his father came to see Hari Krishan in jail, it was evident that the apple had not fallen far from the tree. He asked his son in Pashto how he had missed killing the Governor! It was the rickety chair on which the young man stood while shooting the Governor that let him down. On a separate note, Hari Krishan's brother Bhagat Ram Talwar was the British spy 'Silver' who helped Subhas Chandra Bose escape via Kabul![170]

The three conspirators waited anxiously for the inevitable knock on the door. Having stayed away from the university, they were also trying to gauge if the mission was successful. Virendra came to the *Pratap* office but there was no news. After fifteen or twenty minutes, dejected, he made his way back home. On the street, he passed some students, still in their black gowns from the convocation, and overheard one of them say, 'Governor was definitely injured but don't know how much.'

This was all he needed to know. Virendra came home and quietly went to his room, waiting for the police. His father returned home from the office in the evening and went straight to his elder son's room. 'Have you heard what has happened at the university?' he asked.

Virendra replied that he had heard a bit.

At this, the father asked bluntly, 'Are you also involved? If yes, let me know so that I can arrange for your defence.'

Terrified of his father's anger, Virendra lied, insisting that he had nothing to do with the incident. Mahashay Krishan was no fool. As he left the room, he told his son to gather his things and put them in order. Virendra stepped out briefly in the evening and, when he returned, his mother told him that his father had rummaged through his belongings with a fine-toothed comb.

This incident was as sensational as the attack on Viceroy Hardinge and its news spread as quickly as a paper on fire sizzles into ash. Newspapers commented that when a Governor was not safe, it was a sign for the British Raj to recognize how reviled it was. Punjab and the resistance once again had the country's attention.

The day passed without any more incidents. This time, the police did not want to rush into any action – the failure to catch those behind the viceregal train bombing was still raw. The city transformed into the familiar cantonment and the three friends could not meet. The future course of action was up for discussion, but the CID was closing in. And they did not have to wait long. On 26 December, Ranbir was arrested. Two days later, Durga Das and Virendra were in custody.

Hari Krishan was executed on 9 June 1931. He died so that a country could be free, adding another tier to the pyramid of sacrifices. Brick by bloodied brick, these young men laid the foundation for India's independence. This was not the only commonality he shared with Bhagat Singh. Krishan was also only twenty-three years old, the same age as the legendary freedom fighter was when he was hanged. He was no less brave; yet, who remembers this young man today?

12

Prison Raj: Where the Mind Is without Fear

Lahore had fallen into a deep sleep – the city needed a moment to itself. The streets that looked each day in the eye with unwavering acts of heroism were now silent, besieged by darkness and plunging temperatures. The inhabitants of 41, Nisbet Road had long called it a night not knowing that their beloved city was flattering to deceive. In the late hours, when night flirts with the idea of a dawn, unknown to a sleeping Virendra, the police surround his house. It was 28 December 1930, and five days earlier an attempt was made on the Governor's life.

Mahashay Krishan was an early riser – whether it was Lahore's claustrophobic heat or its turning seasons later in the year, he never missed his morning walk. That morning, as Krishan stepped out of the door, he saw the police. Without exchanging a word with them, he turned around and walked back inside, not stopping until he reached Virendra's room. 'Get ready; the police have come,' were the first words Virendra heard that morning. With no time for emotions, his mother bustled around collecting her son's things and getting his breakfast ready as the police entered the house.

The inspector was a polite man who told Virendra's father of his discomfort in searching the house. If he could be handed over something 'suspicious' by the family, his work would be over. It would also save both from the embarrassment of being the hunter and the hunted. Krishan's response was forthright – he had himself searched his son's room and found nothing objectionable. If the police wanted to, they could go ahead and hunt. Left with no choice, the inspector went ahead and searched his room, returning only with a book of economics. Virendra remembers:[171]

> When I look back, I do find that we came across many young officers, especially Muslims, who had sympathy for us. I do not remember a single instance of any young officer having troubled us. We were either harassed by police constables looking for a quick promotion or by senior police officers, but young police officers seldom caused us any distress.

Virendra makes special mention of two officers – Khan Bahadur Syed Ahmad Shah and Khan Bahadur Niyaz Ahmed – whom he came across in the Shahi Qila of Lahore.

The inspector turned his attention to Virendra's mother, asking her to give her son nashta since when his next meal would be was anyone's guess. The freedom fighter naturally had no appetite – his family was unaware of his involvement in the attack on the Governor, and he alone knew why he was being arrested and what the consequences could be.

A year after his last incarceration, Virendra was back in Borstal Jail and handed over to its deputy superintendent, who quietly said a puzzling khuda hafiz and left. This was his fourth imprisonment and a third Lahore December in prison. Past experiences did not make it easy as Virendra found himself locked up alone. In 1928, he was arrested in the Saunders murder case; in December 1929 he was in the same jail on charges of attempting to blow up the Viceroy's train and now, a year later, in the conspiracy to shoot the Governor.

Freedom fighters preferred prisons to a police station – the atmosphere in jails was more liberal and there were other prisoners to interact with to pass days. Inmates could also move out of their cells to get some fresh air. From where Virendra was in that moment, his past life resembled a bed of roses. He had understood why the deputy superintendent had bid 'khuda hafiz' to him – may god protect you!

Chakki ahata was an area where grindstones were installed. In the earlier days, prisoners sentenced to rigorous punishment were sent to these cells and asked to grind flour all day long. Virendra found himself in a chakki lock-up – although, mercifully, there was no longer any physical labour. Those were the only good tidings. The cell was so cramped that even a charpoy could not fit in, nor was there anyone around for him to speak with. This was solitary confinement at its harshest. Barring half an hour in the morning and an hour in the evening, Virendra spent his days enclosed by shrinking walls. In the brief minutes he was allowed outdoors, all he saw was the sky above and the ground beneath.

At the centre of the jail premises stood a watch tower – a guard was on top screening prisoners like a hawk and nipping any thoughts of scaling the perimeter. A sentry was on duty around the clock and made his presence felt every five minutes by shouting, 'Sab achcha.' It seemed there was a competition for who could shout the loudest. Every warder would stop outside his cell and holler, 'Bol, jawan.' If the prisoner replied, the warder moved on but if there was no answer, his infuriatingly clipped tone went on a loop till a response came.

A result of Bhagat Singh and Jatin Das's hunger strike was that jail staff ceased physically abusing prisoners, but psychological tactics were still used. Repeated calls of 'sab achcha' and 'bol, jawan' made a good night's sleep impossible. For Virendra, even a nap was out of the question – he was imprisoned for a conspiracy to kill the 'laat saab' and, with such serious charges against him, jail authorities were in no mood to show any leniency. He remained confined, with no access to any outsider. On either side of his lock-up were three cells, all empty to keep him isolated. A cat would occasionally drop by, but, other than that, it was just him and his thoughts.

The routine was broken one morning when Virendra was called to the warder's office. Expecting a visit from his family, he quickly wrapped himself in a shawl. The two men who stood waiting for him could not have been further from his family – they were from the CID. Khan Bahadur Syed Ahmad Shah made Virendra sit next to him and, after some small talk, asked directly, 'When did you meet Hari Krishan for the first time?' Virendra was prepared; he had been questioned plenty of times on similar lines and promptly lied saying he had never seen the man. The officer was not ready to let go so easily and changed tack.

Khan Bahadur's son, Nazir, was studying at Government College and was known to Virendra. The police officer brought some emotion into his interrogation: 'There is no difference between the two of you and I do not want any harm to come to you. Tell me the truth, so I can somehow save you.' Virendra did not change his story forcing Khan Bahadur to try another approach – the officer went for the jugular. Durga Das and Ranbir had told him everything, he announced, and, as Nazir's father, he wanted to help his son's friend.

Virendra was torn. If his two comrades had indeed disclosed information, then his fate was sealed. He did not have the conviction to accept his friends' betrayal; yet, Khan Bahadur had spoken so persuasively. Could he disbelieve the police officer? As contradictory thoughts crowded his mind, Khan Bahadur inexplicably stood up. 'You go and rest,' he announced. 'We shall meet again.'

In less than a week he was back; this time, bringing some fruits with him. 'Beta, this is no age to waste in jail,' he began, once again referring to his son and their bond. But his next words gave Virendra some comfort. 'You all were very clever; you even arranged for entry into the university hall. Who got the admit card?' Hearing this, Virendra instantly knew that the police was still groping in the dark, and Durga Das and Ranbir had not confessed. The former knew the admit card was stolen by Virendra. Going forward, the revolutionary stuck unwaveringly to his refrain that he knew nothing about the incident.

Days passed slowly; the cat was still his only company. After a month, Virendra was released on bail, but the petitions of both Durga Das and Ranbir were rejected. A comrade, Dasaundhi Ram, had become an approver and based on his testimony, a case began against Durga Das, Ranbir and Chaman Lal for the conspiracy to kill the Governor.[172] Virendra was freed, but the police could not rid itself of suspicions of his involvement. Durga Das's silence had brought Virendra relief, however temporarily.

Winter meandered on and February brought with it a scent of spring. The nation however was in mourning – Pandit Motilal Nehru had passed away and condolence meetings were being held all over India. On the evening of 10 February 1931, Virendra walked across to his neighbour and family friend, Dr Satyapal's, house to take a lift to the prayer gathering at Bradlaugh Hall. As the men stepped out of the house, Virendra noticed two police officers flanking a vehicle in front of his gate. He was instantly alert, but Dr Satyapal was nonchalant. When the police come to arrest someone, they don't come in twos; they bring a fauj, he casually told Virendra.

The older man had spoken too soon. Khan Bahadur Syed Ahmad Shah stepped out of the vehicle and addressed Virendra,

'We miss you. So, I thought let me see how you are doing. You keep loitering around the entire day, so I decided that you should rest a bit.' He rounded off his sarcasm with, 'I have come to take you.' Out of his pocket came a warrant – one that was as unexpected as it was severe. The arrest was under Regulation III of the notorious section 1818.[173]

The first of its kind in colonial India, the draconian detention act was initially introduced in Bengal in 1818 and later extended across the country. Signed by the Viceroy of India, it allowed for arrests to be made without the legality of a court – setting a dangerous precedent of detentions without trial. If fortunate, the detainee was informed three months later of the reasons for their arrest. When a defence was presented in the high court, a judge took a retrospective call on the confinement's justification. At the time young Virendra was arrested under this stringent act, only eight other people across the country had been put behind bars on similar grounds, notable among them were Mahatma Gandhi and Subhas Chandra Bose.

As soon as he saw the warrant, Dr Satyapal hurriedly accompanied Virendra to his house where Mahashay Krishan was busy writing for *Pratap*. It had only been fifteen days since Virendra was released from his last prison stint – a period of political calm and there had not been anything untoward reported on the streets or in *Pratap*. So why the arrest? The seasoned editor understood that the police had no evidence against his son; instead, a century-old law was being used to settle scores.

Having had her son home for only two weeks, Virendra's mother was disturbed, but she put her feelings aside to pack his belongings, as she had done more than once before. In the homes of freedom fighters, by and large it was the men who were active, and the ladies of the house could only wait and pray for their well-being. In Virendra's case, his mother, his sister and, later, his wife had to all face the consequences of frequent raids and imprisonments.

The severity of this arrest hit the family hard. Regulation III of 1818 felt like an endless ocean with no sightings of a shore – Virendra could languish in jail for as long as the British desired. The constables put his luggage in their vehicle and, leaving his dazed family behind, Virendra retraced his steps back to jail. This time, instead of stopping at Borstal Jail, the police van came to a halt outside Lahore's Central Jail, where Bhagat Singh and his comrades were also in lock-up. This was Virendra's first time here, and it would not be the last.

The college student was taken to the jail superintendent's office, where he was joined shortly by comrade Ehsan Ilahi, who was also arrested under the same regulation. Seeing him, Virendra was relieved – at least he had company. Both had been in custody together twice earlier. Inside the jail, there was another surprise. Fazal Ilahi Qurban had been incarcerated under Regulation 1818 for the past two months. The three were to stay together in a sizeable-sized cell called Diwani ahata, in a civil area. Outside, there was a small courtyard; in one corner, stood a small kitchen and, on the other side, a modest bathroom. This arrest was different. As 'King's prisoners', they were given a monthly stipend of Rs 75 and allowed to wear their home clothes. They could also, if they chose to, get food from home. With their liberal allowance, the three preferred to get food prepared in-house by a cook who was at their service. For the next seven months, this was Virendra's home.

All three settled down, barring one unusual problem. Both Ehsan and Fazal ate meat, whereas Virendra, belonging to the Arya Samaj, was a staunch vegetarian. The former two were keen to get non-vegetarian food cooked, but Virendra, just out of his teens, could not handle the sight of meat. None of them were wrong in their thinking; nevertheless, some anxious moments could not be avoided. Three months later, when Fazal Ilahi was shifted to Multan Jail, Ehsan and Virendra came to a compromise. Twice a week, meat was prepared, but outside in the courtyard and not in the kitchen. On the other days, they ate together.

The prisoners were allowed a visit from their family every fortnight but, with a CID officer permanently stationed in the meeting room, not much was discussed. It was through newspapers that Virendra learned that his friends Durga Das and Ranbir were being tried for the conspiracy to kill the Governor.

In the 1930s, Lahore's society was bustling with several Mahashays and Lalas – honorary titles for men connected to the Arya Samaj. When he least expected it, Virendra received the benevolence of one such gentleman. Mahashay Rattan Chand 'Ratto' was arrested under Martial Law in 1919 and sentenced to be hanged – an order later commuted to life imprisonment. He had spent more than seven years at the notorious Kala Pani, after which he was transferred to Central Jail, Lahore.

As per prison rules, if an inmate was in jail for a considerable period of time without creating any disturbance, he was either given some responsibilities or light work to make his remaining life as comfortable as possible. Mahashay Ratto had a reputation for being an honest man; he was also respected by jail authorities, who made him the prison storekeeper. Ration worth thousands of rupees was purchased for 3,000 inmates and handed over to Ratto who met with suppliers frequently. This gave the older man unrestricted access to any item he desired.

One evening, after Virendra had already spent his first night back in custody, unexpectedly, a prisoner brought him fruits and mithai saying it had been sent by Lala ji, Ratto's name in jail. A couple of days later, when halwa was sent for him, a suspicious Ehsan warned against the generosity of the unknown Lala, cautioning Virendra that it could be a CID man in disguise trying to gain his confidence.

Ehsan Ilahi's words made him think and Virendra returned the halwa. The matter however did not end here; an hour later, the same prisoner returned, this time with a letter disclosing Lala Ratto's identity. It turned out that he was not just a friend of Mahashay Krishan; Virendra, as a child, had played on his lap. Forbidden from meeting the young man, Lala ji had sent him treats through one of his trusted people. His man would visit the revolutionary daily and make sure all his requirements were met – the only caveat was that Lala ji and Virendra could not meet. After that, Lala ji, with his white pagri, would cross Virendra's cell daily without pausing, the inmate would wait to say a silent namaste to him.

Virendra's jail spell stretched seemingly without an end; he had no inkling how long it would be before he was free. The other two, Fazal and Ehsan, were active political workers; nationalism was, in a sense, their only profession. They had no businesses outside nor were they studying in a college. Fazal Ilahi was a worker of the Communist Party and had secretly visited Russia. All his discussions invariably led to Lenin and Marx. Communists were persona non grata and viewed with misgiving by the colonial rulers, and Fazal was arrested on the suspicion of being a Russian agent. Ehsan, on the other hand, was a nationalist and a member of the Naujawan Bharat Sabha. Despite not possessing a college degree, he was a well-read and learned person. The two would often have spirited arguments. Unlike Virendra, their families had no interest in their activities.

Virendra was in his final year of college and the arrest was untimely – it put a question mark on his graduation. Exams were barely two months away and he saw the possibility of appearing for them beginning to fade. Regret was not absolute, however; with frequent jail trips, the student in him had played second fiddle to the revolutionary within and he knew his studies had faltered. In his contemplation, however, Virendra had not accounted for one thing – his father's determination. Krishan refused to let a freedom struggle come in the way of his son's education. For him, the British and a non-graduate son were both equally unacceptable. A BA pass was the minimum qualification for a padha–likha naujawan.

13

War and Peace: Graduation in Jail

When Virendra's thoughts went to the very real possibility that he would never graduate, he felt a twinge of sadness, but he quickly dismissed the feeling. He had resigned himself to forgoing his studies for the country's freedom. In his mind, it was a worthy sacrifice. Mahashay Krishan, on the other hand, was a force of nature who was not prepared for any such compromise, and he was willing to do whatever it took to ensure his son graduated.

With only two months to go for the annual examinations, time was running out. He sent out a letter to the Punjab government asking why his son should be deprived of his right to education. Krishan went as far as to even give two solutions: Either Virendra be released, so he could sit for his exams; or some arrangement be made so the student could appear for the assessments from prison. The father was in full flow, and, while at it, he also demanded that books and copies be allowed in jail for his son to prepare.

The government refused. There was no precedent for relaxing such rules for any captives, including prisoners of the Crown. Krishan, though, was not ready to take no for an answer and he went to meet Jenkins – Virendra's old nemesis. Jenkins had arrested Virendra in the Saunders' murder case and was now a high-ranking CID officer in charge of the prisoners' fate. The meeting, predictably, did not begin well. The men had barely acknowledged each other when a heated debate erupted between them. Jenkins argued that Krishan's son was a dangerous rebel and deserved no concession. The pushback was expected and did not deter Krishan, who countered by asking for proof. 'If you have any, book him and start a case against him instead of detaining him without trial under the 1818 Regulation. But it seems you have no case against him and have kept him to take some kind of revenge,' thundered the father.

This provoked Jenkins. He picked up a heavy file lying on his table and angrily threw it towards Krishan. 'Read,' he shouted. 'You do not deserve to be called a father. You do not know what your son has been doing. See his file.' Krishan had just started scanning the file when Jenkins changed his mind and snatched it back. 'It is confidential!' he snarled. In those brief minutes, Krishan's glance was able to take in letters scribbled by his son and posters, handwritten, that he had pasted on the college notice board. The older man also noticed some CID reports but was not quick enough to catch their contents before Jenkins grabbed the file back.

Curiously, the acrimonious exchange lost steam when Jenkins did a volte-face and agreed to get the government's consent if the university permitted a special case for its student. Jenkins also promised that study books sent by Krishan would reach his son. There was a glimmer of hope; nonetheless, the battle was only half won. After his confrontation with Jenkins, the father went knocking on the doors of Punjab University. He had more than a few friends in the Senate through whom he approached the authorities. That, however, was the easy part. The university was reluctant to accommodate his request – there would be no exceptions for an examination centre for just one student. However, its initial stand changed once it understood that not only was Virendra a special prisoner, the government too was on board with him taking his exams.

The first indication that his father's efforts had borne fruit came when two prisoners turned up at Virendra's cell with books, pencils, a pen and an ink bottle, all sent by Krishan. Soon after, a deputy superintendent informed him that the government had allowed him to sit for the exams. Instead of rejoicing, conversely, Virendra was unsettled. He had given up the thought of appearing for his exams and although there was more than enough time to study in jail, was he in the frame of mind to do so? In a lock-up, mental well-being was as erratic as the cat who appeared out of nowhere only to disappear again during his previous imprisonment. There was the added stress of not getting any guidance for his studies. It was just him and his books. But, could he let his father – who had moved heaven and earth for him – down?

A special examination centre was set up in the Railway Police office at Lahore and plans were in place to escort the student-revolutionary for his final-year assessments – a unique arrangement that was not repeated again. While the logistics were being worked out, Virendra was struggling, both with the shift required in focus and the lack of any assistance. Fazal Ilahi tried to help him solve some exam questions, but Virendra was better off without him lending a hand. Ilahi's answers were influenced by his communist ideology and all roads led to the same answer.

Concluding that he was in this alone and it was an opportunity not to be missed, the student in Virendra finally resurfaced, and, over the next few days, dawn and dusk, became one. Decades later, when his granddaughter was fretting over a school exam he smiled and said, 'If I could pass mine sitting in jail, you will do well. Do not worry too much.'

It was finally the day of the first examination. The lethargic sounds of the morning were just about nudging the prisoners awake when a police van reached the gate of Lahore's Central Jail with an officer and two constables sitting inside the vehicle. At 6 a.m., Virendra was taken to the Railway Police office and chaperoned inside, where a university administrator was waiting for him. Exam paper in hand, he pulled his chair so close that the student could not have even taken a breath without it being counted.

While Virendra drafted his answers, a police officer with a rifle stood guard outside his room, and this became the routine until one day a different invigilator entered the centre. The man was

Mahashay Krishan, *Pratap*'s founder.

Pratap office in Gawalmandi, Lahore.

Virendra (extreme left) after being released from a British jail.

Masthead from the archives.

Virendra and Kiron Das being handed over to the British police from the Congress Seva Dal camp, Lahore, for an attempt to blow up the Viceroy's train; Mahashay Krishan, extreme left.

Raj Lakshmi (standing third from left) as a student of Kinnaird College, Lahore.

Subhas Bose (extreme left) Mahashay Krishan (centre) and Virendra (extreme right) at Lahore Railway station.

The family home on Nisbet Road, Lahore.

Jawaharlal Nehru addressing a press conference at Mahashay Krishnan's house in Lahore. Virendra sits behind him.

Actor Prithviraj Kapoor visiting the family at their home in Jalandhar.

Virendra as a jail inmate.

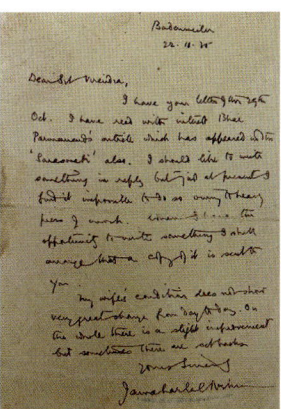

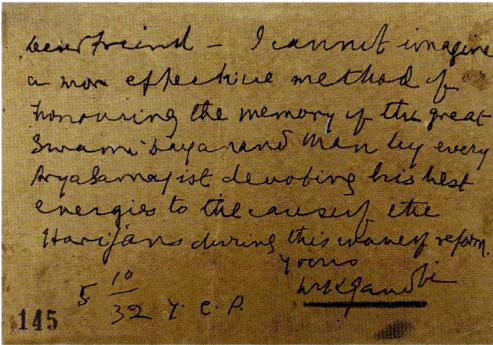

Mahatma Gandhi's postcard to Virendra.

Nehru's letter to Virendra from Badenweiller in Germany during his wife Kamala Nehru's treatment.

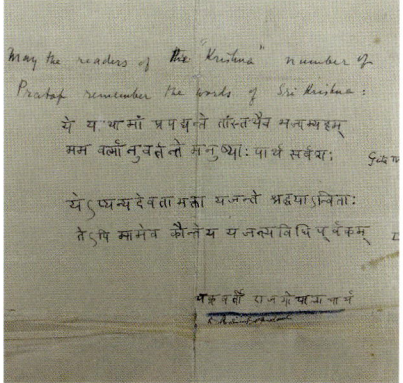

Letter by C. Rajagopalachari, last Governor-General of India, to *Pratap*.

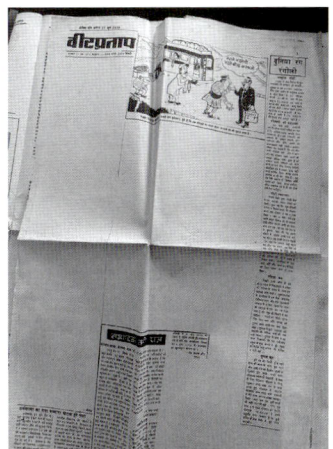

Vir Pratap editorials left blank during Emergency.

Pratap editorials left blank during Emergency.

Virendra with his kalam.

The cover of the parcel bomb sent to the *Pratap* office in 1983 that killed two people.

Punjab chief minister Beant Singh paying homage to Virendra at the family home in Jalandhar after he passed away on 31 December 1993.

kind enough to tell Virendra that if he was carrying a book, he could check his answers while the man himself looked away!

Meanwhile, Mahashay Krishan's customary morning walks were ongoing, but with a slight alteration. He changed his route towards Lawrence Gardens and would stand at the chowk when the police van ferried his son to the makeshift examination facility. One day, the police inexplicably changed its route and Krishan waited for three hours that day for a sight of his son – worried if all was well.

Krishan was made to pay a sum of Rs 120 by the Home Department, Punjab, as a cost 'necessitated by the special arrangements which had to be made for the Degree examination of Virendra during the period of his internment under Regulation III of 1818'.[174] The government refunded this amount to him in 1931.

Once the exams were over, which meant his outings had also come to an end, Virendra was back to being a prisoner. In the evenings, the three young men strolled in the small courtyard overlooking the high prison walls and, when restricted to the indoors, they read books or passed time by simply lying on their charpoys. Living in such proximity for months without a link to the outside world occasionally fired up tempers, especially between Ehsan and Fazal Ilahi. Both were Muslims but had a complicated relationship with religion – more so, Fazal Ilahi, who, as a staunch believer in communism, was anti-religious. Ehsan was not opposed to faith but had scant interest in it. It was only when Fazal Ilahi was shifted to Multan Jail that a calm fell over their lock-up, although the gated existence strained their relationship as well on some days, and it was the handsome monthly stipend and Mahashay Ratto's generosity that kept them going.

After several months, Virendra was given a chargesheet and, on his behalf, a reply was filed in the high court which was rejected. Within six months, as was the law, he was sent another chargesheet. This time, he covertly sent it outside to his father, who had a lawyer prepare the reply. It was sent back to him in jail for his signature through Mahashay Ratto's clandestine network.

The response was brief – Virendra had been in Central Jail for six months, hence the question of his indulging in any political actively did not arise. If there was any evidence to the contrary with the government, he should be informed so that he could respond suitably. As expected, the police had no case.

It was late July, and Virendra was taking an afternoon nap when the jail superintendent walked in, followed by two helpers. The prisoner was woken up and asked to pack his bags. 'Where to?' he asked. 'Multan Jail,' came the prompt reply. The thought of leaving Lahore saddened Virendra. His family visited him every fortnight, which would be impossible in Multan, a city more than three hundred kilometres away. He was also distressed to part with Ehsan Ilahi – the initial unpleasantness had given way to a strong friendship between the two.

The young man wanted to inform his family about the shift, but the jailer was non-committal. There was no such provision; still, he promised to consider the request. 'You can pack your stuff without hurrying, there is time for the train,' he added on his way out.

The farewell was emotional. Virendra left most of his worldly belongings for Ehsan and, as the two hugged each other, the tears that rolled down were as much for the separation as for anxiety of the unknown. The prison helpers carried his luggage to the jailer's room where the young man was made to sign papers. 'Let's go,' prompted the jailer.

'But the police have not come. With whom are you sending me to Multan?' questioned Virendra.

The jailer smiled and said mysteriously, 'Arrangements have been made.'

As Virendra stepped out of the enormous steel gates of the jail, he was taken aback by the sight that met his eyes. Instead of a police van, his luggage was being stowed on a horse-driven tonga. The jailer waved his hand. 'You can go now.'

'But go where?'

'Home,' came the answer.

And it finally dawned on him.

After seven months, Virendra was a free man. His face showed his confusion. He was intentionally misled – perhaps to spare Ehsan Ilahi's feelings, for the other man's confinement remained indefinite. Hoodwinking his friend brought mixed feelings with it until the enormity of the events began to sink in. Home and liberty – it was going to be the best tonga ride he had ever taken!

Virendra headed home as fast as the horses' legs could carry him. Krishan was not at Nisbet Road, but his mother came out running and, in their excitement, the matriarch and son forgot to collect the luggage from the horse carriage. Fortunately, they were able to retrieve it later. When Krishan walked in, he did not look surprised to see his son. If he had any prior knowledge of his release, he had hidden it well from his wife to save her from disappointment if events did not go as planned. Or, as a stern father, he simply hid his emotions.

Krishan looked at his son and addressed him with a mix of resignation and laughter, '*Aa gaye par kitne din ke liye* (You have come, but for how many days)?'

His words were to prove prophetic. Virendra's fifth imprisonment had ended but the preparation for the sixth had already begun.

14
Chaar Aana: The Brave and the Cinema

The year 1931 was harsh on the revolutionary movement – it was the year the Trimurti-led crusade came to an end. On 27 February, Chandrashekhar Azad – the only remaining leader who was free, was killed in a police encounter in Allahabad's Alfred Park. Bhagwati Charan Vohra tragically died earlier while making a bomb and the incarcerated Bhagat Singh embraced the gallows less than a month after Azad's death.

Till his dying moments, and despite limited resources, Azad continued to inspire a fizzling revolutionary movement and it is widely believed that Bhagat Singh's popularity during his lifetime was in no small measure due to the efficient propaganda machine of the Hindustan Socialist Republican Association (HSRA). An award of Rs 50,000 on Azad's head was sweet persuasion – a comrade betrayed his location to the police. For a revolutionary, Azad though had survived insurmountable odds. 'He was a relentless revolutionary. He was also restless; when one plan failed, he came up with another one,' remembers Virendra.[175]

Influenced by Mahatma Gandhi's non-cooperation campaign, Chandrashekhar Tiwari was barely fifteen years old when, along with some friends, he picketed Sanskrit College in Varanasi. He was arrested and his questioning was to irrevocably alter the nature of the revolutionary movement. It was also the baptism of his name, Azad.

Name? – Azad.

Name of Residence? – Jail.

Father's name – Swadheen.

The punishment of fifteen lashes was curtailed as he was still a minor. With each blow, instead of cowering down, the boy's voice rose a notch higher to bellow proudly, 'Bharat Mata ki jai, Mahatma Gandhi ki jai.' Bleeding profusely, he pledged there and then to take revenge on the British – an oath that was to consume him till his last drop of blood. As per jail rules, Azad was handed three annas for his return ticket; he flung the coins on the ground disdainfully and walked off.

It was a meeting with Ram Prasad Bismil that proved to become the defining moment of Azad's personal journey as a freedom fighter, and he joined Bismil's revolutionary organization HRA (later known as the HSRA). Living as a celibate under the Arya Samaj's influence, fitness was Bismil's one big interest and his enthusiasm rubbed off on Azad, who, in his free time, was also found working on his strength and masculine image. A renowned poet – wrongly credited at times for the iconic '*Sarfaroshi ki tamanna*' penned by Bismil Azimabadi – Bismil was hanged in the Kakori Conspiracy Case, while Azad escaped and went on to live several lives within a single lifetime as he played hide and seek with the police.

As far as he was concerned, Azad had dedicated himself in service of India's freedom and his family – his father was a gardener, his mother, a homemaker – willingly or otherwise had to be content with whatever leftovers came their way. The deeper Azad submerged into the organization, the more tenuous his bonds became with the family. Ganesh Chander Vidyarthi, Azad's mentor, learned of their financial distress and handed the revolutionary Rs 200 to give to his parents. Instead of sending the money home, Azad passed it on to his party. When Vidyarthi inquired, Azad replied, 'Vidyarthi-ji, my parents will manage somehow but there are some young men in my party who sometimes must sleep on an empty stomach. The country needs them more than my aged parents.'[176]

Azad's most abiding image – the one that endures in periodicals and newspapers – is of him twirling his moustache. Virendra goes beyond this popular imagination and gives an insight into the man behind the photograph. Azad unwittingly built a reputation as an attractive personality, a fame that was at odds with his revolutionary persona. His daring acts too worked as a magnet, and he began to attract the attention of women who found him as challenging as he was appealing.

Azad was not impressed by this turn of events. A revolutionary could not divide his love – either it was the country or a woman. He was transparent about his commitment to freedom. His friends, on the other hand, were not as strong-willed and the leader did not forgive his comrades for their relationships. In his mind, they weakened the struggle. His distaste for personal engagements with the opposite sex became so rabid that, one time, Azad had to be restrained from shooting a freedom fighter who, he felt, had crossed this Lakshman Rekha. A revolutionary must resist three temptations – women, alcohol and cigarettes – he insisted, believing they had the potential to destroy men. He was the same man who was to encourage women to join the revolutionary group during the British resistance.

Chandrashekhar Azad was equally non-compromising when it came to crowdfunding his movement. He was adamantly against the misuse of public money for personal gratification or any kind of careless spending. As the leader, he distributed four annas daily to each comrade and this included a food allowance.

Bhagat Singh, on the other hand, enjoyed watching movies. In the enormity of his sacrifice and ideological stance, it is easy to overlook that he was only in his early twenties when he was hanged. It was his love for cinema that revealed his youth. Intentions apart, for him to reach the hall to watch a film was not straightforward, and it was not merely about the distance. Azad predictably refused all requests for an additional allowance to watch movies and instead reprimanded Bhagat Singh – cinema was frivolous and did not behove a revolutionary. (There are views that Azad himself went to the cinema when working in the squalor of a dockyard in his early teens.) The leader further chastised his comrade, telling him that money given by the public was to be returned by their blood and not spent in trivial pursuits. A stalemate ensued causing some friction between the two, but Bhagat Singh was also clear in his mind who the leader was. It was not him.

There were quite a few young ladies in Lahore who were similarly smitten by Bhagat Singh's personality. The young man's status among Lahore's fairer sex was further boosted after the Assembly bombing and his concise, fearless views in the Lahore Conspiracy Case. By then, however, he was out of reach, incarcerated in a British prison.

While he was a free citizen, Bhagat Singh – despite his respect for Azad – was temperamentally miles away from living the ascetic life of his senior comrade. He enjoyed listening to music, but cinema was his big love. As soon as his eye caught a movie's poster, Bhagat Singh's first instinct was to head out and watch the film till he remembered that money was in the 'Brahmachari's' hands – Azad's nickname by his comrades. The older man never tired of repeating, 'You will be caught sitting in a cinema hall and I will keep waiting for you.' Full of life – ironically even as he stepped to his death – Bhagat Singh opposed these restrictions. '*Maut se pehle kyun marna* (Why die before death comes)?' So, he begged and he cajoled, chipping away at his elder comrade's patience till he found his way to the movies.

While wandering around Lahore planning their next move after Lala Lajpat Rai's death, Bhagat Singh noticed a billboard advertising a new release. He immediately made up his mind to watch *Uncle Tom's Cabin* but with char anna in his pocket and meals still to be eaten, he could either watch the movie or get some food. Regardless of his resistance, Singh was scared of Azad's anger, especially over the wastage of precious funds.

Even so, the call of the movies was stronger and the revolutionary was soon inside a cinema hall. He was able to watch the movie without a hitch. However, he felt immensely guilty on his return. He admitted to violating the code, omitting any mentions of foregoing his meal and staying hungry. Azad saw through his tale and sensed his predicament; Bhagat Singh was given another four annas and explicitly told to eat. He was also given an earful on how a revolutionary can ill afford to lead a life of luxury and pleasure. Azad worried that Bhagat Singh's film craze was no secret and taking advantage, the CID could swoop down on him any day in a darkened movie hall.

These differences apart, their affection for each other was abiding. The day Bhagat Singh threw a bomb in the Assembly, Azad was in Agra. Reading the news in the papers, Azad became emotional – his comrades considered him hard-hearted – as it struck him that he may never meet his protégé again. He recalled a conversation the two had on a lighter day about how they would meet their ends. Unhesitatingly, Azad had told his younger comrade the inevitability of being caught watching a movie. Laughing, Bhagat Singh had replied that finishing him would be easy for the police but to hang Azad, they would need very thick ropes – one for his neck and another for his stomach!

'Although the entire revolutionary movement has not got the kind of recognition it deserves, Azad has been especially neglected,' says historian Prabal Agarwal,[177] adding that there is a lack of understanding about the true nature and historical role of the Indian revolutionary movement. Azad's leadership and Bhagat Singh's ideological mentorship changed the revolutionaries from being mere anti-colonialists to fighters for an egalitarian and progressive society. 'It went on for fifty years, and was led by several extraordinary men and women whose lives still need to be explored.' The dominance of Punjabis in the Hindi film industry after 1947, in the historian's opinion, played a role in keeping alive a selective Bhagat Singh memory in the public.

Azad was advised to flee to Russia; it was understood that once arrested he would be marched straight to the noose. He dismissed the suggestion outright – he was not interested in going to 'Roosphoos, I will die only in the mitti of my motherland'.[178] And so it was. In February 1931, he was shot dead in Allahabad's Alfred Park. Azad had pledged never to be caught alive – he lived and died fulfilling that pledge.

Sukhdev Raj describes Azad's last moments:[179]

> On 27 February, after breakfast, I left on my bicycle. On the way, I met bhaiya Azad and both of us headed towards the park. As I had come from Burma, he enquired about that country and chatting together we entered the park. There we saw a man sitting on the bridge brushing his teeth with a datun, he was looking towards Azad who pointed that out to me. By that time, the man had turned his face. That was some sort of a signal because shortly [after that] a vehicle came and stopped near the entrance to the park. A British officer and two plainclothes men got out and came near us asking who we were and what were we doing there. Still talking the British officer's hand reached for his pistol, at once bhaiya's hand went for his pistol which he always carried with him, and my hand went for my pistol. Both Azad and the officer fired at each other, but the British

officer was quicker. Azad was hit in his leg and the British officer in his shoulder. Both kept firing. One bullet entered the lungs of Azad but profusely bleeding he kept on firing. The British officer was hit on his wrist, and he tried running towards his vehicle, but Azad was able to puncture the tire. He took shelter behind a tree and so did Azad. In between bhaiya ordered me to leave. Because of excessive bleeding, he fell there and became a martyr.

The bullet-stricken body lay on the ground; no one came near him. At last, a constable was asked to move closer and check if there was any movement. Finding him unresponsive, other officers finally inched in and the body was placed in a truck which sped away.

Virendra passed away on 31 December 1993. Early in the new year, the family received a letter from Nilokheri, Haryana. 'It was on Virendra's asking that I shot at Khan Bahadur Abdul Aziz, DIG, the prosecutor in Bhagat Singh's case,' its contents read. It was signed by a Dev Vohra. He was eighty-seven years old then and happy to meet the son of an old comrade when Lalit visited him.

Back in 1929, Virendra and Dev Vohra were in the same college, and they shared the same desk. Vohra lived in a hostel where Virendra kept a cyclostyling machine that churned out seditious material regularly.

One day, while we were sitting in class, Virendra said that they wanted Abdul Aziz, the police prosecutor to be shot. 'Can you do it?' he asked me. I had been in Officers' Training Corps [OTC], something like the present-day NCC [National Cadet Corps], and had been handling guns and was considered a good marksman. I agreed. But we needed arms and, to get these, we needed money. So, one Lekh Ram from UP and I raided the Gadodia Store near Chandni Chowk in Delhi, and, with this money, I went to Peshawar and bought two guns and a few bullets. One of the guns I gave to Chandrashekhar Azad and this was the weapon he used in his last battle with the police in Allahabad.[180]

Virendra never spoke about this incident with anyone in the family just as he as he never repeated the statement where he said he made bombs in pre-Partition India. Information from his former colleagues and outside sources has contributed to joining the dots of his past. Was this voluntary silence a common link of that generation – whether it was those involved in India's freedom actively or the ones who became refugees?

Chandrashekhar Azad was cremated before his body could be claimed by his comrades. Purushottam Das Tandon and Kamala Nehru were able to collect his ashes and give the fallen leader the respect that he deserved. Two days later, at a meeting held in Allahabad, as tributes were being paid, the wife of famous revolutionary Sachindra Nath Sanyal declared, 'People kept ashes of Khudiram Bose and put it in a locket around the necks of their children so that they became as brave as the revolutionary. With the same emotion, I have come to take a pinch of Azad's ashes.' Hearing this, the public smeared Azad's ashes on their forehead and the rest were immersed in the Ganges at the Triveni. Historians believe that Azad's recognition in history books as commander-in-chief of HSRA falls short in the face of the defiant and defying role that he played in India's freedom struggle.

> It is like remembering Marx and forgetting Engels or paying our homage to Che but ignoring Fidel ... Azad was the leader of the revolutionary movement of which Bhagat Singh became the most popular icon. Also, Azad and Bhagat Singh had a three-decade-long legacy of revolutionaries behind them which should not be forgotten. From Aurobindo and Hardayal, this legacy passed on to Sanyal, Bismil, and Ashfaq and finally came to Azad and Bhagat Singh who not only carried it forward but took it to newer heights ...[181]

As in life and so in death, the revolutionary touched many lives – although, initially, he was not comfortable with recruiting women. As far as he was concerned, some experiences with the opposite sex had been unpleasant and it would be foolhardy to open those doors. Yet, he did exactly that and is credited for paving the way for women revolutionaries – some of whom became indispensable to the movement.

Historian Prabal Agarwal says:[182]

From being a brahmachari and an ardent follower of the Arya Samaji Ram Prasad Bismil, by [the] late 1920s, Azad recognized the critical role women had to play in the revolutionary movement. Under his leadership, revolutionaries of North India moved away from their earlier emphasis on celibacy to camaraderie with women associates. He recruited Durga Devi Vohra, Sushila Mohan, Prakashwati Pal and several other women into the revolutionary fold, and gave them major responsibilities in the party.

Azad's regard for Durga Bhabhi was not unfounded. Despite grave setbacks –including the deaths of her husband and her mentor – she did not lose sight of the larger cause. For her, Bhagat Singh was a much-beloved younger brother and, while saving the freedom fighter from the noose was becoming increasingly hopeless, she channelled her every day towards avenging the judgment.

She and two others – Sukhdev Raj and Baba Prithvi Singh, who had replaced Azad as their leader – decided to assassinate Lahore's police commissioner. The plan looked watertight and, as soon as they reached the officer's residence, Durga Bhabhi would take over. Being a woman, it was hoped that she would not arouse any suspicion and, using this to her advantage, once inside the house, she was to shoot the officer. On standby, Prithvi Singh and Sukhdev Raj were to wait outside, and tackle any attempt to follow or shoot Durga Bhabhi.

The ground reality was not so kosher.

For one, it was impossible to enter the police commissioner's residence – security was tight with men in khaki patrolling the house. Seeing this, Sukhdev Raj and Prithvi Singh suggested aborting the idea for, if Durga entered, an escape looked unlikely. The woman, despite the dangerous mission, would have none of it. She had already done the hard part by leaving her son behind with relatives. If she was killed, he was to be looked after by them.

Prithvi Singh understood that there was no shaking Durga Bhabhi's resolve and the plot was tweaked. He parked a car in front of the Lamington Road police station. Alert, they waited. A vehicle soon pulled up, and two British men and a woman stepped out. They had barely taken a few steps when shots rang out; both Durga Bhabhi and Sukhdev Raj had shot at them. A man was injured, while the other two lay down on the ground and managed to save themselves. As the shots broke the day's calm, police officers charged out from the station and gave the three fleeing in their car a chase. They escaped but were declared absconders.

Durga Bhabhi had not given up. Despite going underground, one day she turned up at Mahatma Gandhi's doorstep and introduced herself. But Gandhi already knew of her. At the time, the Congress and the British were involved in negotiations, which were later to be known as the Gandhi–Irwin pact. The leader presumed that Durga Bhabhi wanted his help for herself and told her to surrender with the promise that he would take care of the rest. She instead appealed to him to save the three men on the death row, imploring him to make their release a condition for the pact. Gandhi turned her down. 'They all believed in violence;

I cannot help them,' he told her. Durga Bhabhi returned home dejected and was to live a retired life in independent India. She did not ask for any pension or honour for herself – all her sacrifices were for the country.[183]

In Virendra's book *Veh Inquilabi Din*, I.K. Gujral writes about the dilemma of the youth for whom the call of duty was absolute. At the same time, attempts to clarify their actions were almost pedantic.[184]

> Virendra and his colleagues suffered the pangs of this predicament. The Gandhian method soaked in our cultural ethos, was subtle and remote. The path of violence that Bhagat Singh and his comrades were blazing was heroic and direct. Virendra, like many of his generation, shifted from one to the other. To them, it was not an academic pursuit nor the subject of a seminar. They jumped into the fast-moving torrents.

Revolutionaries claim that Gandhi refused to actively intervene in favour of Bhagat Singh and his two comrades. Was it an unfortunate appendix to the history of our independence movement? Did the Mahatma err here?

15

This War Did Not Start with Us: Inquilab Zindabad

On 5 March 1931, Lord Irwin and Mahatma Gandhi signed a pact and, as its ink dried, Bhagat Singh stopped shadowing the gallows. His death was now not just defined, the execution was also imminent. The Indian National Congress was to suspend the Civil Disobedience Movement in return for the release of all political prisoners. There was a caveat – the definition of a prisoner extended only to those arrested during the Congress agitation. There was to be no freedom for members of the revolutionary club languishing in prisons, including Virendra who had still not been released from his confinement with Ehsan. He and his fellow revolutionaries read the writing on the jail wall: It was the end of the road for Bhagat Singh, Rajguru and Sukhdev.

On the day of their release, some of the 'political' prisoners, all heavyweights, came to meet the young revolutionaries, and, not surprisingly, the ones left behind, including Virendra, were in no mood to engage, 'I did not talk to them,' he remembers. It was not about them – there was a great sense of betrayal over the failure of the Congress leadership to get the three death sentences commuted. Virendra remembers his cellmate, Ehsan Ilahi, as particularly belligerent; those standing outside the iron grills sheepishly had no response to him.

In jail, Bhagat Singh and his comrades had company; young prisoners arrested in the Meerut Conspiracy Case were also told that freedom wasn't theirs for the taking. Their predominantly communist leanings had convinced the government of Russia's influence in the conspiracy. Outside the imposing prison walls, Gandhi, like the dying embers of a fire, remained the last and only hope for the revolutionaries orphaned by Chandrashekhar Azad's recent killing. There was an overwhelming belief, not just within the group but also in the country at large, that a pardon was possible. All it required was Gandhi to speak the language that the British heard. The hanging, a national issue both emotive and cohesive, was looming large like the curtain call of a final act – the great Mahatma, though, the revolutionaries felt, was not in the audience.

'It seems cruel to inflict this letter on you, but the interest of peace demands a final appeal ... popular opinion rightly or wrongly demands commutation,' Gandhi penned to Viceroy Irwin on the morning of 23 March 1931.[185] How confidence-inducing was this last-minute communication when Gandhi's conviction to his ideals remained like a weathered rock on a seafront?

Says historian S. Irfan Habib of this time:[186]

> We should realize that the British government had put a condition before Gandhi that the talks about the release of prisoners, which were in huge numbers, [would] take place only if he agree[d] not to include the release of the three revolutionaries. Despite this caveat, Gandhi began the negotiations and raised the question of Bhagat Singh and his comrades' release. But the colonial government was committed against their release.

The three men were staring at the hangman's knot. The Privy Council[187] – the highest court in the British empire based in England – had rejected their plea. There was one final recourse, if they so chose, and it was to appeal to the Viceroy for mercy. For Bhagat Singh, the proposition was almost laughable. He and his two comrades were going to die martyrs and nothing was going to come in between. Virendra writes that the twenty-three-year-old was 'almost as excited as a groom at his wedding'.

Building blocks, painstakingly placed one on top of the other, created the matrix of India's imperial battle. At times, the blocks were from the non-violent camp, and, on other occasions, the revolutionaries added their stamp. In this instance, three young men wanted to set a precedent by leaving behind a prototype of valour for freedom fighters to follow. They were immune to any momentary or last-minute weaknesses; their last block was far from shaky. These young men, Virendra says, were India's pride. 'The government did not quite know how to deal with people who had no fear of death and whose conduct was designed to secure not their acquittal, but maximum publicity for their cause,' he remembers.

The pressure to appeal, though, was unrelenting. Bhagat Singh finally asked for time to think. It was a ploy to shake off both the coercion and expectation, and his lawyer, Pran Nath Mehta, was the first to wise up. Two days later, when Mehta met Singh for discussions on the petition, he was surprised to hear that the plea was already forwarded to the Punjab Governor. Mehta, who was also Bhagat Singh's friend, asked for a copy and what he read jolted him. There was no appeal whatsoever for clemency – instead it was a warrant for death. The three wrote:[188]

To
The Punjab Governor

Sir,
With due respect we beg to bring to your kind notice the following:
That we were sentenced to death on 7th October 1930 by a British Court and that the main charge against us is of waging war against H.M. King George, the King of England. The above-mentioned finding of the Court pre-supposed two things: The first is that there is a war between Britain and India. And second, we have taken a deliberate part in

it therefore we are now prisoners of war. This is an extreme view, but we consider it an honour.

We would like to dwell in detail on the first charge. We are constrained to go into some detail. Apparently there seems to be no such war as the phrase indicates. Nevertheless, please allow us to accept the validity of the pre-supposition taking it at its face value. But in order to be correctly understood we must explain it further. Let us declare that the state of war does exist and shall exist so long as the Indian toiling masses and the natural resources are being exploited by a handful of parasites…

No matter, if once again the vanguard of the Indian movement, the Revolutionary Party, finds itself deserted in the thick of the war. No matter if the leaders to whom personally we are much indebted for the sympathy and feelings they expressed for us, but nevertheless we cannot overlook the fact that they did become so callous as to ignore and not to make a mention in the peace negotiation of even the homeless, friendless and penniless of female workers who are alleged to be belonging to the vanguard and whom the leaders consider to be enemies of their utopian non-violent cult which has already become a thing of the past; the heroines who had ungrudgingly sacrificed or offered for sacrifice their husbands, brothers, and all that were nearest and dearest to them, including themselves, whom your government has declared to be outlaws. No matter, if your agents stoop so low as to fabricate baseless calumnies against their spotless characters to damage their and their party's reputation. The war shall continue.

It may assume different forms. Sometimes it may be open sometimes it may be underground. At times it may become as fierce as a matter of life and death. The choice of the course, whether bloody or comparatively peaceful, which it should adopt rests with you…

We are sure the decisive battle is very near. The days of capitalist and imperialist exploitation are numbered. This war did not start with us, nor will it end with us… Our lives are a mere page in the chapter of our freedom struggle accurately beautified by the unparalleled sacrifice of Jatin Das, and the most tragic but noblest sacrifice of Comrade Bhagwati Charan, and the glorious death of our dear warrior Azad.

You have decided to hang us at the gallows which you will surely do. You have got the power in your hands and the power is the greatest justification in this world. We know that the maxim 'Might is right' serves as your guiding motto. The manner in which our trial was conducted is proof of that. We did not plead for mercy during the trial proceedings and neither do we intend to do it now. But we do wish to state that since we are charged with waging war, therefore we are prisoners of war. And we claim to be treated as such, instead of being hanged, we should be shot dead.

It rests with you to prove that you really meant what your court has said. We request and hope that you will very kindly order the military department to send its detachment to perform our execution.'

Yours,
Bhagat Singh

The three comrades unflinchingly stared death down; yet, many were disheartened by their move and, with the great Mahatma. The reference to the neglect of women revolutionaries was also a direct attack on the leadership of the Congress party.

It is lamentable how, in seventy-five years, the ethos of our freedom struggle has been replaced by the vilification of leaders who facilitated the march of almost 8 million refugees into a new dawn. It is lazy and opportunistic to judge their actions through the lens of hindsight; in those extenuating circumstances, India was privileged to inherit the leaders of the stature that it did.

The inability to draw icons from the independence movement based on ideology has also allowed for a certain disdain of the freedom movement at large, or perhaps it is as simple as the generational ease of living that is now far removed from recollection or nostalgia. Bhagat Singh, mercifully, stays as the hardware on the mantelpiece of India's youth and remains the gold standard of how sacrifice is not conditional. A mercy appeal may have changed the fate of the three to that of life imprisonment, but would the legend of Bhagat Singh have survived then?

Abandoned by the country's leaders, Bhagat Singh, Rajguru and Sukhdev waited. The end was not far, and shorn of escapism and denial, the inevitability of it consumed British India.

Koi dum ka mehman hoon aye ahl-e-mehfil,
Chirag-e-sehar hoon bujha chahta hoon.

O members of the gathering, I exist only for a few moments,
I am dawn's lamp, I want to be extinguished.

Bhagat Singh's last letter to his brother Kultar Singh was poignant and telling.[189]

A question does arise here: Can a person eager, nay impatient, to become a martyr be saved? A conversation that the three prisoners had with lawyer Pran Nath Mehta gives a sense of their state of mind. This is believed to be their last exchange with anyone from outside the jail premises.[190]

Pran Nath Mehta: Gandhiji is trying very hard to save you. He can succeed if you help him.
Rajguru (with irritation): What kind of help?
Pran Nath Mehta: No need to get upset. You all agree that the day of Independence is not very far.
Bhagat Singh: We are living for that day.
Pran Nath Mehta: Independent India will require your services. Who can help better in reconstruction than you?
Sukhdev (with anger): What kind of Sheikh Chilli talk is this? We are only the foundation. The building will be built by people who come after us. We don't have to worry about that.
Pran Nath Mehta: My friends! You laid the foundation of this building. An engineer who lays the foundation alone knows how to make it strong. (Getting emotional) Do you three have a right to your lives or do you think your lives are in the trust of your country?

Bhagat Singh (smiles): Yaar, stop this lawyer talk and tell us what you want.

Pran Nath Mehta: That your lives belong to your country and are not yours to give away. The people want that, to strengthen Gandhiji's hand, you should write a mercy petition to the Viceroy.

Hearing this, Rajguru and Sukhdev became a little aggressive, but Bhagat Singh (calmly): What kind of mercy petition do you want?

Pran Nath Mehta: At this moment, I cannot tell you. A group of lawyers are preparing the draft. Rest assured, there will not be anything demeaning for you.

The next day the three comrades informed Mehta that their plea had already been sent – martyrdom was calling and Bhagat Singh was waiting with his arms wide open. This was the quintessential revolution he had been chasing in his short but enlightened life, and for one final time he spelled it out to his comrades in jail who asked him why he didn't want to be saved. His reply:[191]

Comrades!

It is natural that the desire to live should be in me as well, I don't want to hide it. But I can stay alive on one condition that I don't wish to live in imprisonment or with any binding.

My name has become a symbol of the Hindustani revolution, and the ideals and sacrifices of the Revolutionary Party have lifted me very high – so high that I can certainly not be higher in the condition of being alive.

Today my weaknesses are not visible to the people. If I escape the noose, they will become evident and the symbol of revolution will be tarnished, or possibly be obliterated. But to go to the gallows with courage will make Hindustani mothers aspire to have children who are like Bhagat Singh and the number of those who will sacrifice their lives for the country will go up so that it will not be possible for the imperialistic powers or all the demoniac powers to contain the revolution.

And yes, one thought occurs to me even today that I have not been able to fulfil even one-thousandth part of the aspirations that were in my heart to do something for my country and humanity. If I could have stayed alive and free, then I may have had the opportunity to accomplish those, and I would have fulfilled my desires. Apart from this, no temptation to escape the noose has ever come to me. Who can be more fortunate than me? These days I feel very proud of myself. Now I await the final test with great eagerness. I pray that it should draw closer.

Your comrade,
Bhagat Singh.

The letter was dated 22 March 1931. The 'final test' was to come a day later.

A cocktail of anger and gloom spilled onto the streets – in Subhas Chandra Bose's words 'poignant grief that stirred the country from end to the other'.[192] Bose was on his way from Calcutta to Karachi when news of the hangings scorched India; Gandhi and Sardar Patel had also departed from Gujarat together for the Karachi session.[193] At the Karachi station, the Mahatma faced a backlash from the very people who idolized him, and was greeted with black flags and calls of 'Gandhi, go back', which he handled with stoicism. As timings go, this was perhaps the most ill-timed Congress session in its history – it was taking place less than a week after the hangings.[194] Who would have thought that the forty-fifth session of the Indian National Congress would be convened when India's cities and countryside were in mourning?

The Congress's collective conscience tarred, Jawaharlal Nehru's words echoed the common man:[195]

> Though I am saddened by the hanging of Sardar Bhagat Singh I have deliberately kept quiet. He was loved by all of us. His unparalleled bravery and supreme sacrifice have inspired millions of youths in the country. How sad it is that India could not save these young people. The country will shed tears of sorrow on this helplessness.

His principles of non-violence notwithstanding, Nehru's admiration for the revolutionaries was not a form of sympathy for an anti-hero. In his respect, there was both an understanding of Bhagat Singh's ideological convictions and an acceptance of a mind that was ahead of its time.

Yashpal, who planted the bomb under Lord Irwin's viceregal train, sarcastically commented, 'Gandhi considered it moral to put government pressure on the people for prohibition, but he considered it immoral to put people's pressure on foreign government to commute the death sentence on Bhagat Singh.'[196]

In the outpouring of tributes, Sardar Patel joined the chorus. 'I cannot identify myself with their methods. Political murder is no less reprehensible than any other, but the patriotism, daring, and sacrifice of Bhagat Singh and his comrades command my admiration. The heartless and the foreign nature of the government was never more strikingly demonstrated than in their determination to carry out the execution ...'[197]

Here, the great 'Iron Man of India' is trying to run with the hare and hunt with the hounds.

Subhas Chandra Bose was blunt. He writes in *The Indian Struggle*:[198]

> Pressure was brought to bear on the Mahatma to save the lives of the young men, and it must be admitted he tried his best. On this occasion, I ventured the suggestion that he should, if necessary, break with the Viceroy on the question because the execution was against the spirit, if not the letter, of the Delhi Pact ... But the Mahatma who did not want to identify himself with the revolutionary prisoners would not go so far. And it naturally made a great difference when the Viceroy realised that the Mahatma would not break on this question.

Bose adds, 'So far as the Mahatma was concerned, he had to make his conscience somewhat elastic.'[199] In response to the Viceroy's concession that at best he could do was to delay the hanging till after the Karachi session, Gandhi replied that if executions must happen, let them take place before the Congress congregation.[200]

Was Gandhi compelling in persuading the British to take another look at the death sentence or was the pact with Lord Irwin so all-consuming? It is common knowledge that he was willing to take a longer route to independence rather than compromise on his ideals. Historians differ in their outlook, but there is a line of thought that while Gandhi tried to save the men, he did not owe the revolutionaries enough to jeopardize the pact and the release of political prisoners.

Says historian Mridula Mukherjee:[201]

> Nehru, Gandhi and Bhagat Singh were all men of enormous integrity. None of them did something they didn't deeply believe in. Revolutionaries had their own understanding and methods, but the Congress didn't believe in them – although Nehru admired Bhagat Singh, who faced the consequences of following one kind of thinking. But it was not Gandhi's method and to ask him to keep the settlement on hold was unreasonable ... To doubt his sincerity is extremely insensitive. He tried but it was not in his hands, and he never said anything he didn't agree to. Both he and Bhagat Singh had equal rights to follow their own path.

There are also conflicting interpretations on whether Gandhi's letters to the British to commute their death sentences were mere tokenism. Some scholars say that he remained comfortable with the suspension or postponement of the inevitable.[202] Bose writes, not very charitably:[203]

> Lord Irwin was the Viceroy and Governor-General of India, and he was farsighted enough to realise that if an understanding was to be arrived at between the Government and the Congress, it was desirable to do so while the Mahatma was the leader of the latter body, for according to some Britishers, 'Gandhi was the best policeman the Britisher had in India.'

To his credit, the Mahatma never made a secret of his disapproval of the methods used by revolutionaries. 'There is a romance around the life of Bhagat Singh,' he once remarked while acknowledging grudgingly or otherwise, that his courage was indisputable.[204] But any praise was a backhanded compliment, imploring the youth in the next breath to not 'follow his path',[205] and calling the men 'misguided'.

Three young lives were at stake; would it be too harsh to say that Gandhi disregarded a nation's collective emotions? A moment lost, which – if it was seized – could have been transformative for India's history. Admittedly, the revolutionaries infringed on the principle of non-violence that the pacifist Mahatma held sacrosanct, but is the act of hanging a man condemned non-violent? The trial itself was a farce of epic proportions – '… coercive colonial legalism was used to convict and hang three freedom fighters, who would otherwise have gone free.'[206] The men were hanged but, in its failure, to get amnesty for them, the Congress leadership allowed the British to divide and conquer once again – pitting the Gandhian path against the extremist stream – and coming out as the only victor. In the end, Bhagat Singh's words remained unheard, 'We are next to none in our love for humanity. Far from having malice against any individual we hold human life sacred beyond words.'[207]

So were their lives.

Says the co-founder of Indian History Collective, Rishi Majumder:[208]

> The desire to transform Gandhi into an all-on-the-right-side-of-history god (more parmatma than mahatma) has led him to people, during his time and after, imagining and talking of versions of him which didn't really exist. This is, I feel, because Gandhi was and is our bulwark against so many ills and disasters, and people need [him] to be perfect. [In] my mind, even if it isn't perfect, the bulwark still holds. But in the mind of Gandhi, there was a quest for perfection, and this was passed on to the people who loved him. Only while Gandhi knew he was imperfect, in the minds of his followers that quest was auto-fulfilled. Gandhi, for those who love him, must be ideal: in private and public life; in ends as well as means.'

In this all-encompassing image, Gandhi's role as a politician has been relegated to a footnote – to speak of him in the same breath as contemporary politicians is after all unthinkable.

Coming in for countrywide criticism after the hangings, Gandhi called a press conference with both Indian and foreign correspondents in attendance. Inevitably, the question was asked and his declaration of helplessness over jeopardizing the pact did not make a dent in the nation's gloom. The backlash was unabated as the public grappled with the death of three promising young men lost to the swinging pendulum of non-violent politics and ideological violence. Faced with such antagonistic sentiment, Gandhi made Nehru prepare a resolution: 'This Congress, while dissociating itself from the disapproving of political violence in any shape or form, places on record its admiration of the bravery and sacrifice of the late Sardar Bhagat Singh and his comrades… with extreme bravery and daring they continued on the path they had chosen. They felt it was an honour to become a martyr. Bhagat Singh is no longer with us today. Let us be martyrs in the struggle for independence and non-violence with the same honour as Bhagat Singh.' [209]

Did he have misgivings about the resolution he drafted? He added, almost as an afterthought, 'I find that the qualifications of the resolution have been forgotten and the praises have been exploited.'[210]

His defining figure notwithstanding, the Mahatma was a politician and read the pulse of the people. A statement was also released, saying: 'These heroes had conquered the fear of death. Let us bow to them a thousand times for their heroism But, we should not imitate their act … Our dharma is to swallow our anger, abide by the discipline of non-violence, and carry out our duty.'[211]

Unbending, even in the face of overpowering public opinion, Gandhi set a lofty example, but the martyrdom of the three men, some say, remains a blip in the Mahatma's otherwise impeccable service to the nation. Unlike Bose and Nehru who visited them in jail,[212] Gandhi was reticent and kept his distance.

Historian Chaman Lal shares:[213]

> Gandhi visited Meerut Conspiracy Case communists in jail, but not Bhagat Singh and other revolutionaries. Though Gandhi did refer to the Viceroy for clemency, he asked his permission to make it public. (To save his public image). He did not stand up to his own principled position of being anti-capital punishment and, somehow in this matter, he showed moral weakness. This does not undermine his other positive aspects, such as [being] a true anti-communalist and votary of strong brotherly Hindu–Muslim ties, for which he gave up his life.'

Chaman Lal's reference to clemency is in Viceroy Irwin's records, 'As he was leaving, he asked if he might mention the case of Bhagat Singh, saying that he had seen in the press the intimation of his execution for March 24th.'[214]

Virendra adds that Gandhi told Lord Irwin that if the death sentence was withdrawn, it would create a healthy atmosphere in the country. With much reluctance, Irwin agreed to reconsider the decision. Events, however, escalated as soon as this assurance became public, and he faced a revolt from his own officers and senior government officials who threatened to resign if the three men were granted freedom.[215] The fate of the other political prisoners was irrelevant to the British.

Gandhi's philosophy of non-violence in any form of political movement was binary; the revolutionaries, on the other hand, inhabited a world of grey. Violence didn't give them an adrenaline rush and they were at pains to ensure that their actions were not acts of terrorism. The door to a revolution in its truest form – which 'did not necessarily involve sanguinary strife' – that Bhagat Singh dreamt about was still bolted, but they were knocking. 'Let me announce with all my strength, that I am not a terrorist, and I never was, except perhaps at the beginning of my revolutionary career.'[216]

The Mahatma's failure to secure commutation provides his critics with a convenient weapon to attack him as they failed to understand that he had more to gain by saving the lives of Bhagat Singh and his comrades, writes Chander Pal Singh. 'If Gandhi had succeeded in saving the lives of Bhagat Singh, Sukhdev, and Rajguru, it would have been seen as the victory of nonviolence over violence and moral victory of Gandhi over the revolutionaries.'[217]

In their lifetimes, Gandhi and Bhagat Singh were rail tracks that ran parallel to one another, although they were more similar than either would have cared to admit. Uncompromising ideology churned their wheels, oiled in no small measure by a disregard for their lives and popularity. Ironically, their paths converged when both Gandhi and Bhagat Singh sacrificed their lives in the service of the nation.

As in life and so in death, Bhagat Singh challenged Gandhi's principles. While the leader mobilised masses through his campaigns, the obsessively well-read and erudite Bhagat Singh simultaneously explained his actions to the public at every step. He wasn't ashamed of his doctrine, only in its interpretation, and deliberately chose to be an open book. In his own way, Bhagat Singh was as effective as Gandhi.

How do historians interpret the actions of the revolutionaries, outliers in India's independence struggle and yet indispensable to freedom's calling? Is the tag of 'radicals' exaggerated when quite a few of their actions seem almost amateurish in hindsight?

Scholar A.G. Noorani declares:[218]

> If those men, and their likes in those days, were less skilled than the wielders of the gun today, they were far more idealistic and practiced in their own lives a far sterner code of personal morality. To no small extent was what Nehru called 'the phenomenon of Bhagat Singh' due to the man's spotlessly clean life, his lofty vision, and a selflessness that defies belief.

Violence by the revolutionaries was nuanced and far removed from the kind of aggression that engulfed both sides during and in the aftermath of Partition. Equally, scholars draw a distinct buffer between revolutionary actions and the casual interpretation of heroism today. Says historian S. Irfan Habib:[219]

> Bhagat Singh's definition of a revolutionary was based on ideas, to bring about a foundational change in society. Terrorist was the label used by the British; even Bhagat Singh wrote in his statement once that [he] did have faith in terror to counter the imperialist terror, but it was only in the beginning. Terrorism today has no meaning at all if we compare the two. They never believed in indiscriminate killing to spread fear among the people, as we see today.

Surprisingly, the one leader who sympathized with Bhagat Singh and his comrades, despite their differing politics was Pakistan's founder Mohammad Ali Jinnah. Speaking in the Central Assembly on 12 September 1929, Jinnah asked, 'Do you wish to prosecute them or persecute them?' Pakistan's founder also had strong words for the British, and the trial in absentia while Bhagat Singh and other prisoners went on a fast in jail, a defence that finds scant mention in history books:[220] 'The man who goes on hunger strike has a soul. He is moved by that soul, and he believes in the justice of his cause.' The irony, A.G. Noorani says 'is the weapon which Bhagat Singh and associates used, and which was to win them acclaim was distinctly Gandhian. It was the hunger strike.'[221]

In the course of history, the exploits of the two men who defined India's freedom struggle with actions that were a nod to the country's pluralism continue to co-exist. While Gandhi took his last breath promoting communal harmony and remains a fulcrum for the downtrodden and the persecuted, Shaheed Bhagat Singh defies seasonal politics to remain deeply entrenched as a cult icon for successive generations of young Indians.

In his letters to political workers, Bhagat Singh praised Gandhi as a leader but with a postscript that his views were idealistic and impractical. Once the revolution petered away after his and Azad's deaths, it was the Gandhi-led movement that was to prevail till the end. Interestingly, during the year-long farmers' agitation witnessed in India in 2020–21, the ideals of Gandhi and Bhagat Singh coalesced again – while keeping the revolutionary's photos and the misguided yellow turbans, the farmers sat for a very Gandhian dharna.[222] In V.S. Naipaul's words, 'India was set on the way of a new kind of intellectual life; it was given new ideas about its history and civilization. The freedom movement reflected all of this and turned out to be the truest kind of liberation.'[223]

What kind of leaders arise from this land of ours in the future is challenging to predict. It can, however, be safely assumed that another Gandhi or a Bhagat Singh is nigh impossible. Their legacies, contrasting yet enduring, continue to stand tall.

On 13 April 1919, hundreds of unarmed Indians were shot in cold blood at Jallianwala Bagh – a place of abiding pilgrimage for Punjabis and nationalists. The fading red-brick walls marked with shots fired more than a century ago tell the story of unimaginable excesses of the British Raj; a tragedy brought back into the headlines in March 1940 by Udham Singh, a revolutionary with roots in the Ghadar Party. By then General Dyer, who ordered his troops to fire on innocent civilians after blocking the only entrance and exit at the garden, was dead.

The man responsible for the firing, Punjab's Lieutenant Governor Sir Michael O'Dwyer, however, was in London where Udham Singh tracked him down and assassinated him. Legend has it that Singh was present at Jallianwala Bagh on that fateful day and swore revenge, but there has been no confirmation of this claim. After the shooting, Udham Singh surrendered, and the revolutionaries had made a sensational comeback.[224]

Praises poured in, particularly from Punjab, and while the press remained circumspect,[225] the British were at pains to portray the killing as an isolated incident with no connection to the massacre.[226] One man, however, was angry. Mahatma Gandhi bitterly criticized Udham Singh, calling his act 'insanity'[227] and a blow to the freedom struggle. His words in *Harijan* were uncompromising, 'I would like every Indian patriot to share with me the shame of the act and the joy that the lives of the three distinguished Englishmen were saved ... it fills me with shame and sorrow that for some time every Indian face in London will be suspect.'[228] Virendra remembers that in civil society, Gandhi's statement did not find much support. Punjab had waited more than twenty years for closure after the massacre.

Gandhi was ambiguous when it came to Bhagat Singh and his comrades' hangings – for Udham Singh there was outright condemnation. But, in both instances, capital punishment by the British did not receive absolute opposition from a man whose dharma was non-violence. Udham Singh was not to know; the killing made him a household name and led to an awakening in the colonialists that their expiry date was close. Seven years later, India was free and Udham Singh lives on as Shaheed-E-Azam.

16

A Day of Hangings: An Eyewitness Account

Virendra's affair – not quite one of mutual love – with British prisons took him on a roller-coaster ride of jails of Rawalpindi, Multan, Sialkot, Shahpur, known as Punjab's Kala Pani, and Lahore, the city where it all began. On 8 August 1942, Mahatma Gandhi launched the Quit India Movement at the Bombay Congress session and, a day later, as he, Patel, Nehru and other prominent leaders were arrested, Virendra released a special edition of *Pratap*. That very evening, the colonial police showed up and he was back in custody; this was his ninth arrest and, as it turned out, his final one. Joining him within days at the godforsaken Shahpur Jail – Mahashay Krishan wrote that if Kashmir is jannat on earth, Shahpur Jail is the narak – were both his father and brother, and it was left to *Pratap*'s employees to take out the newspaper every morning (by now it was no longer an evening paper), which they did efficiently.

Virendra and his cellmates at Shahpur Jail, many of whom went on to hold high public offices in independent India, received the *Tribune* newspaper officially in jail. Additionally, they smuggled *Pratap* into the prison to stay informed of the rapidly changing political climate. That the newspaper was held in such high esteem by Indians was underscored during the Lahore Conspiracy Case proceedings. Historian A.G. Noorani writes:[229]

> There was a mild affray in court. With the permission of the Government Advocate and in his presence, a press representative handed over copies of the *Civil and Military Gazette*, *The Tribune*, the *Bande Mataram*, the *Pratap*, and certain other local newspapers to the accused to enable them to read the previous day's proceedings of the case. A police constable took exception to this and roughly handled the press representative who, in turn, gave a rattling blow under the lower jaw of the constable. This created a commotion in Court.

All newspapers barring a copy of the British mouthpiece *The Civil and Military Gazette* were confiscated from Bhagat Singh.

Appropriately, Virendra's final incarceration was in the city of Lahore, where he returned after a year and nine months to a jail whose dingy corridors were a witness to the making of a revolutionary thirteen years ago. Among those incarcerated with him, this time, was Biju Patnaik – Orissa stalwart and later its chief minister. The two ate several meals together not just in each other's jail cells but also while both were unwell in hospital during their imprisonment.

Virendra's last spell in jail was for a long three years and he was released in 1945. 'It took me a few days to get used to freedom. Much water had flowed down the Ravi,' he writes in his book.

Among his defining memories from jails in undivided India is one from Sialkot, the place of Virendra's penultimate detention. His cell was in proximity to the pen where convicts were hanged and, just before his discharge papers were handed over, he came in close contact with three inmates on the death row. His encounter with these men took him back to a time when three brave hearts had walked, heads held high, to the gallows.

23 March 1931: Virendra was at Lahore's Central Jail, detained under the stringent Regulation III of 1818. The air in the prison and on the streets was loaded with a sense of unease – the die had been cast. It was the morning that the three fearless revolutionaries were to meet their end. 'The day Bhagat Singh, Rajguru, and Sukhdev were hanged it was my fortune or misfortune to be in the same jail,' says Virendra, in his historic first-person account.[230]

> After their appeal was rejected by the Privy Council and especially after Bhagat Singh refused to petition for mercy, we knew it was only a matter of time ... There was this barber who used to go to shave Rajguru and Sukhdev and come to us also. [Bhagat Singh by then had started growing his hair again.] We got all our information through him,

and he came on 20 March and told us that the end seemed near. He felt that the jail authorities were preparing for such an eventuality …

In front of where we were lodged, there was an open ground. The jail authorities had started collecting wood there. We thought that after the hanging the three would be cremated here. We tried to enquire from whichever jail official we could meet but received no satisfactory reply. No official was ready to open his mouth on this issue but there was an unusual bustle in the jail …

Outside the prison gates, Lahore was ill at ease and hardly noticed that it was spring. The hearts of its citizens were frozen with the certainty that doom was impending. A dust storm the night before had settled down as though it too was bowing to the inevitable.[231] All that was left was for the family members of the three men to say their goodbyes and they were expected to come shortly to meet their sons – for one last time.

Virendra writes:

Newspapers on 23 March reported that relatives of the three revolutionaries had been informed that the hanging would take place the next day, 24 March so [they] could have their last meeting on 23 [March]. As per prison rules, the time of hanging was 7 a.m. in the summer and 8 a.m. in the winter months. Additionally, as per jail rules on the day of a hanging, other prisoners were to be kept locked up in their cells till the body was taken out of the jail compound.

Virendra and his fellow prisoners had no reason to believe otherwise. But an unassuming jail employee, Barkat the barber, was to shake him and other inmates out of their mournful stupor.

> So, we thought that the hanging would be on the morning of 24 [March]. But on 23 March, at about 2 p.m., the prison barber came running to us with tears in his eyes, and in a quivering voice said, 'Sab kuch khatam ho gaya [Everything is over]. The Sardar is saying that they would probably be hanged today itself. He has conveyed Vande Mataram to the two of you.'

On hearing Barkat's words Virendra and Ehsan Ilahi were distraught. They had accepted the hanging with drooping shoulders, but were not willing to see the intrepid revolutionaries die any sooner than they had to. Thoughts raced through their minds questioning the insidious move by the British to bring forward the execution by a day. With passions running high in the city, the British had quietly advanced the hangings by twelve hours.

Bringing his emotions under control, Virendra requested Barkat to go back to Bhagat Singh and ask him for a keepsake that the two young men could treasure as a remembrance. Half an hour later, the barber returned – in his hands were a black fountain pen and a comb. 'On the comb, Bhagat Singh had carved his name with a blunt instrument. Ehsan Ilahi kept the pen and I, the comb.'

Time was moving and, yet, it felt like it had stood still. It was late afternoon and police officers were camping outside the gates of the Lahore Central Jail.

> Every evening at 7 p.m., chief warder Chattar Singh would lock us up, after securing all other prisoners. That day, he came at 4 p.m. When we asked him why he had come three hours early, he became emotional and could not speak. After several minutes, he composed himself and said the end had come; the three would be hanged that evening at 7 p.m., there was nothing that could be done to save them now.

The warder left after locking the prisoners in, 'we sat on our cots, totally silent'. Virendra and Ehsan Ilahi were accompanied by another undertrial, who was tasked to help them. They told him not to cook anything that day. Anguished, the men could only wait. The silence – theirs and of the other inmates – swept through every corner of the sprawling Lahore Central Jail.

> The three who were to be hanged were kept in ward number 14. There was a furlong between that ward and where we were. Thus, we could not gather immediately what was happening but lodged next to number 14 were [the] accused in the second Lahore Conspiracy Case and they had a clearer picture.
> Just before 7 p.m., Bhagat Singh, Shivaram Rajguru and Sukhdev Thapar were brought out and taken towards the phansi ghar. As they walked, they loudly shouted, 'Inquilab

Zindabad!' Hearing it, the other accused in the conspiracy case responded with equal gusto. Soon, the entire jail was reverberating with loud cries of 'Inquilab Zindabad'. We too joined them. It spread even to the non-political prisoners, who started shouting the same slogan and it echoed across the jail. Then, there was deadly silence. That night, no one ate in the Central Jail of Lahore. And no one slept.

All the prisoners were overcome with thoughts of the final moments of the three extraordinary men and desperately sought information from anyone who would have it.

Only the chief warder Chattar Singh could tell us [about the hangings] as he was present at the spot. We waited for him to come and at 7 in the morning, he finally opened our locks. We had many questions to ask about how the three revolutionaries had approached death. Singh could not speak and then he burst out crying. With tears streaming down his face he said, 'I am a government servant and I have seen many hangings, but I have never seen such bravery in facing the gallows before.'

The chief warder went on to tell Virendra and Ehsan Ilahi an incident that occurred shortly before the execution of Bhagat Singh. After wearing the uniform for the hanging, when the revolutionary came out of his cell, Chattar Singh made a request.

He said to him that as there were only a few minutes left of his life, he should remember Wahe Guru. Hearing him,

Bhagat Singh laughed saying, 'Sardar-ji, throughout my life I have never remembered him. Looking at the atrocities against the poor and the downtrodden, I may even have reprimanded Him sometimes. Now, with death standing right in front of me, if I remember Him, He will say that this young man is both dishonest and a coward. But if I do not change my views about Him, He would say that this young man was both honest and brave.' Saying this, Bhagat Singh started his walk towards the phansi ghar.

Bhagat Singh's niece Virendar Sindhu provides more details of his dying moments.[232]

Sitting in his cell Bhagat Singh was reading *The Life of Lenin*. A few pages were left when the lock to his cell was opened, and he was asked to get ready for his hanging. Bhagat Singh replied, 'Wait. Let me read a few more pages. A revolutionary is going to meet another revolutionary.' He completed [the] book and then told the jail officials, 'Chalo, let's go.' The jail officials were all downcast, not so the prisoners who were being led to the gallows. There was no trace of fear or sadness on their faces. Bhagat Singh requested that they not be handcuffed, and their faces not be covered. The requests were accepted. By that time Rajguru and Sukhdev also came out of their cells. They saw each other and hugged – Bhagat Singh in the centre, Sukhdev on the left, and Rajguru on his right – and with arms locked with each other they began walking. They stopped for a second and then burst out singing a song written by Lal

Chand Phalak, '*Dil se niklege n mur kar bhi watan ki ulfat, mere mitti se bhi khushbu-a-wafa aayegi.*'

Led by the warder and surrounded by jail officials the three walked towards their end. One warder opened the door to the phansi ghar; the deputy commissioner of Lahore and a jail official named Muhammad Akbar were already inside. Bhagat Singh walked up to the British officer and said, 'Mr Magistrate, you are fortunate to be able to see today how Indian revolutionaries can embrace death with pleasure for the sake of their supreme ideal.'

No magistrate was willing to witness the hanging – Bhagat Singh as India's most admired son had monopolized the shrine of the greats. It was Nawab Muhammad Ahmed Khan Kasuri who did what others before him refused – he became an honorary magistrate and signed off on the execution. Uncannily, he was killed more than forty years later at the same spot where Bhagat Singh was hanged.[233] Calling themselves prisoners of war, the three revolutionaries had asked to be executed by a firing squad. Their demand was rejected and Kala Masih – his son, Tara Masih, who later hanged Prime Minister Zulfikar Bhutto of Pakistan – stepped up as the hangman.[234]

> The three then climbed the platform where the noose [was] hanging and went and stood under them. With their own hands, they put the noose on their necks. Bhagat Singh had some difficulty in putting [on] the noose, so the hangman came forward and adjusted it. And then the wheel turned, and the board parted. And the three fell into eternal sleep at the feet of Mother India.

The time of death was 7.33 p.m. Bhagat Singh was twenty-three years, five months, and twenty-six days old.

As a crowd began congregating outside the jail, the bodies were sneaked out in the darkness from a back gate. The remains of the three brave men had been chopped up into pieces and filled into sacks. These sacks were then loaded on a truck and taken to the banks of the Sutlej River in Ferozepur for a hasty cremation from where the half-burnt bodies were collected by Bhagat Singh's sister and Lala Lajpat Rai's daughter, among others. Final respects, befitting India's bravest, were paid to the three martyrs in Lahore on the banks of the Ravi – an evergreen backdrop of India's defiance against the Raj.[235]

Virendra remembers in his book:

> As per jail rules before his hanging, a prisoner is allowed to meet his relatives. On 23 March, Bhagat Singh's father was informed that [his] son was to be hanged the next day, so they [his family] could come and have the last meeting with him that day. Sardar Kishan Singh reached the jail with all his relatives, including the grandparents of Bhagat Singh, and his uncles and aunts, but was told that only he and his wife, the mother, could meet him. He tried to persuade the jail authorities to allow all relatives to meet him but was informed that the orders were to allow only the parents to meet him. Sardar Kishan Singh refused to meet his son [–] after all, he was also the father of Bhagat Singh and did not

want to show any weakness. They all returned from the jail gate without meeting their son.

In the evening, a huge public meeting took place near Mori Darwaza in Lahore, where Sardar Kishan Singh told the gathering about how he and his family came away without meeting with their son. As he was speaking, a man came to him and whispered in his ear that the three had been hanged. Sardar Kishan Singh fell silent for a moment, then controlling himself, he told the crowd, 'I have just learned that what was to be done has been done. I am going to claim the body of Bhagat Singh. All maintain calm and peace. There should be no protests.' But who was prepared to listen to him? And how could he have claimed the body of his son? It was on its way to Hussainiwala to be consigned to flames on the banks of the Sutlej.

And that ended a glorious chapter of our revolution.

17
Empires Crumble, Ideas Survive

Was Bhagat Singh the bravest freedom fighter as popular imagination would have us believe? During the Raj, there was almost a profusion of heroes – known faces and nameless citizens all joined by a common thread: A fierce burning for independence. They willingly went to the gallows or took torture on their chins, sacrificing the defining years of their lives. Yes, there were also notable exceptions who succumbed – compromising and surrendering to temptations.

In the debt India owes to those who withstood unimaginable torture only to find it was a step towards the noose, would it be unfair to single out Bhagat Singh for greatness? Eulogized and idolized with born-again popularity, Bhagat Singh rightly has his place in contemporary debates. Similar admiration, however, does not extend to his partners – Rajguru and Sukhdev – both of whom stared down death equally fiercely. What makes Bhagat Singh stand the tallest in the pantheon of the tall?

Says Professor Chaman Lal, author and honorary advisor to the Bhagat Singh Archives in New Delhi:[236]

> In every movement there are martyrs. And while freedom fighters like Azad and Bose are prominent names, only Bhagat Singh was given the title of Shaheed-e Azam by the people. There were other young ones who daringly embraced death. Azad's bravery was no less – his last moments were spent fighting – and Rajguru was maybe even braver. It is said when the three went to the gallows, it was Rajguru who put the noose around himself first.

Could Bhagat Singh's three hunger strikes have played a role? 'Many people broke the strike, but he was the one who sustained it till the end and, when the revolutionary Jatindra Nath Das became a shaheed, it is said that his head was on Bhagat Singh's lap.' Das passed away after a sixty-three-day hunger strike to protest the treatment of political prisoners. Bhagat Singh continued on, finally calling off his fast at Lahore Central Jail on 4 October 1929. He had been on a hunger strike for 110 days.[237]

A freedom fighter with an intellectual disposition, Bhagat Singh was no enigma, yet not everyone sees through his layers to fully understand the reasons behind his enduring legacy, says Chaman Lal.

Additionally, he penned down his thought process – something, unseen by any shaheed earlier. There were only a handful of letters from Bismil, Ashfaq, Azad and a few others. All revolutionaries just wanted revolution, and it was an abstract idea to throw out the British and replace them with Indian rule. They wanted to break the shackles on Bharat Mata as seen in Tagore's painting. Anything beyond had not been thought out. Bhagat Singh was the one with a proper idea and the first freedom fighter who had an ideological orientation.

Bhagat Singh's timeless appeal is much more than his youthful defiance, including the fact that he went to his hanging with his smile and charisma intact. He evokes raw emotion not just for embracing martyrdom but also for his act of inviting and welcoming it with open arms. For the freedom fighter, it was a longing – a man who was more than his exploits.

Jawaharlal Nehru writes: [238]

Bhagat Singh did not become popular because of his act of terrorism but because he seemed to vindicate, for the moment, the honour of Lala Lajpat Rai, and through him of the nation. He became a symbol, the act was forgotten, the symbol remained, and within a few months each town and village of Punjab, and to a lesser extent in the rest of northern India, resounded with his name. Innumerable songs grew about him and the popularity that the man achieved was something amazing.

The director of the Intelligence Bureau, Horace Williamson, noted just days after Bhagat Singh's execution, 'His photograph was on sale in every city and township and for a time rivalled in popularity even that of Mr Gandhi himself.'[239] Bhagat Singh's idea of a revolution was far removed from the popular image of a man who prescribed openly to violence. Conversely, he opposed bloodshed and believed that sacrifice for sacrifice's sake was futile. 'It is very easy and very fatuous to condemn persons or acts without seeking to understand the springs of action, the cause that under-lie them,' says Nehru on the phenomenon of Bhagat Singh.[240]

Historians point out that the revolutionary regretted Saunders' killing. The only other violent incident involving Bhagat Singh was the harmless Assembly attack for which the intensity of the bomb was already assessed in Agra for minimal harm. Says historian S. Irfan Habib:[241]

> We romanticize people like Bhagat Singh ... Even well-meaning people who are not ideologically motivated romanticize the martyr. A question that has confronted me all these years is, what is Bhagat Singh's legacy that we recognize today? His popular legacy is not the real one. The legacy of shahadat, martyrdom, is there, and you cannot argue with that, but for me it is incomplete. We cannot celebrate by overlooking what sort of India he conceived, his vision of independent India, and what he thought as an active revolutionary. Only the inheritance of his martyrdom is left as it's convenient to commemorate – only put flowers and then forget about him. The British hanged him once

but we kill him every day by ignoring his legacy and the vision which he left behind for India.'

Bhagat Singh, the intellectual, is often overshadowed by his actions and the defiance he demonstrated against imperialism. It is an upcycling of an image that is far more glamorous than that of a rationalist espousing his thoughts on an egalitarian society, a persona endorsed and exaggerated by a lazy, commercial Bollywood. Singh questioned the role of religious dogmas; his nationalism was authentic and far removed from the muscular version that has become associated with the term in recent times. For one, he was not stingy in his criticism of his motherland when required: 'Our country is unique where six crore people are called "untouchables", and their mere touch defiled the so-called upper castes.'[242]

It is worth taking a moment to assess how he would have sized up India if alive. Historian Chaman Lal has this to say:[243]

He cannot be put in the dustbin of history; there is a compulsion there. After 2014, Gandhi's name has been kept as a showpiece. There is no [real] belief in Gandhi, and similarly with Bhagat Singh. The Mahatma's name is internationally renowned, so it is complicated, otherwise even Gandhian thought and history [would] have been let go. The RSS's name came up in Gandhi's death and the regime does not outright discard Godse; it indirectly patronizes him. Nehru is being targeted [currently], while other names like Bose and Ambedkar are being used to target him. So, appropriation of historical figures is through the 'WhatsApp university' or we [through what we] call religious fundamentalists. For them, history is nothing. It is mythology that they create themselves.

He points out that in the old Parliament's gallery of portraits for national heroes, Bhagat Singh was not included. Interestingly, he says, a portrait of Savarkar – a man whose mercy plea to the British remains controversial – was hanged directly opposite that of Gandhi.

Despite political compulsions, Bhagat Singh remains relevant as an ideological symbol that gives strength against oppression, as witnessed in the year-long farmers' protest in Delhi (in 2020–21). 'You can fool all the people some of the time and some of the people all the time, but you cannot fool all the people all the time.'[244]

Embracing death was not Bhagat Singh's endgame and azadi for him was more than just freedom from the British. He wanted to arouse passion for liberty through thoughts an independent India he hoped would adopt. For that, the revolutionary needed to set an example – one that galvanized the country's youth into action. Even as a teenager, immersed in the idea of revolution – he wrote his first article at seventeen on universal brotherhood – he displayed no youthful recklessness. His only weakness was watching films!

Says S. Irfan Habib:[245]

Merely replacement of the British with Indians was not his end goal. Communalism and casteism were a big issue for him, as was the role of students in politics. He wanted that the 98 per cent should rule, not 2 per cent. One feels ashamed that he is relevant today. He should not be as those issues should have been resolved and [should have] become almost non-existent today. But no one bothers to look at his idea of nationalism. He conceived composite nationalism – a country that was not divided on caste, religion and language ... There was no exclusion. In his idea of universal brotherhood, he conceived of a world where there would not be any 'other'. Today, we look at othering people in our [own] country, forget the world.

The historian emphasizes that as long as the idea of nationalism is shaped by political expediency, freedom fighters like Bhagat Singh and Subhas Chandra Bose – who was close to Bhagat Singh and his ideas – will continue to be usurped for political gain.

A voracious reader, writer and thinker, the revolutionary's chief demand in jail was for political prisoners to have access to books and newspapers. It had helped shape his worldview in the brief time he lived. Bhagat Singh's supply of literature – Marxist, revolutionary and ideological – from admirers outside was endless and he sent his list of books – Dostoevsky to Dante and Omar Khayyam to Tagore – to be delivered from libraries in Lahore.[246]

His last years, spent in jail, were not filled with despondency. On the contrary, inside the tiny walls of a jail cell, Bhagat Singh rested his revolutionary persona and gave his intellectual side a chance to flourish. It is admirable that the philosophical writings and clarity of thought belong to a twenty-three-year-old, the age at which he was hanged. 'If religion is separated from politics, then we can all come together in politics even if we belong to different religions,' he wrote.[247] Or take his seminal essay, 'Religious Riots and their Solution', which clearly foresaw how a tear in the country's pluralistic fabric would be disastrous. 'The condition of Bharatvarsh is indeed pitiable today. The devotees of one religion are sworn enemies of the devotees of another religion. Merely to belong to one religion is now considered enough reason to be the enemy of another religion … under these conditions, the future of Hindustan seems very bleak.'[248]

One of the few surviving members of the Naujawan Bharat Sabha, Comrade Ramachandra, aged ninety-four, told Lalit:[249]

> Bhagat Singh was a very bright lad. He was barely in his ninth class when his father brought him for admission to National College. Normally, this was not possible unless one had passed matriculation. But the college was not affiliated with any university, so rules could be bent, and Bhagat Singh was two years junior to me in college. When we set up the Naujawan Bharat Sabha I was the President, and he was the General Secretary. He wrote most of the handouts and was a voracious reader. That is why he could express himself so cogently.

In jail, Bhagat Singh penned his famous essay, 'Why I Am an Atheist'. This, along with other writings, give an insight into the man whose ideas were ahead of time.

Born in Pakistan's Lyallpur (now Faisalabad) into a Sikh family that was influenced by the Ghadar Party and the Arya Samaj, Bhagat Singh's journey of discovery started as a child. His uncle, Ajit Singh, was a revolutionary and part of a group that started an agitation on land alienation in Punjab. 'Bhagat Singh transcended caste, creed and class, and was hero-worshipped by Punjab's peasantry for his anti-bourgeoise struggles,' remarks Razi Ahmed, founder of Lahore Literary Festival.[250]

His life, however, unfurled in all its glory in Lahore. It is also the city where he was martyred – a burden that has few parallels. Author Haroon Khalid writes:[251]

> Sometimes there are tangible traces of that other city: an abandoned Hindu temple standing like an anomaly in the middle of a crowded market, an old colonial structure surrounded by glass-fronted plazas. Mostly, however, that city exists in folk tales, stories, and legends. These stories are scattered all over Lahore, at its junctions, around its monuments...

One of those historical roundabouts is on Shadman Road and is vacuously named Fawara Chowk. Constructed over what was once Lahore Central Jail, it is here that Bhagat Singh, Rajguru and Sukhdev were hanged. For years, Fawara Chowk has tried to shrug off its anonymity but has failed to reclaim the identity of a man whose deeds were not big enough to overlook his Sikh roots in a Muslim nation. Civil society almost succeeded – a decision was taken by the local government to rename the roundabout

Bhagat Singh Chowk but there was a slip between the cup and the lip. Last-minute opposition and court intervention stayed the decision; peace activists, civil society and intellectuals were attacked by right-wing groups and Fawara Chowk stays, destined for tragic obscurity.

18

Remarriage Rumours: An Aeroplane for Mr Nehru

By November 1935, Virendra had been actively involved in *Pratap* for almost two years, a period that coincided with him also joining the Congress. Despite the odds and his lack of preparation, he had cleared his Bachelor of Arts degree in jail. However, two months before his master's examination, he found himself imprisoned again. Fortunately, or fortuitously, he passed this as well. At only twenty-two years of age, he was already a veteran of jails and arrests. When he finally tasted freedom, Virendra found himself within a different set of walls – he started working at *Pratap* under his formidable father, Mahashay Krishan.

One day, an article by Bhai Parmanand criticizing what he termed the Congress party's 'appeasement of Muslims' caught his attention. Without giving it a thought, and not expecting a reply either, Virendra forwarded the article to Jawaharlal Nehru. He had not met the leader – when Nehru presided over the Lahore session, Virendra was in jail. Which was why he was pleasantly surprised to receive a reply.

Nehru's mail to Virendra was from the health resort of Badenweiler in Germany, where his seriously ill wife, Kamala, was receiving treatment. In his correspondence, Nehru wrote, '… I have with interest read the article by Bhai Parmanand … I would like to say something in reply, but not just yet. Because of some other preoccupation, it is impossible for me to write anything now.' In the postcard, Nehru further elaborates, 'My wife's condition does not show very great change from day to day. On the whole, there is a slight improvement but sometimes there are setbacks.' Kamala's condition would go on to worsen and she did not return to India alive.

While he was abroad, attempts were on to re-elect Nehru as the Congress president. But with his wife's precarious condition, the leader did not give his assent to take on the mantle once again. He was unwilling to leave Kamala and told his supporters not to consider him for the post. 'Life was pulling at me again,' Nehru remarked when, despite his opposition, he received news in January of being elected for the second time. The session was to convene in April and he was not completely surprised. 'I was expecting this as friends had forewarned me, and I had even discussed it with Kamala. It was a dilemma for me: to leave her as she is or to resign from the presidentship.'[252] Kamala herself cleared the path for him. She died on 28 February 1936, in a sanatorium in Switzerland's Lausanne. Nehru returned with her ashes to Allahabad, to take over the mantle of the Congress president once again.

This was a phase when the party was not in a strong position in Punjab, where the Muslim League and the Akali Dal were giving it a fight. But it was the powerful zamindars of the Unionist Party, Sir Sikandar Hayat, Fazl-i-Hussain, Sir Sunder Singh Majithia, and Chaudhary Chotu Ram – also later bestowed with a knighthood – who posed the biggest challenge.

These luminaries were supporters of the colonial rule, while Congress owned the struggle to oust the Raj. This clash of ideology had heated political temperatures and there were expectations that the two parties would play out the real contest in Punjab. The Unionist Party had one big advantage: It had the resources and backing of the government.

Despite the demanding circumstances, the Punjab Congress was not ready to throw in the towel without making a go at all possibilities. Staring at an unpleasant outcome, they went straight for the jugular. Pandit Nehru was to be invited to Punjab and the man deputed to go to Allahabad to request the leader to visit was Virendra.

With only respect for a stalwart to go with, Virendra reached Allahabad as delegated. From the railway station, he took a tonga to Anand Bhavan – the Nehru family's ancestral house. If he had thought convincing the leader was not going to be easy, Virendra had not accounted for Mr Upadhyay. At Anand Bhavan, he was confronted by Pandit Nehru's secretary, who told him unceremoniously that the leader's programme was fixed for the next month and a half. Nehru was to tour the country, so there was no chance of him heading to Lahore. Upadhyay added, not as an afterthought, 'Panditji has no time to meet you either.'

Virendra was carrying the hopes of all the Congressmen in Punjab and, even if he so desired, he couldn't return without making another attempt at meeting Nehru. His persistence finally paid off and he was asked to come again at three in the afternoon. At the appointed hour, Virendra was taken to Anand Bhavan's upper floor, where Pandit Nehru was sitting in the veranda, busy writing. He was surrounded by books and a typewriter.

The leader asked Virendra to sit and, after what seemed a couple of minutes, he probed about the situation in Punjab, particularly Lahore. He then inquired from the younger man the purpose of his visit and when Nehru understood the reason, his rejoinder was a quick 'impossible'.

Virendra had not come this far to give up so easily and disputed the statement: 'You cannot ignore Punjab.' Nehru's opinion was that even if he spent a month in the state, the chances of a Congress majority were negligible. On the other hand, there were states where a visit of even three days could make a significant change in the situation. As far as Nehru was concerned, Punjab was a lost cause and the Congress was in a hopeless position to form the government. 'So why should I waste time?' he argued.

The meeting was almost over when Virendra threw one final ace that at long last had Nehru thinking. 'Whatever happens in Punjab also affects the neighbouring states, especially the North-West Frontier Province,' he said. This counter-offensive finally had the leader's attention. He was greatly impressed by the struggles of Abdul Ghaffar Khan and his brother, Abdul Jabbar Khan, known popularly as Dr Khan Sahib. Even though he could not tour the Frontier Province, Nehru recognized that events in Punjab could impact the neighbouring state. Urdu newspapers published from Punjab had a big readership in this region.

Interested, he asked Upadhyay to bring his programme schedule. After perusing it, he looked up. 'I may be able to come for two days, but can you people arrange an airplane to take me?' He continued, 'If you can organize one, wire me and I will make a programme for two days.'

With a fervent promise to try, an ecstatic Virendra returned to Lahore. Nehru's popularity was at its peak and paralleled even the great Mahatma, and Punjab erupted in jubilation after his successful trip. But there was still an outstanding task, one that could make or break the trip: The issue of hiring a plane. Along with Gopichand Bhargava, Virendra contacted a private company that rented small airplanes. The charges were high, but they had no choice. Plane booked, they wired Pandit Nehru who promptly replied. He was coming to Punjab.

This was probably the first time a plane had been chartered for an election campaign and it had a further electrifying impact on the state. Nehru added to the excitement by sending a message to the people of Punjab. 'Due to paucity of time, I have come by plane,' he announced. Next, the problem arose of accessibility to the leader. Every Congress candidate worth a constituency wanted to visit the man whose charisma made international headlines. This, however, was downright impossible in a two-day visit.

One constituency that Nehru was keen to visit was of independent candidate Mian Iftikharuddin. The Mian had studied at Oxford and, though a rich landlord, he was known for his progressive views. He was also Nehru's friend. The Mian joined the Congress a year later and became its Punjab president. This was when Nehru stayed at his Lahore kothi, as did Indira on her first visit to Lahore after marriage. So, half a day of Pandit Nehru's tight schedule was already taken and a visit to his friend's constituency was scheduled. Incidentally, Mian Iftikharuddin switched to the Muslim League just before Partition.

Nehru's itinerary was meticulously prepared. He personally combed through the fine print and did not tolerate even the slightest disturbance or mismanagement. The leader was famous for his short temper, and, although it cooled off equally swiftly, no one was willing to be found short and on his wrong side. Virendra did find himself on the receiving end, but, by then, they were no longer strangers.

At that moment, a lingering question was on who would escort the popular leader around Punjab. Dr Satyapal suggested Virendra's name – he was behind the successful invitation, so it was befitting that he chaperoned Nehru, he declared. This did not stop the jostling for the prestigious duty and, on the first day of the trip, Nehru was escorted by Lala Jwala Das Sikri to Ferozepur. The next morning, responsibility was handed over to Virendra but by then an incident had occurred which made Virendra himself apprehensive to face Nehru.

A fortnight after Virendra's return upon convincing Nehru, he received an interesting wire from *Pratap*'s correspondent in Allahabad. There were strong rumours in the city of Pandit

Nehru re-marrying, and while much was not known about the woman in question, it was believed she was a graduate. This report put Virendra in a spot – if it was true and *Pratap* published it, it would create a nationwide sensation. On the other hand, if it was circulated without credibility, the newspaper would not only lose the trust of thousands of readers, but they would also be blamed for defaming a beloved leader. After deliberating for twenty-four hours, Virendra dashed a cable to Jawaharlal Nehru: 'Our Allahabad correspondent informs us that you are about to remarry. Please confirm.'

A response, an angry one, came as early as the next day. 'Fantastic nonsense. Who is your correspondent?'

Virendra was relieved. It was a timely save from what could have been a blunder of historic proportions. Since Kamala Nehru's death, rumours around Nehru's personal life floated generously. Not only was he handsome and charismatic, but he was also India's best-loved son. Some women intentionally exaggerated their association with him and his opponents further amplified the baseless gossip. In reality, Nehru plunged headlong into the freedom struggle after his wife's passing and put all personal matters in the background. Virendra did not respond to Nehru's wire for he did not want to expose his reporter to the leader's famous temper.

A few days later, Jawaharlal Nehru landed in Lahore. After visiting Ferozepur district, the leader was in the city for the second and last day of his trip. As Virendra reached to escort him, he was caught on the back foot. 'Why have you not replied to my inquiry?' This confrontation was Nehru's opening remark. The Congress leader wanted *Pratap*'s Allahabad correspondent's name, but Virendra successfully diverted him and once again avoided answering.

It was the month of February and Punjab was facing a frigid winter, but it didn't stop Nehru – accompanied by Virendra carrying a thermos of hot water – from addressing at least ten meetings a day in different cities. From Lahore, he left by plane to Sialkot. Indians were not allowed to enter airports – so, only the local Congress candidate Krishan Gopal Dutt and his brother were there to receive him. For all that, the airport was packed. Britishers, in large numbers, had come to catch a glimpse of the man who was leading the fight against them. It was the same story when he departed from the airport.

Before leaving for Sialkot, Virendra organized fruits and sandwiches for the leader but Nehru submerged himself in an endless round of meetings and ignored his meals. Dutt had arranged lunch at his Sialkot residence; Nehru refused this as well, retorting that he was not in the city for pleasure. It was only on the flight back to Lahore that he ate, asking Virendra simultaneously for details of the next gathering. When Nehru was informed that he would be addressing the public outside Mori Darwaza, he had an idea and asked if the plane could glide over the venue. Virendra marked the distance to Mori Darwaza from Anarkali and the pilot, in unprecedented scenes, did indeed fly over the large assembly of people gathered on the ground.

Lakhs had come to hear or simply catch a glimpse of Pandit Nehru. This large crowd pleased and energized him immensely, and Virendra remembers his speech as one that was full of josh.

Frank Moraes, editor and author, wrote:[253]

Very early in his political life, dating from his first contact with the peasants of Pratapgarh in 1920 Nehru lighted on the discovery that the masses acted on him like tonic, and that while he transmitted to them something of his energy and mental fire, they gave in return renewed strength, courage and vigour.

It had turned out to be a successful day and, soon after his last address finished, Nehru sat in a car with Virendra, and they left for Amritsar. On the road, as they were nearing the town, a beautifully lit up house caught the leader's attention. Virendra speculated that it was likely because of a wedding, to which Nehru responded wistfully, 'I also got married on Basant.'

Saying that, he fell silent.

Nehru was still in Punjab when another episode put Virendra in a tight spot. His father, Mahashay Krishan, was an uncompromising editor and, ignoring his son's position as an active member of the Congress, in an editorial, he slammed the party for what he called 'Muslim appeasement'. He complained that both the British and the Congress were pampering the Muslim League. It reached Nehru's ears that *Pratap* was critical of the Congress and he questioned Virendra about it. 'My father's editorials are independent of his son's,' responded Virendra, adding that he was not involved with the policy of the newspaper. To his credit, even in the future, Nehru did not hold Mahashay Krishan's views against Virendra. As a side note, his visit helped most of the Congress candidates win in Punjab that year.

Nehru visited Lahore two more times. On one occasion, he stopped in the city on his way back to Allahabad. He had not been allowed to enter Kashmir and was arrested by the maharaja's government, which forced him to turn back at the border. Finding him unexpectedly in their city, the local Congress wanted to take out a procession in Lahore. It was, however, a move that required government permission and no one was willing to try getting it. To get around the stipulations, a plan was made to drive him around Lahore in an open car, while discreetly informing the public about his route. They could line the roads with flowers and garlands.

Virendra had a German Adler car – it was a convertible and it fit the criteria. He decided to drive it with Nehru as the only passenger. Two people driving around town did not constitute a 'procession' and therefore there were no grounds to stop them. That day, from Shah Alami Darwaza to Lahori Gate and onwards, they travelled the length and breadth of the city. People on the streets in large numbers tried stopping them, but they carried on, not wanting to give the authorities any excuse to clamp down. As the crowd swelled and people threw flowers inside the car, Virendra started to get nervous. He had been quiet about one fact – he had only recently learned how to drive! But he, his fabled passenger and the car – overflowing with flowers – all made it back safely. Nehru, who strongly believed in being among the people, was ecstatic at the enthusiastic reception he received.

On another visit to Lahore, Nehru stayed at Virendra's neighbour Dr Satyapal's house. Satyapal was in jail then, so his wife requested Virendra to look after the esteemed guest. Nehru's non-stop tours had finally caught up with his health and, with a bad throat, he fell ill. For someone who was always on the move, this was not easy, and, in the evening, he complained to his visitor Lala Achint Ram about being confined to the house. A compromise was reached and the men decided to go out for a late-night spin – this would allow Nehru to get some fresh air and he would not be mobbed.

Virendra took out his car once again and drove Jawaharlal Nehru, with Achint Ram sitting in the back. Both were of the same age and had known each other for a long time, and some frank conversations took place as they were driven from Nisbet Road to Lawrence Garden. Once they reached Canal Road, Nehru asked Virendra to halt the car and the three men sat quietly for a while on the banks of the canal. People and vehicles passed them by but, in the darkness, no one recognized India's tallest leader sitting quietly on the muddy ground. Returning home, Nehru confessed, 'It is after a long time that I was able to relax; otherwise, people do not leave me.'

19

Of 'a Clogged Brain' and 'Conceited Arrogance'

The Unionist Party of Sir Sikandar Hayat Khan was in power in Punjab and Mahashay Krishan had definite views about it. The party's atma is English, it is just dressed up in Unionist colours, he would say. To be fair, there was an attempt – at least initially – at forming a secular government with Hindus, Sikhs, Muslims and Christians invited to partake. The party tried to gain popularity by concentrating on economic issues, but it was through and through a product of the Raj, just as Sir Sikandar himself was. Before becoming the premier, he was the Reserve Bank of India's deputy governor where he was constantly surrounded by British officers and had no independent say, forcing him to look over his shoulder perpetually.

Sir Sikander carried this feeling of insecurity even as Punjab's Premier, until finally one day, he found an outlet. *Pratap* was at its receiving end. By now, the newspaper was firmly entrenched among its readers. Sir Sikandar, however, had no respect for reputation. Routine censorship and forfeiture of security apart, in 1942, *Pratap* was also forcibly closed for forty-five days. By then, the editor-proprietor and his family were, if not indifferent, at least inured to the daily harassment they faced.

Ironically, the most heated confrontation between the Premier and the editor was about a war being fought thousands of miles away, World War II. This clash lasted a month and a half and was a milestone in pre-Independence journalism.

'Jung Ka Rang' was a daily column by Krishan on the war that he wrote between 1941–42 when the conflict was at its peak. At that time, the Allies were not doing very well – Hitler was successful in Europe and his army had entered Russia. On the other side, Japan had joined the war, and its forces were able to reach Burma after devastating Pearl Harbour and overrunning Indonesia, Singapore, and Malaya. The editor records, 'The British did not want [that] I should write about the defeat of the Allied forces lest people get this feeling that the Allies were on their last legs. They wanted I should give the message that the Allies were progressing. This I could not do.'[254]

The last straw for the British was an article raising a question about the public's response if the Japanese entered India. Mahashay Krishan answered the question himself with an anecdote. During World War I, the chief justice of the Calcutta High Court asked legal luminary Sir Rashbihari Ghosh (the revolutionary who attacked Lord Hardinge was Rash Behari Bose) what he would do if the Germans entered India. He replied, 'We will do what we have been taught to do. We will welcome them.' Surprised, the chief justice asked what they had been taught to do. Ghosh answered, 'We have been taught to welcome the invader. We will be loyal to them. We will stand on the shore at Bombay and, when the Germans land, we will be there to welcome them with garlands.' Krishan concluded by saying as things remained the same, and there was a glaring incapability to resist foreign invasion, there was no option but to welcome the Japanese with garlands if they entered India.

Then, all hell broke loose. The home secretary censored the newspaper once again – this time, with an additional rule to submit its copy for prior vetting. The government expected the paper to compromise for a peaceful resolution. Instead, *Pratap* stopped publication. For twenty-five days, no one from the paper approached the government. Ultimately, Sir Sikandar was forced to make the first move.

Krishan was later to write about Sir Sikandar Hayat Khan, 'His entire life was spent in the servility of the British. Whatever he achieved was due to the largesse of the government. But he was in the public eye and public response also mattered to him.'[255] With newspapers all over the country coming after him, Sir Sikandar – who cherished the reputation of a liberal, progressive administrator – informed Bill Bustin of *The Civil and Military Gazette* of his desire to meet Krishan. *The Civil and Military Gazette* was an English daily founded in British India as a colonial mouthpiece, with Rudyard Kipling as one of its employees. The *Pratap* editor, however, was a tough nut to crack. He demanded a written invitation, or otherwise 'people will say I went to ask for forgiveness and for censorship to be lifted'.

Cornered, Sir Sikandar sent him a written invite but if he expected matters to ease up after that, he had underestimated Krishan. The meeting lasted two hours and the editor recounted it in the paper as '*bahut garma garm baat hue* (it was a heated discussion)'.

> Trying to put us on the defensive, Sir Sikandar at the outset said the justification for the censorship is not in consideration here. Are you ready to give an undertaking that in future you will be more careful? [He asked.] Equally animated, I replied, 'Definitely not. We have come because you invited us, and you must take back the censorship order unconditionally.'[256]

Sir Sikandar realized that he had met his match. He told the editor, 'You need not express regrets in writing, just whisper in my ear that in the future you will not write on the war. It will be a gentleman's agreement, and no one will come to know of it.' With this, he brought his ear towards Krishan. To his mortification, the editor refused to even move, let alone whisper in his ear. He ended the two-hour-long meeting with this Urdu saying, 'Tu bhi badal phalak ki zamana badal gaya (You also change Falak [the name of a poet] as times have changed). 'I also told him that *Pratap* was ready to wait till the end of the war, but the censorship order will have to be withdrawn unconditionally.'

The ice had been broken with that. Sir Sikandar had understood that public opinion was with *Pratap* and instructions were sent to the home minister to withdraw the censorship orders unconditionally. A statement was prepared but before the Premier could sign it, there was another twist. An announcement by Jawaharlal Nehru appeared, criticizing, in extraordinarily strong words, the censorship order on *Pratap*. Sir Sikandar flew into a rage and issued a strong rejoinder in turn; it marked the beginning of a bitter personal feud between him and Nehru.

As far as timing goes, Nehru's intervention pushed back the clock on *Pratap*'s censorship. In a bitter exchange, Nehru accused the Punjab government of having a 'clogged and panicky brain'. Getting personal, Sir Sikandar commented on not just Jawaharlal Nehru's language but also about his 'conceited arrogance that ill becomes the son of that great gentleman and patriot'.[257]

Things rapidly went downhill from here.

On his way to Kangra with a newly married Indira, Nehru met Virendra at a dinner in Lahore, where he promised to release a few words on the government order against *Pratap*. The next morning at seven, before leaving for his vacation he was ready with a statement, reproduced here:

May 11, 1942

During my present visit to Lahore, I have had the occasion to see the order against *Pratap*. This is a remarkable document for anyone who knows anything about the workings of a newspaper. It enjoins pre-censorship of every matter, including headlines connected with the war, the international situation, internal security or civil defence measures or any other matter relating to the prosecution of the war taken by the Government …

This is a remarkable order which only the clogged and panicky brain of the Punjab Government could have devised. It is obvious to even a tyro in journalism that no daily newspaper can possibly be published under these conditions and restrictions. Further, no intelligent reader wants to read what the Special Press Advisor wishes to impose on him. It is added that no reference of any kind must be made in the paper that any news, article, photograph, or drawing will be or has been submitted for examination to the Special Press Advisor, or has been withheld, or in any way curtailed, altered, or modified by him. Evidently, the Special Press Advisor is a shy and retiring individual and wants to hide his shining light under a bushel. He wants all credit for his hard work to go to the editor. The editor and the publisher have rightly refused to issue their newspaper subject to these conditions. There is no other honourable and sensible course open to them. To accept such conditions is to dishonour the profession of journalism and fool and betray the public …

—Jawaharlal Nehru

That very day, Sir Sikandar issued his rejoinder.

I was pained but not surprised at Pandit Jawaharlal Nehru's statement regarding the imposition of pre-censorship on the *Pratap*. The statement bristles with misstatement of facts and seems to have been based on tainted or biased information. The Punjab Government was forced to take the step as the *Pratap* despite repeated warnings persisted in a policy prejudicial to the successful prosecution of the war … It is a malicious untruth that I suggested to the emissary of the Press Committee that the Pratap should support the policy of the government.

The Premier added that he had no intention to comment on Nehru's language but goes right ahead and does exactly that.

Such conceited arrogance ill becomes the son of that great gentleman and patriot who was an outstanding example of Indian culture and who won the esteem of his countrymen irrespective of caste and creed by his unfailing courtesy and generous hospitality.
—Sir Sikandar Hayat

The row caught the attention of other leaders. Bhim Sen Sachar, a Congress leader in the Assembly, upbraided the Premier for insulting 'a gentleman of the high and distinguished position of Panditji'. Nehru, though, was not done, nor was he willing to let the matter slip.

May 19, 1942

The Premier has said that what I have said bristles with misstatements of facts, and it is a malicious untruth to say that he [the Premier] suggested to the emissary of the Press Committee that the *Pratap* should support the Government.

It would have been helpful if the Premier had pointed out exactly what the misstatements were ... The principal fact I was concerned with was the order served on the *Pratap*. This is, I believe, a public property and each person can judge for himself whether my criticism was justified or not. The central committee of the Newspapers Editors Conference, which consists of both English and Indian editors unanimously condemned the order. *The Civil and Military Gazette* of Lahore which cannot be charged with a bias for India's nationalism or freedom, calls it 'obnoxious.' I shall be glad to know from the Premier if he thinks it is possible to issue any daily newspaper in terms of his government's order ...

The Premier has specifically denied having asked for an assurance that the *Pratap* should support the policy of the government. I am glad to have the denial ... I received my first information on the subject in Delhi. This was derived from a telegram received from Lahore by the President of the Newspapers Editors Conference after the interview with the Premier. When I came to Lahore it was confirmed. In the course of a letter that conveys the results of the interview with the Premier, an eminent English editor wrote to the publishers of the *Pratap* as follows: 'He [the Premier] declared himself willing to rescind the order against the *Pratap* only on the assurance from the Pratap undertaking to fall in line with the government and the public opinion in the province regarding the war.

My limited knowledge of a foreign language prevented me from appreciating the essential difference between supporting the government's policy and falling in line with the Punjab Government. But I should have hoped that in any event, this linguistic difference did not proceed with malice. The Premier has reminded me of my failings and how unworthy I am to be the son of my father. I appreciate his gentle admonition realising fully that I err frequently, and in many ways. But I have the satisfaction at least to be conceited and arrogant in a right cause. Inefficiency and incompetence in high places irritate me, and it is notorious that New Delhi has become their chosen abode. The Punjab government walks more and more in the long shadow of the imperial capital. In my previous statement, I made no reference to the Punjab Premier or any other individual. I refer to that impersonal thing, the government. I didn't even know what part the Premier had played in the matter, nor did I accuse him personally of anything. If the Premier wishes to assume fully the responsibility of the order on the *Pratap* and the subsequent occurrences connected with it, I have no desire to deprive him of that honour.

— Jawaharlal Nehru

Sir Sikandar issued a statement swiftly in response:

May 20, 1942

Pandit Jawaharlal Nehru has asked me to elucidate my statement and point out the misstatement of facts in his first statement. He has asserted in that statement that the request made on behalf of the All-India Newspaper Editors

Conference by their emissary met with a flat refusal. This is not correct. Mr F.W. Bustin, who was the emissary, has since made this clear in his article published in *The Civil and Military Gazette*. Pandit Nehru also alleged in his statement that it had been demanded of the *Pratap* that it should 'support the government's policy'. This again as I said in my previous statement, is a malicious untruth. While saying so I do not mean to convey that Panditji included the untruth in his statement maliciously, but that his informants misled him by introducing this lie out of sheer malice against the administration. Surely there is a world of difference between 'supporting (or falling in with) the policy of the government' and 'undertaking to fall in line with the [policy of] Punjab Government and the public opinion in the province regarding the war' ...

My surmise that Panditji has been misinformed by interested and biased partisans has proved correct, as is evident from his reference in his second statement to the correspondence between an 'eminent English editor' and the *Pratap*. It is obvious and not surprising that the persons who sought Panditji's backing in their attempt to justify *Pratap*'s attitude conveyed to him a garbled version of the affair and withheld information that did not suit their purpose ... His statement was issued from Lahore. I wish he had taken the trouble to verify the facts by referring to me before issuing it and avoided this unpleasant controversy ... We are not strangers, as I have had the privilege and pleasure of meeting him before.

As for the concluding portion of his statement, let me hasten to assure Panditji that far be it from me to even think of admonishing a public man, much less a leader of his eminence and position. It would have been sheer presumptuousness on my part to do so, and even my worst detractors will tell him that I am temperamentally incapable of any lapse of this kind. It was the tone and the language of his first statement based on incorrect and one-sided information which actuated me to remind him of the unique cultural traditions of his community and his family, and the unfailing courtesy and generosity of his illustrious father who will always be remembered with esteem and affection by his countrymen. I hope that Pandit Ji will forgive me if I do not share his views or satisfaction as expressed in the following sentence in his recent statement, 'But I have satisfaction at least to be conceited and arrogant.' Conceit and arrogance are inexcusable in any individual at any time and even less excusable in a righteous cause.

—Sir Sikandar Hayat

Back from his visit to Kangra, Nehru met the press at 41, Nisbet Road where he tried to bring the original dispute back on track. Nehru dismissed both his and *Pratap*'s relevance in front of what he considered the non-negotiable issue of the freedom of the press. On the side, he told Virendra, 'You turned out to be very clever. You have hung your own problem around my neck.'

May 24, 1942

On my return to Lahore today I have seen the second statement issued by the Punjab Premier about the *Pratap* case. Perhaps it is more correct to say that the statement is about me, as unfortunately, I figure more in this connection than the *Pratap*. I have no desire to discuss my personal matters as the subject is distasteful to me and in any event, I can hardly look upon myself objectively. For all the good advice the Premier has quite unsolicited given to me, I am duly grateful, and I hope that I shall profit from it. It will be my misfortune if I cannot live up to the high standards that are required of those who may have to deal directly or indirectly with the Punjab government's activities. But it does not really matter what I am. For individuals should not count in a discussion of a public issue. Even the *Pratap* as such has only secondary importance. The real issue was and is how a government should treat the press. Was the order passed on the *Pratap* a proper order and is its continuation justified?

The Premier stated previously that my first statement bristled with misstatements and in particular one remark was malicious falsehood. I have carefully considered his list of such misstatements and falsehoods. As far as I can make out, there are two mentioned by him. The first is my statement that the request made on behalf of the All-India Newspapers Editors Conference was rejected by him. This the Premier says, is incorrect because he sent a long telegram to Mr Srinivasan. May I inquire whether it is not a fact that the request was refused, and the refusal persists even now? The sending of a telegram or any negotiations that might have taken place in between does not make the slightest difference to the final act of refusal. The fact that the order against the *Pratap* still continues is itself final evidence of that refusal. I must confess that I have failed to discover anything even remotely resembling a misstatement in what I said. It is true that I did not refer to certain correspondence and negotiations. They made no difference to my final conclusion.

The second statement which is also said to be a malicious falsehood, is my remark that the government demanded of *Pratap* that it should support the government's policy … What the government actually did was to ask *Pratap* to fall in line with the government's policy in regard to the war. I appreciate the difference, but I am amazed that the Premier should not realise that the policy in regards to the war covers practically every conceivable thing that is important today. In wartime, there is no essential difference left between a government's general policy and its policy in regard to the War. The latter governs or should govern, if a war is properly conducted, everything. Certainly, I was not thinking of the price of potatoes or any such matter, when I wrote my first statement. I was thinking definitely of war policy and its far-reaching consequences. It covers a multitude of errors and absurdities; it is the parent of the Defence of India Act, and its ugly progeny, the Defence of India Rules. It leads to internments without trails, to exorbitant salaries and allowances to officials and to hundred and one other unsavoury consequences.

It is malicious falsehood, that this is a list of misstatements which are said to have been abundant in my statement. It is obvious that the Premier's standard of public criticism and his choice of language are very different from mine. But the real question still remains: was the order on the *Pratap* justified? I repeat it was a fantastic order, impossible to obey. This has got nothing to do with what the Premier thinks of the Pratap. Every journalist and, I venture to say, every reasonable and responsible person considers the order and its continuation obnoxious. Why not deal with this matter directly instead of dealing with personalities?

—Jawaharlal Nehru

The order to withdraw censorship was kept pending while the two leaders slugged it out against each other in print. Another fifteen days passed. No one from the paper approached the Premier or reminded him of his promise, but he had had enough and wanted to end this controversy. There was another, a not altogether altruistic, motive behind it – Sir Sikandar wanted to visit a hill station and was eager to end the fracas before his departure. He made a delegation of journalists visit him and 'request' him to withdraw the censorship order on *Pratap*. This was finally done and, after forty-five days, *Pratap* made a triumphant reappearance. Mahashay Krishan was back with his series on the war, 'Jung Ka Rang'.

The era when truth was sacrosanct, and press freedom was fought for fiercely is perhaps long gone. Back then, it was not just journalists but also political leaders who didn't shy away from being in the firing line. When asked to bend, there was no question of them crawling – journalists prided themselves on speaking truth to power and were ably supported by a political class on which the sun has long set. Nehru once memorably told the famous political cartoonist Kesava Shankar Pillai, 'Don't spare me, Shankar.' And Shankar didn't, generously lampooning India's first Prime Minister in the 4,000 works he is believed to have featured Nehru in.[258]

Debates in pre-Partition India, barring the odd Sir Sikandar riposte, were intellectual, and respect was seldom compromised. Disagreements were threshed out with academic clarity; the high-pitched filth of present-day politics was beneath the stature of stalwarts who were additionally politicians.

Scholarly, yet filled with conviction, their speeches continue to age well and are a reference point not just for students of history. Says author Tripurdaman Singh:[259]

> One only has to look at Nehru's great debates with his contemporaries and opponents to see how civil and polite political engagement in India once was. Even in the rough and tumble of public politics, when furious debates ensued, politicians chose to engage with each other directly and civilly, without the malice and rancour we see today. The inability to speak directly to each other and the use of below-the-belt punches to score points in public settings

is causing the standards of public discourse to fall rapidly. Whether this can be arrested or not remains to be seen.'

Krishan, for his part, fiercely defended his profession. In his eyes, there was only one way to be a newspaper editor.[260]

> 'Are journalists merely vendors of news? If so, then there is no difference between them and other traders, and they have no right to demand any extra respect from society. However, a journalist is not the same. He not only sells news, but he also dedicates his life to a cause. He is given the responsibility of raising his voice against oppression. He must speak for the oppressed. He must be prepared to incur the wrath of the authorities. A journalist must voice the grievance of the people, to speak clearly and loudly to the government, to advise it, and, if it does not pay heed, to wage a struggle against it.

This particular episode in *Pratap*'s history was a ringside view into how there was no letting up of pressure on the press in pre-Partition India either. Rather, the British heckled vernacular newspapers, clamping down on anti-colonial information that could make the masses restless. As far back as 1878,[261] the British passed the Vernacular Press Act to curb press freedom and immobilize dissent, but it made men like Bal Gangadhar Tilak defiant. Tilak ran two publications, *Kesari* in Marathi and *Mahratta* in English, both openly rallying for Swaraj. After a particularly biting report, Tilak was arrested on charges of sedition.

The draconian Sedition Law, Section 124A of the 1860 Indian Penal Code, is a colonial relic. Enacted in 1870 it was labelled, 'the prince among the political sections of the Indian Penal Code designed to suppress the liberty of the citizen'[262] by Mahatma Gandhi. While historic cities and iconic avenues like Rajpath and Mughal Gardens have been re-named to wipe out a colonial hangover, more than 150 years later, the Bhartiya Nyaya Sanhita (BNS), 2023 that replaces the Indian Penal Code 1860 (IPC) only expands the definition of sedition. Ironically, Britain itself repealed sedition as a criminal offence in 2009.[263]

In 1949, the East Punjab High Court Special Branch in 'Pratap (Petitioner) vs Crown case' under the Press (Emergency Powers) Act (1931) ruled:[264]

> ... The outpourings of aggrieved persons who pray for redress instead of being appeased are sought to be smothered with the handy weapon of the law of sedition. We do feel that the law of sedition in our country should no longer be left in the nebulous state ... it is desirable that the safeguards let in by the Federal Court in its judgement in Niharendu Dutt Mazumdar's case should be incorporated in our law of sedition and our Press Act, for these very proceedings, very clearly demonstrate to our mind that people still require protection against the Executive Government even though it is the National Government.

In 1945, Virendra was asked by the Punjab Congress to go to Delhi to meet Nehru and get his directions about the approaching elections. Nehru was staying at the Hardinge Avenue residence of his cousin R.K. Nehru and, when he reached, Virendra found a huge crowd already waiting to meet Pandit ji. Spotting him, the leader called out to Virendra and spoke to him briefly. As Virendra took his leave, Nehru said, '*Abhi ruko, aur baat karni hai* (Please wait, we need to speak some more).'

He was taken to a room where Nehru complained that *Pratap* was opposing the party's Kashmir policy and that he was also being personally targeted. Virendra again explained that the editor of the paper was his father, and that he did not and could not interfere with the editorial policy of *Pratap*. Nehru then went on to explain the reasons for his support of Sheikh Abdullah. His words are significant as even today India's first Prime Minister is criticized for his handling of the Kashmir issue. Nehru frankly told Virendra, 'To save Kashmir from going into the clutches of the Muslim League, it is essential to strengthen the hands of Sheikh Abdullah.' And then he told Virendra that if he thought fit, he could convey his views to his father.

This was Nehru's gentle side, but Virendra writes that he also faced that infamous temper. It was around 1946 when Nehru visited Lahore and stayed with Diwan Chaman Lal. The political climate in the state was keyed up with Akali Dal candidates contesting against the Congress and things came to a head in Lyallpur, where the Akalis created a ruckus in a Congress meeting and tried to burn the pandal. This upset Nehru immensely. On his return to Lahore, when Virendra and Pratap Singh Kairon went to meet him, he exploded. Holding the local Congress responsible for his discomfiture, he shouted, 'You are not doing anything to counter the Akali menace.'

The two, with their heads bowed, tried to explain their position but Nehru would have nothing of it. Then just as abruptly he calmed down and said, '*Batao, kaise aana hua* (Say, how have you come)?'

Virendra replied, '*Iss waqt aap gusse mein hein batane ka koi fayda nahin hoga, hum phir aayenge* (At the moment you are angry so it is pointless to tell you, we will come again).'

His tone changed. The storm had passed. Calmly, he asked, '*Baki hulkoan mein kya haal hai* (What is the situation in the other constituencies)?'

That was Jawaharlal Nehru – much maligned by some sections these days, but one of India's greatest sons. And, after the Mahatma, the most beloved leader of the time. He was to lead and hold together a battered and bloodied nation into the dawn of freedom.

His tryst with destiny continues on.

PART 4

20

Jinney Lahore Nai Vekhya: Azadi

'The day we had been waiting for finally arrived. Yet, it was a day that produced mixed feelings among the people – joyous for some, sad for others and tragic for many.'[265]

And so, the day broke.

15 August 1947: It was the morning of a new dawn – and everyone imagined it would come with a generous sprinkling of fairy dust. Instead, the city's face was raw with bloodshot eyes, and a visceral repugnance for lifelong neighbours and childhood friends. It was a moment, one struggling moment, culled from a raging cry of insanity. And yet it was poignant, for Lahore was a city that had promised the most. Was the parting shot by the British the most lethal? In any case, Virendra found he was still in Lahore.

Raj Lakshmi and the two children, six-year-old Lalit and one-year-old Chander were at Subathu, a cantonment hill station, for the holidays. The yearly summer retreat was at Waverley, a family cottage generously covered with creepers. On one side of the lodge, zinnia flowers in full bloom laid out a charming carpet and, tucked a little further away, were pear trees that were still sharing their abundance. Not too far in the future, Waverley – along with its British-era furniture – was requisitioned by the army and never returned to the family. An antique wooden sideboard is the only keepsake and it continues to hold pride of place in the family home.

When Raj left for Waverley, there was unease in the city but no whispered rumours yet – and she was oblivious to the fact that it was a one-way ticket. She was not to return to Lahore. Raj had packed only for the holiday months – her belongings, memories and everything she owned, in the meantime, became the possession of another country.

As violence singed Lahore, Virendra was home alone with his younger brother, Narendra, and their domestic staff. Their once bustling neighbourhood, whose residents knowingly or unknowingly became a part of Virendra's journey, had gone quiet. The silence was desolate. Families had fled, some with just the clothes on their backs. Down the road, the majestic brick building of the Dyal Singh Public Library, that the Punjabi philanthropist Dayal Singh Majithia had willed, stood stark against the sky with all its lights off. By the eve of Independence, Nisbet Road was like a muslin curtain incinerated by fire.[266]

That evening there was a deadly silence in Lahore. At night, we could hear little except the barking of the dogs. Fires were still burning in some areas, and I could see their glow from the roof of my house. At midnight, India's freedom was to be announced. It filled one with a sense of pride, but the atmosphere all around was enveloped with feelings of desolation and fear, an overwhelming silence of the cremation ground.

August had wiped out Lahore; it had made the city – that once blossomed with its petals of pluralism – unrecognizable.[267]

At the beginning of August, the Hindu and Sikh houses and shops in the Shah Alami Gate area were set ablaze. For several days, we could see the flames over the Lahore skyline. Anyone trying to put the fires out was shot or otherwise incapacitated. The Shah Alami fire was like a final warning to the non-Muslims to leave Lahore.

For Virendra, this absolute rupture would have been unimaginable barely two years earlier when, in the summer of 1945, he walked out of prison gates for the last time. A year after his final spell in jail – and by then he was working full time at *Pratap* – he was elected to the Punjab Assembly from the Muzaffargarh constituency (now in Pakistan) on a Congress ticket. Virendra stayed with the party till the 1960s, when he resigned over corruption in the state under Chief Minister Pratap Singh Kairon. Coincidentally, Kairon and Virendra once shared barracks at the Sialkot Jail. After Partition,

Kairon had stayed at the outhouse of Virendra's new home in Jalandhar.

By March of 1947, Lahore was volatile. Disturbances in several pockets of the city had forced a wave of exodus. On the second day of March, Punjab Chief Minister Sir Khizar Hayat Tiwana switched sides and resigned,[268] assuming it was prudent to patch up with Jinnah. This, Virendra noted, made the Muslims in Lahore audacious while the other two dominant communities dug their heels in deeper. The next day, as Hindu and Sikh members of the Assembly gathered, a heated Akali leader, Master Tara Singh unsheathed his kirpan and announced belligerently that he would never accept Pakistan.[269]

Virendra remembers stepping out of the Assembly that day to be accosted by a mob yelling pro-Pakistan slogans. Tensions had reached boiling point; an equally aggressive group of people gathered to answer the crowd. That evening, Hindu and Sikh leaders met again and gave fiery speeches, pouring oil – as Virendra remembers – onto a city already on the boil. Two days later, thirteen people were killed when the police opened fire on a procession that clashed with the Muslim community.[270]

In the words of Virendra, this had a deleterious effect on the entire province. Riots started everywhere. The Governor wanted to take over the administration after Sir Khizar resigned but the Muslim League forced him to appoint one of his nominees, the Nawab of Mamdot, as chief minister. Once that happened, Punjab was on fire.

This is the same March that Om Prakash Bhutani, who retired as director general, Indo-Tibetan Border Police (ITBP), also remembers. In 1947, he was a third-year college student in Lahore.[271]

> I saw people being stabbed, bombs being thrown and, to safeguard ourselves, every evening, we would put a bati, a utensil with a broad base and narrow sides, on our head and tie it with a cloth as a way of protecting ourselves. That year, colleges closed early for the summer. So in May 1947, we went to Delhi for the holidays. We never came back.

'If I am the chief of sinners, I am the chief of sufferers also,' goes the famous quote in *The Strange Case of Dr Jekyll and Mr Hyde*. Lahore, it felt, was facing the brunt of this.

The British were no more the enemy – the adversaries were from within. A defining consequence of Partition, Pakistani writer and journalist Majid Sheikh says, was that suddenly from a multi-cultural and multi-religious population, a communal-minded city emerged. With other religions not there to oppose its dominance, within the Muslim population, the various sects showed their 'belief muscle' and instead of a city with a 45 per cent Muslim population, it became a 95 per cent Muslim city.

'The very culture of the old city changed overnight. The same was the case with educational institutions of Lahore, where a majority of teachers were non-Muslims. Take the example of the famous Government College. It lost almost 70 per cent of its teachers, including a Nobel Prize–winning physicist,' says Majid Sheikh.[272] During cross-migration, Sheikh points out that inside the Walled City, Amritsari traders took over the entire Shah Alami area – before 1947, a Hindu-majority area – and whose gateway was knocked down. 'These displaced new occupants needed bricks for construction, and they vandalized the old Akbar-era walls, and the result is that today no wall exists.'

Noted Urdu novelist Abdul Hameed, a refugee from Amritsar who settled across in Lahore, also observed a cleansing happening in Lahore.[273]

> There were 300,000 Hindus and Sikhs living in Lahore as Independence approached. By August 19, 1947, that number had sunk to 10,000, and by the end of the month to just 1,000. The majority moved to India. Many were killed, though there is no knowing their number. Some neighbourhoods of the city were entirely Hindu and Sikh, others were mixed, while some were solely Muslim.

Lahore did not empty at the stroke of midnight on 14 August 1947. Rather, freedom was a fluid August date and Hameed's numbers reflect this staggered exodus. Physically, leaving the city, as Virendra experienced, was a test of faith and, as for the emotional cord, for a few, it has not yet snipped – even now. For these 'Lahoris' who crossed the border, the city remains their tomb of eternal khwahish – where the past is romanticized, but, like a festering wound, the Punjabi on either side does not forget. What is it about Lahore that has had so many takers but even more loyalists? Those who crossed over recall the times when the city was bigger than any man-made boundary and those who stayed behind remember when Basant – marking spring's arrival

– was the city's most precious festival, and kites – now banned – dotted the skies, its riot of colours emblematic of Lahore's cultural amalgamation.

Is this an elitist emotion?

> Almost every household had a person with some interest in the finer arts. In the garden opposite the Lahore Fort, as also in the gardens around the Walled City, groups would gather every evening and traditional folk episodes would be narrated. In the houses of such poets, 'mushairas' were held, and poets like Iqbal and Faiz and others would read their latest writings. Outside the ancient Lahori Gate was a street where printing presses churned out the latest books and pamphlets. Even Waris Shah's *Heer* was first printed here. All these activities of scholars, teachers, and creative persons gelled together the entire population.[274]

One can safely say, Majid concludes, that Lahore is an emotion, a subject that lies deep in the subconscious of those who have experienced it. 'Even Pandit Nehru loved visiting his in-laws' city and spent long hours with creative people, enjoying their work and the food provided.'

With furtive glances and quickening steps, families fled towards the railway station. As fast as they ran, they were still not quick enough. People, desperate and scared, were slaughtered before they could hear the promised sound of a train engine.

The cauldron of sectarian violence had left Lahore naked – there were no rules left any more, of humanity or those known to man.

And just like that, Virendra's revolutionary past now belonged to a bygone era, one that had not prepared him for the next chapter of unfiltered ethnic cleansing, where the hunter and the hunted had, in the recent past, broken bread together.

'One day, I was standing in front of my house when a truck laden with corpses, coming from the station side, drove past sending a chill down my spine,' he writes in his book.[275]

What rambled into the Lahore station from across the border was no less barbaric. 'Corpse trains rolled into Lahore, dripping with blood, their carriages filled with hacked-off limbs, women without breasts or noses, disembowelled children,' records Nisid Hajari.[276]

Raj's sister, Saraswati Talwani, fondly called Shabto, was also in Lahore with her husband, a seven-year-old son, Pradeep and a domestic staff, Harbhajan. They lived in a barsati that was accessed by a twenty-five-foot-high staircase built along the outside wall at the rear of the house. Much like Om Bhutani, they too had to innovate to keep themselves safe.

Although there were curfews imposed on the city of Lahore, after sundown we could hear mobs of anti-Hindu and Sikh protestors shouting in the streets below. To protect ourselves during the evening hours, we kept a stack of bricks and boiling water to thwart the efforts of anyone trying to ascend the stairs.[277]

The Radcliffe Line had not yet been officially revealed but the people of West and East Punjab sensed it was a jagged edge.

The Talwani family made it securely across the border, but one urgent task remained. Their caretaker, Ferozedin, who looked after their household goods and cattle in the border town of Ferozepur wished to join his family in Pakistan. [278]

> It was not safe for him to go to the border of India and Pakistan with his long beard, coloured orange with henna, and dressed in a tehmet usually worn by elderly Muslims. He would have been easily identified as a Muslim in a Hindu town rife with tension between the two communities. To help him travel safely, my father gave him one of his kurta pajamas, and trimmed and washed the orange out of his beard. He then drove Ferozedin to the border and towards safety.

The story of Partition that is being narrated these days is that everyone was a victim and that there were no perpetrators, points out Ravinder Kaur, a historian of contemporary India.

> When we speak about forced displacement and of refugees, the story that comes across is only of loss but in times like these there are different actors. Punjab was a mixed population before Partition, but we continue to perpetuate this myth that everyone was a victim. Who was doing the ethnic cleansing?[279]

Pakistan was born and Gopichand Bhargava was elected East Punjab's first chief minister. Virendra called on him before he left to take charge in Shimla. Both men were despondent – the circumstances of their forced departure had brought about a feeling of dejection. Bhargava had also forgotten to take one particular matter into account – the fear and frustration of non-Muslims who were still in Lahore. Before he could make a move, his car was surrounded and a furious mob demanded to know who would look after those left behind. Lost for words, Bhargava stood helplessly as people lay down in front of his car, and it was left to Virendra and others with him to move them aside to allow for the CM-designate to make his way to Shimla.

Against this backdrop of riots and curfews, there was one impending decision and, at a personal level, it could potentially change Virendra's life forever. There was a gnawing uncertainty of who would get the prized possession of Lahore and so Virendra waited. The city was home and held too many memories to be left without giving it a last chance. In the end, it was but a final glance.

'Virendra, who was called Punjab da Nehru, had a car, and we would all get into it and drive down from Lahore to Amritsar to eat poori at the famous Thandi Khooi shop,' reminisces Vijay Chopra.[280] He added that before Partition 'Mahashay Krishan ke editorials ko padhne ko duniya paagal thi (there was a craze to read Mahashay Krishan's editorials).' That Krishan's editorials packed a punch the British knew, but his real connect was with the reader. Navin Suri, chief editor of the Urdu daily *Milap* – another newspaper that migrated from Lahore – says that when he started learning Urdu for journalistic purposes, he was advised by his grandfather to read editorials written by Mahashay Krishan, who had 'transformed journalism into literature'.[281]

Religion, bloodshed and monochrome images of trains filled with corpses form a ready-made mosaic in the canvas of Partition. In that painting, Independence is the predominant colour. Once the trauma settled and families were rebuilt, a new portrait was needed – one brushed not by collective but personal strokes. It was not just the land that was forsaken, but clubbed together under the subset of 'refugees', millions lost their identity as they became anonymous data points.

With time, writers are now correcting these shades. Recognition of the severity, the broken edges, and the uncertain boundary of Partition allow us a standpoint that was perhaps unavailable to an earlier generation of writers of a nationalist Indian history, says Gyanendra Pandey in *Remembering Partition*.[282] 'How much violence and intolerance has it taken to produce the "successful" nation-states of the twentieth century? How many partitions did it take to make the partition of 1947?' he asks. Pandey finds that partition and violence are interchangeable for those who lived it, partition is the violence and the 'somewhat mild and, in the Indian context, hackneyed term, partition' does not reflect the gravity of the subcontinent's suffering.

Perhaps it is also about the silence of the stakeholders. Just as Kamala chose to bury her revolutionary phase, family elders spoke of their past life with much circumspection. Virendra cited making bombs but never elaborated and, over the years, the family understood that he wasn't always forthcoming about his days in British India. This studied stillness is, as Pandey says, in individuals and communities rebuilding in 'radically altered settings where they struggled to overcome new fears, to gradually rebuild faith and trust and hope and to conceive new histories – and new "memories" that are, in some reckonings, best forgotten. Partition survivors sometimes say there is no point in telling today's children about these things.'[283]

But their own memories were in the smallest things. A carnage forced Pakistani travel writer Salman Rashid's family to flee Jalandhar and he remembers his mother saying that his father never wept. On a wintry day in the late 1960s, his father asked for boiled potatoes, sprinkled them with salt and black pepper, and bit into them, still piping hot.

> As he was eating the potatoes, he casually mentioned how his own father had loved them like this. Later, my mother said she had seen his eyes mist. This was the only indication of grief associated with the memory of Partition, the home in Jalandhar, and all those who had once lived there and had failed to make it across Radcliffe's line.[284]

There was no one-size-fits-all for closure – emotional healing, a rung after, was more ambivalent – and it reveals in the different nuances of how the past is told.

Says historian Ravinder Kaur:[285]

> What surprised me is that there is a very dominant mode of storytelling and yet, very few became the face of that storytelling. Also, there were immense differences in how loss was experienced – some witnessed direct violence, and many didn't. Likewise, some lost everything while others

were able to recover through compensation schemes, so there was also a distance between what they experienced and what they were sharing. Moreover, not all were remembering it in the way the recent wave of memories is portrayed.

So, is pre-Partition nostalgia also conditional? Like Virendra, Pran Neville too lived on Nisbet Road and to keep his memories of Lahore intact, he visited the city only in the 1990s after writing a book that speaks of and to a city whose composite culture was once its heartbeat. 'There is an old saying that my grandfather used to say, "To every bird, its nest is best," says Anshuman Neville. 'He was overpowered by nostalgia.'[286]

Could other refugees with different outcomes and journeys afford this wistful yearning?

Independent India was two days old and Virendra was still in Lahore. He looks back to that day:

> I did not know really what I should do – stay there for some time or leave? And how to exit from Lahore? I learned of a group of people leaving for Amritsar on 17 August. We joined them and, in the evening, reached an unknown place on the way to the city. We spent the night in an abandoned factory shed. The next morning, we were advised that the road ahead was not safe to travel. So, we returned to Lahore.[287]

Lahore was only 50 km from Amritsar, but a line had been drawn and Virendra was not the only refugee to make more than one attempt to safely cross over.[288] At least a million were dead as Punjab's cities and countryside merged into killing fields.

The brothers' – Narendra and Virendra's – hold on the city was meanwhile becoming tenuous. Lahore was still under curfew.

> I could not stir out, nor did I know if any of my acquaintances were still in town. Almost half the city had already been vacated. There was not a soul in our neighbourhood. The only regular traffic on the road consisted of troops and fire engines. Surprisingly, the telephone was still in working order, but it wasn't of much use to us. Most calls I received were anonymous ones that warned me to get out or face dire consequences. A few Muslim friends also called and advised that I leave immediately and return when things calmed down.[289]

The announcement finally came and it was to irrevocably change the course of Virendra's thinking. Lahore was given to Pakistan, while Calcutta remained with India. Virendra knew he had to leave immediately; time had run out.

> I had my car and toyed with the idea of making a break for the Wagah border. But what if we were waylaid on the way? Before I could come to any decision, I learned that the staff of *The Tribune* had arranged a military escort. I requested them to let us join their group. They agreed. I locked up our

house, packed a few clothes and on 21 August our convoy left Lahore for India.

It was not just a house that Virendra locked up – he also bolted away for posterity, or anonymity, footprints of a historical journey in its every corner, all twenty-two of its rooms, large and small. They surrounded a central courtyard, and, in the days when Lahore belonged to one and all, hawkers made their way to the enclosure where they haggled with ladies on the upper storeys of the house. Once a price was fixed, a basket was lowered with money and then raised back with the goods. Parked outside the house was the Adler car, which saw its own role in history.

Narendra, Virendra's younger brother, returned to Lahore as quickly as possible after Partition. Anil Narendra narrates:[290]

I remember my father mentioning that when he went back to the office, a huge mob collected outside, and it wanted to attack the office and probably kill my father. But a Muslim employee came to his rescue and took my father [out] from the back door, and then asked him to take his cycle and flee. With his help, my father escaped.

Chander Mohan was a year old when India became independent (his passport still says that his place of birth was Lahore). He visited the city with Prime Minister Atal Bihari Vajpayee's press entourage in 1999.

When the plane carrying the Indian entourage landed at the airport, there was a thunderous applause – I was in Lahore, or as we say in guttural Punjabi, Lohr aa gaya. The trip was not entirely a pleasant experience; there were Jamat-I-Islami protests. Our aircraft was taken to one corner of the Haj terminal, and our shuttle buses were then escorted by machine gun-mounted jeeps through a mud road. In the time that I did manage to spare, I tried to retrace the steps of my family's history. I soon discovered that our house on Nisbet Road no longer existed, replaced by a market, but our office in Gawalmandi was still there. There were so many restrictions during the trip that I could not see the Lahore that I had heard in the stories told by my parents.

Any attempt to go back and retrace the family history remains unfulfilled. The next time Chander Mohan wanted to visit – for an event commemorating Bhagat Singh – his visa was rejected.

As in any other bursting metropolis in India, where buildings are expanded by encroaching on vacant public space, the old home at Nisbet Road has also seen changes in the recent past. The market is now a haphazard shopping complex with tangled, exposed wiring hanging from its front. Inside, it has offices of everything from a bank branch to a children's academy. The lawn of the old house has also been constructed over.[291]

Radcliffe wasn't strong enough to wipe away the similarities!

The scene on the route was terrifying. Houses were on fire. Corpses lay along the road. With God's name on our lips, we reached Amritsar that evening. The moment we crossed the Wagah border, all fear and depression seemed to vanish.

The fact that we were finally on the soil of our own free country brought a strange feeling of elation.[292]

The family settled down in Jalandhar – barely two hours away from Lahore. Sometimes, the shortest distance can make for the longest voyage.

'It had been a fateful journey. For a moment, the riots, the arson, the genocide, the desolation, and the fact that I had left my hometown, probably forever, did not matter. What mattered was that a dream had come true.'

> *Ilahi woh bhi din hoga jab apna raj dekhenge,* (God – there will be a day when we will see our reign)
> *jab apni hi zameen hogi aur apna aasman hoga.* (When it will be our land as also our sky)[293]

21

From the Raj to Punjab: Jalandhar

It was the lull after the storm. Partition was tangible, India was independent and Virender, along with his family, were at Dimple Lodge in Shimla. At the behest of Chief Minister Bhargava, he joined the government pro bono as Director, General Public Relations, a job that did not last long. In due course, all roads led to Jalandhar (Jullundur during the British period) – an old town two hours away from the home they left for good. But there were still some hiccups. They were asked to vacate the allotted property to make way for All India Radio station. In the first flush of Independence, patriotism was an overwhelming sentiment and so, no questions asked and they did as they were told.

Pratap

On the move again, and this time, only the rear portion – the janana end – of a brick-coloured bungalow was given to them. An iron archway led to a garden that fanned out replete with majestic mango trees dominating a lonely, outstretched jamun tree. A government officer and his family were already residing in the mardana section, segregated during a Muslim family's stay in the bungalow before Partition. Between the two buildings was an open area that gave the families some privacy. All bathrooms of the divided bungalow opened towards the outdoors and Raj Lakshmi sneaked out from hers every so often to noiselessly enter the one belonging to the daughter-in-law to feed her some eggs. The young woman was being treated improperly by her family.

The family soon sold out and the two parts, with their high ceilings, lattice work and jaali doors became a whole. The veranda, with its sandstone-coloured pillars in the front of the house, was enclosed, as was the exposed expanse in the middle which became Virendra's office. Surrounded by sprawling land, there were no neighbours; a well, a murgikhana and a kabristan completed the dwelling. These were later sold.

Before Punjab split, all this was the property of Mian Ehsan ul Haq. The Dewan of Bikaner state was also a cricketer of some repute and was the foremost Indian to play in the first-class for Middlesex in 1902. The photo of Haq, who was to become one of Pakistan's most notable judges, still hangs in the Lords' Long Room. The Haq family abandoned their home overnight, leaving behind estates in Jalandhar and Dalhousie. 'My grandparents left at Partition with pretty much nothing, but they had land in Lyallpur, so everyone went there. My father was in boarding school in Panchgani, so he stayed in India until he finished in

1951. Two of my aunts who were married stayed behind,' shares Ayesha 'Tammy' Haq, his granddaughter.[294] She promises to visit her ancestral home as soon as visa formalities allow!

Sometime in the early 1950s, Virendra saw a gentleman standing in front of the house. He was Justice Haq. Virendra took him inside what was once his own home and, as he was leaving, asked him to come back. Haq replied honestly: 'Even though I want to, my sons don't.'

One man did make a special trip to Jalandhar. With a grainy photo in hand, Pakistani travel writer Salman Rashid walked across Wagah border to make a personal pilgrimage for what he says was the fulfilment of family pietas of very long-standing. He was in search of Habib Manzil, his grandfather Dr Badaruddin's house, and, through it, answers on the fate of five immediate family members. He writes in his book, *A Time of Madness*:[295]

> I headed home for the first time in my life. I was fifty-six years and a month old. I was going to a home I had never known; a home in a foreign land, a land that state propaganda wanted me to believe was enemy territory ... This was the home where the hearth kept the warmth of a fire first kindled by a matriarch many hundred years, nay, a few thousand years, ago and which all of a sudden had been extinguished in a cataclysm in 1947.

The calamity that Rashid mentions did not have closure. As an iron curtain dropped, his grandparents, a great-grandfather and two aunts did not make it to Pakistan – they simply disappeared and were never heard from again. The writer's ancestral home still stood on Railway Road in Jalandhar, but it was an encounter with a man, Mohinder Pratap Sehgal, who asked for forgiveness, that brought clarity sixty years later. Sehgal's father had led a mob that 'slashed with daggers and swords' ten people, including Dr Badruddin's family, hiding in a small room. The doctor was killed with a shotgun blast through the eye while the two-year-old child of the family servant, Eidu, was flung to his death from the terrace. 'In 2008, when I was in Jalandhar for the first time, I had thought my demons would be exorcised and with the story of my family getting closure, I would be at peace. It has only increased the grief. The grief of dividing a timeless land and its peoples.'[296]

As for Dr Badruddin's son and Salman Rashid's father, apart from the odd memory that food triggered, tragically, he too inhabited the silos of silence that many in his generation lived. In the absence of any sharing, the past is the elephant in the room. How do local communities and their non-disciplinary 'histories' deal with the painful moment of violence even as they seek to dismiss it, questions Gyanendra Pandey.[297] The loss in Jalandhar that Salman Rashid's father never spoke of translated in Lahore where he refused to buy a house of his own. 'Fools build houses, wise men live in them,' he told his son.

In 1956, for the first time since Partition Virendra, Raj and Chander, now ten years old, along with driver Dharamchand drove across in their Vauxhall car to Lahore. Accompanied by journalist Kuldeep Nayar, they were warmly received in the city but found Nisbet Road vastly changed from their time there.

Seven or eight families were living in their old house and they followed a woman up to a room on the upper floor where she opened a wooden cupboard to show them Raj's old photo tucked inside.

Writer Majid Sheikh says:[298]

Once the troubles subsided, Lahore was almost an empty city. Over half the houses were unoccupied and, amazingly, a lot of the Muslim neighbours had promised to take care of the old non-Muslim houses till such time that they returned. The common perception was that this was a temporary [situation] and once the communal frenzy subsided people would return. That never happened. As refugees from India, mostly from the Amritsar and Punjab areas, flocked towards the new Pakistan, most of them Punjabi speaking, they were provided with temporary housing in the unlocked houses of non-Muslims. Each house which formerly held six or seven persons of one family now held two or three families with an average of fifteen to twenty persons per house.

After the sentimental visit, Virendra's family headed to an India–Pakistan hockey match. Despite the batwara and the wars, the border was not rigid, and citizens on both sides circulated freely for weddings and cricket matches. Before 1947, Sameer Mehra's family from Amritsar owned a film distribution office in Anarkali.[299] Even after Partition, their old relationships were not boxed in. 'We went to weddings, especially in Punjabi communities where we spoke a similar language and sang the same wedding folk songs. I will be honest; from Amritsar, we also went to Delhi for holidays and people were welcoming but hospitality in Lahore was on a different level.'

Sameer remembers listening to the execution of Zulfikar Ali Bhutto in 1979 on a clear radio Lahore frequency in Amritsar. An hour further down, in Jalandhar, the television signal was a dodgy black and white but, in early 1982 on a good reception day, the Pakistani drama *Sona Chandi* had a dedicated audience.

By then a new way of life had found its own quotidian rhythm. Virendra's kalam was moving again – *Pratap* went back into print in 1952 from Jalandhar, with an edition from Delhi run by his brother, Narendra. Resuming from where it left off, it began selling 13,000 copies – higher than usual – and, in early 1956, *Vir Pratap*, a Hindi daily was launched. A figure hard to miss in his Nehru achkan and Gandhi topi, Virendra or Vir ji as Punjab knew him, was back to his non-compromising journalism. In 1977 – a crucial political year when Indira Gandhi called off the Emergency – he became president of the All-India Newspaper Editors Conference.

A year after the 1965 Indo-Pak war, Chander Mohan was in Prague on a five-month scholarship with the Czechoslovakia news agency Ceteka. As he entered the training facility in the small town of Roztez, its director pointed to a room saying his friend was waiting for him. Taken aback, as he was not familiar with anyone in the country, Chander entered. Dressed in a black sherwani in the bitter European cold, a bespectacled Abdul Subhan from Karachi was waiting patiently and, in the following months, the two became close friends. The war sentiments between the two countries had not died down and, in a motley crew of twenty others, including two quarrelling Afghans, the unlikely friendship of an Indian and a Pakistani stood out. 'One of our assignments at Ceteka was to write on the war; he wrote his version, and I wrote mine. And that was that.'[300]

The two men last met in 1967 in Moscow, when the gentle Pakistani carried his friend's suitcase to a waiting taxi. After that, a few letters were exchanged – in one of them, Subhan informed his friend that he was to be married. Correspondence, though, wasn't easy and it sadly died down. 'Despite the ravages of time and war, Abdul Subhan has remained the warm memory I choose to recall on cold December days when an Indian and a Pakistani met in Prague.'

The pages of this particular story were re-opened half a decade later after another visit to Prague when memories resurfaced and Subhan's whereabouts were traced when Chander Mohan wrote an article about their friendship for Pakistan's *Dawn*.[301] There was such an outpouring of response from the Pakistani public that letters to the newspaper were discontinued.

But this is not how two friends are supposed to meet after fifty years – by then, Subhan was paralysed and bedridden, and the video received of a dishevelled man was heartbreaking. When his nephew, Salman, read out the article to Subhan, he told Chander '*Woh bahut roye* (He cried a lot).' Over a phone call, Subhan's wife graciously invited the family to visit.

I was hoping to plan a visit and was even prepared to fight for the rejected visa, but now I am uncertain if I am brave enough to make that attempt. Why didn't I contact my friend earlier? To say that I was disappointed with myself would be trivialising it. Now I was helpless. I had traced my friend down, only to learn that we could not even have a simple reunion conversation. All I could say was: Bahut takleef hui.'[302]

The story captured the imagination of the Pakistani public to such an extent that an artist used his medium of storytelling to put it up as an exhibition at the Karachi Press Club.

The trajectory of both countries is divergent and they can never coalesce now. Regardless, we can learn to live like good neighbours so that in the future, it does not take fifty years for someone to contact a friend across the border.

PART 5

22

Truth and Dare: The Midnight Knock

On Delhi's Fleet Street – Bahadur Shah Zafar Marg – electricity was abruptly cut off. Despite nightfall, the sweltering summer heat was oppressive as newsrooms panicked, unaware that this was just the beginning. The next morning, 26 June 1975, India woke up changed.

The President has proclaimed the Emergency. This is nothing to panic about. I am sure you are all aware of the deep and widespread conspiracy, which has been brewing ever since I began to introduce certain progressive measures of benefit for the common man and woman in India.[303]

With these words on All India Radio, Prime Minister Indira Gandhi chaperoned the nation into an era whose dregs still shadow her inheritors. On a momentous midnight, her father had held India's hands as he promised the country its tryst with destiny. Just before the stroke of another midnight, while the country slept, his daughter took away the civil liberties of her people, 'advising' President Fakhruddin Ali Ahmed to sign the Emergency proclamation and suspend democracy. Historian Gyan Prakash writes that on 25 June 1975, at 11.35 p.m., a pajama-clad President handed his secretary a 'top secret' one-page letter from Indira Gandhi, and a little later, after signing the draft Emergency proclamation, the President swallowed a tranquilizer and went to bed.[304]

Egged on by a tight-knit coterie led by her elder son, Sanjay, in four years, Indira went from embracing greatness – 'Empress of India' and 'Iron Lady' among monikers generously bestowed on her – to erring into the arms of authoritarianism. After a shaky start in 1966, she had learned quickly on the job, commanding control and populism to dismiss the contemptuous Opposition, who called her 'Gungi Gudiya (a mute doll)'. All this, only to allow absolute power to corrupt her absolutely.

The year 1971 belonged wholly to her; Bangladesh was liberated, a landslide win shored up by the election slogan 'Garibi Hatao' was a victory straight from the heart of the masses, and the 'D' word – Goddess Durga – uplifted her persona by mythical degrees.[305] Was Atal Bihari Vajpayee among those who compared Indira to 'Durga'? In his biography of the former prime minister, Abhishek Choudhary refutes it as fiction and writes that Vajpayee was missing from Parliament on the evening he allegedly called

Indira a goddess reincarnate. Choudhary also quotes Mrs Gandhi's friend Pupul Jayakar posing the same question to Vajpayee and receiving a vehement denial.[306] The assertions that he indeed praised Indira Gandhi so loftily[307] however stick and Vajpayee's flip-flop reputation ensures the jury is still out on who called her 'Durga'.[308]

The only way for Indira to go was up. Until it wasn't. And the fall was debilitating. The Emergency knocked out an unsuspecting India, enacted thirteen days after the Allahabad High Court declared Indira's 1972 election from Rae Bareli null and void. She was also disqualified from holding any office for six years – a judgment upheld by the Supreme Court on 24 June. The next day, Jayaprakash Narayan's call for an anti-government rally wasn't answered by the usual bandobast – rather, hours later, the Emergency was imposed, and key Opposition leaders were either in custody or floundering around to find a safe hiding place. The rest is history and extensively written about in history books.

'It is wholly wrong to say that I resorted to Emergency to keep myself in office. The extra-constitutional challenge (of the JP movement) was constitutionally met ... Emergency was declared to save the country from disruption and collapse ...' With the domestic media muzzled, Ramachandra Guha quotes Indira from *Sunday Times of London*, among the many interviews she readily gave to the international press.[309] She also told the *Saturday Review of New York* 'that what has been done is not an abrogation of democracy but an effort to safeguard it ...' 'These were the signs,' writes Guha 'of a creeping dictatorship, like military men who seize power via a coup, Mrs Gandhi claimed to have acted to save the country from itself.'[310]

Was Indira's Emergency sui generis to her power cult – a one-off blip in her political career – or had it been a process in the making? Gyan Prakash traces its origin to an offset of democratic complications and a political culture that continues to remain alive in the present.[311]

> In traditional accounts, the Emergency is represented as a deviation from the normal trajectory of Indian democracy – solely attributable to Indira Gandhi's desire to remain in power. Such a view prevents scrutiny of democracy's history and leads to a self-congratulation of India's commitment to democratic functioning. In my view, the Emergency was declared against a background of India's long-standing history of state centralization and attacks on citizen rights. Indira's declaration of the Emergency drew on this long history to manage the crisis of her regime posed by the JP movement and the Allahabad judgment.

The Opposition crackdown and a call from the Ramlila Maidan to overthrow the prime minister didn't even make it to the news. Delhi and India's fourth estate – barring two newspapers that briefly benefitted from a fortuitous slip – had been immobilized. No newspapers were published from Bahadur Shah Zafar Marg the morning after democracy was attacked. Press freedom was not just curtailed – in the coming months, it was caged and foreign correspondents were expelled or forced to leave.[312]

The orders were draconian – regional and vernacular press across India's towns were raided with gusto, and newspapers, in bundles, were seized. The Justice Shah Commission of Inquiry set up by the Janata government to probe Emergency excesses notes:[313]

> The government disconnected electricity to the newspaper offices on the night of June 25, 1975, when an Emergency was imposed. Shri B.N. Mehrotra, who was the then General Manager of Delhi Electric Supply Undertaking was given oral orders on the night of June 25, 1975, by the Lt. Governor of Delhi, Shri Krishan Chand, that electric supply to the newspaper offices in the city should be disconnected ... According to Shri Kishan Chand, the then Lt. Governor of Delhi, the instructions for disconnecting power supply came during one of a series of meetings at the Prime Minister's House on June 25, 1975, but he was unable to recollect as to who gave the specific orders.

The Commission further notes, 'The illegal act, however, was the only way before the regime to prevent newspapers reporting the detention of almost all opposition leaders and the declaration of the Emergency.[314]

In June 1975, journalist Coomi Kapoor was with *Indian Express* and wrote:[315]

> The electricity on Bahadur Shah Zafar Marg kept flickering on and off. By afternoon there was a newsflash from the agencies, declaring that censorship had been imposed and nothing could be printed without prior official clearance. By evening, the electricity supply to Bahadur Shah Zafar Marg was disconnected for the whole night so that the

> *Times of India, Indian Express, Navbharat Times, Patriot, National Herald, Daily Pratap* and *Vir Arjun* [*Vir Pratap*'s sister publication from Delhi] could not bring out their editions. The newspapers would not be printed for another two days.

On 28 June the *Indian Express* took out a blank page, along with a front-page apology for not publishing for two days.[316]

> The newspaper carried a blank space instead of the first editorial, while its sister publication, *Financial Express*, reproduced lines from Rabindranath Tagore's famous poem: 'Where the mind is without fear and the head is held high.' It concluded with the prayer, 'Into that heaven of freedom, my Father, let my country awake.'[317]

A fresh set of guidelines on 13 July issued by the Centre promptly warned editors against leaving editorial columns blank or using quotations from great works of literature or by national leaders like Mahatma Gandhi, Rabindranath Tagore and Jawaharlal Nehru.[318] From jokes to birthday greetings for Morarji Desai, the snip of the scissors was arbitrary and as distant to any internal security concern as the Emergency was to democracy.

At the *Pratap* office in Jalandhar, events had unfolded as they had in Delhi – if not a touch sooner. As both the Hindi and Urdu newspapers were being put to press, the midnight knock came and a stranger's booming voice cut through, ordering the printing of the papers to stop with immediate effect. A clueless newsroom erupted in pandemonium – Indira's address to the nation was still several hours away.

'I quickly called up journalist Kuldeep Nayar who was a family friend and he straightaway got on the line cautioning others which is how leaders like George Fernandes were forewarned and went underground,' recounts Lalit.[319]

The press was in chaos, the fundamentals of news-making were jettisoned and what fell within legally permissible levels of publishing was not even on the table. Virendra's pushback against the Emergency proclamation was to put his kalam down. The columns that should have held his editorials in both *Pratap* and *Vir Pratap* were left blank. Censored reports were withdrawn, but no replacement was sent. And Pratap Bhavan was not inclined to fill in the white spaces. Unsurprisingly, within days the government knocked on the doors again and there was a clampdown on its protest; the two newspapers were informed that leaving middle-page spreads blank was unlawful.

During this time, Virendra and his sons were forced to engage with low-ranking government officials who acted as censors. Their knowledge of press workings was laughable but that didn't deter them or dampen their determination from clamping down on press freedom. These men had clear instructions and erred on the side of caution; some of their actions were borderline ridiculous. But they had been flung from dreary bureaucratic anonymity to what was entirely an unexpected moment – an indefinite one – in the sun and, in that power play, there was no questioning them. A protest was as far as complaints by the press could stretch – and all objections were overruled as predictably as the scorching sun that June in Punjab. Every line that went to print was stamped upon with the censors' signature. By then, a central Censor Room was functioning from the first floor of Parliament House. The Shah Commission report states:[320]

> Censors worked there in two shifts from 10.30 am to 3 pm and 3 pm to 10.00 pm. It was also decided that there would be no name board affixed on the door to show that it was the Censor Room … the actual work of censorship on a day-to-day basis went even beyond the scope of the guidelines. Orders were arbitrary in nature, capricious, and were usually issued orally.

Jalandhar in 1975 published ten newspapers in three different languages – Urdu, Hindi and Punjabi. Says Lalit of this time:

> The censors were from different government departments like labour and excise, among others, and they didn't understand the media business. [They] were told when in doubt, cut. This went on till somehow, they got fooled by their own propaganda and started easing up after elections were announced which is when we went all out against the government.

Having remained staunchly defiant in the face of colonial torture, Virendra was as unmoved by the Emergency diktats as he was adamant. 'I didn't get any editorial censored during the Raj, I am not going to do it now,' he declared. Once the government clamped down on his blank editorials, his kalam simply went silent. It was months later that he took a call to publish daily snippets of his past – a composite of many lifetimes – instead of allowing his writings on the present to be censored. It is this collection that later formed the basis of his memoirs *Veh Inquilabi Din*.

> I stopped writing editorials for our two newspapers, *Pratap* and *Vir Pratap*, as I was not prepared to submit them to the censors for clearance. For about eight months, I did not write a single line. Friends suggested that since no one could predict how long the Emergency would last my total withdrawal from writing was not advisable. Therefore, from 29 February 1976 I started writing a series of articles in which I narrated the events of the two decades before Independence which though connected with my personal life and work, were of some political significance too.[321]

'You were asked only to bend, but you crawled,' L.K. Advani famously said of the press during the Emergency – words that have a life of their own fifty years later.[322] Then, as is happening in the present, the role of some newspaper owners was questionable. Media barons, like industrialist K.K. Birla played ball – he reportedly sacked *Hindustan Times*' editor B.G. Verghese on the office staircase for being critical of Indira and her son, Sanjay. Incidentally, as an exception *Hindustan Times* took out an edition on the morning of 26 June 1975.[323] The Delhi Electricity Supply Undertaking (DESU) cut power along Bahadur Shah Zafar Marg, where most media houses were located, but failed to take similar measures in Connaught Place, where the offices of *Hindustan Times* and *Statesman* were located.[324]

Along with the *Indian Express* in Delhi and Virendra in Jalandhar, *Statesman* also defiantly printed blank editorials and announced that the issue had been censored. Among the most critical voices at the time was that of Arun Shourie, whose scathing pieces in the *Indian Express* were cyclostyled and distributed to those underground.

> By 1976, the environment was without hope. The popular movement had died down and people had reconciled to the new state of affairs. Political leaders were in jail and people like Chaudhary Charan Singh and the RSS chief had started writing letters to Gandhi – all were trying to come to an accommodation. It was individuals who were fighting and that is how I came in touch with Ramnath Goenka at the *Indian Express*.[325]

Voices of dissent were buried; the cacophony of sycophants was shrill and capitulation was wholehearted – the media, the elite and corporate India broke ranks to prostrate and support the subversion of the Constitution. Indira's constitutional misuse through amendments included removing the Emergency from the ambit of trial as it was a 'waste of public money', a move accepted without a whimper. Her son Sanjay Gandhi, the de facto leader, became an extra-Constitutional authority and carried out mass forced sterilization drives in the millions and slum clearance programmes in the Walled City area of Turkman Gate in Delhi, predominantly inhabited by Muslims.[326] In just twenty-one months, a political tsunami hit the country.

Perhaps this is a democracy's Achilles heel – a periodic churning with only the lead protagonists changing. From Shiv Sena supremo Bal Thackeray to noted journalist Khushwant Singh and industrialist J.R.D. Tata, Indira Gandhi's snub to the Constitution – which included her father's imprint – had its supporters, if not admirers.[327] By the middle of August 1976, harsh pre-censorship rules were in place and a newspaper went to print only after government representatives minutely poured through its contents. Print media was categorized as A: Friendly, B: hostile, and C-: Neutral. These categories were further indexed. While A+ was 'positively friendly' and included *Amrita Bazar Patrika* among others, B+ was 'continuously hostile' and both *Indian Express*, Tamil Nadu, and *Vir Pratap*, Punjab, were prominently classified in this list.[328]

Barring a couple of newspapers, Arun Shourie doesn't see any other print media asserting itself in the present either. 'During the Emergency, some persons stood up but today hope is not with the big paper. What is the use of reading the same damn thing? Yet, make no mistake, print is prosperous – look at the advertisements. But it is not a medium for anyone to get facts.' Shourie's faith is from 'new journalism on the internet', which he says is not just the future but also the mainstream. 'The truth will be sustained only by small groups, and the government and states will be swatting them. It is a race of cat and mouse.'[329]

Indira Gandhi's Emergency is a self-goal that gifted opponents of the Congress a political opening with endless lives. What is often overlooked is how it was also an embarrassing chapter for the Sangh with questions over the role of the RSS and some prominent leaders of the Jan Sangh. Vajpayee is widely believed to have spent a better part of the period not in jail but at home on parole after giving 'written assurances' to not oppose the government.[330] Journalists say this is true, but, as he was unwell and under house arrest, his intentions were not as malicious as addressed.[331] The role of RSS chief Balasaheb Deoras and his 'letters of apology' to Indira Gandhi from jail have also been the subject of much speculation among critics.

While the response from the political class to the Emergency was multi-layered, one stream of thought that political analysts have flirted with was how the Congress and the Sangh were not boxed into their respective corners as each liked to believe of the other. Ravi Visvesvaraya Sharada Prasad, whose father H.Y. Sharada Prasad, was Indira's information advisor, says:[332]

> The relations between the Congress and the RSS were not always antagonistic; there were numerous shades of grey and, at the time of Independence, many top Congress leaders were sympathetic to the Hindutva ideology, and the RSS reached out to them to work together in the national interest.

This would fit into Indira's staunch Hindu credentials. Ironically, the Emergency is seen as a gift horse whose mouth the RSS did not look away from.

Newspapers like the *Indian Express*, *Statesman* and *Vir Pratap* that refused to be cowed down found the going tricky. Retribution was swift through advertisements, which were used as a carrot-and-stick policy by the government. The Shah Commission notes that it was evident that political considerations were one of the criteria for giving commercials.[333]

> The Government during this period utilised its advertising policy as a source of financial assistance or denial of financial assistance in newspapers, etc., in complete variance with the policy which it had enunciated on the Floor of the Parliament. Newspapers and journals that were critical of the Government's policies were denied advertisements whereas others like Amrita Bazar Patrika and National Herald which were regarded as being supporters of Government policies were given advertisements beyond their legitimate due.

At Pratap Bhavan, the problem was more existential. *Vir Pratap* and *Pratap* were the only papers in the bustling media hub of Jalandhar that protested by refusing to publish an editorial – the most essential of newspaper ingredients. Day after day, the space was filled with serialized mythology that the editors knew would bore even the censors into quiet obeisance. Pushed to a corner, it also solved the dilemma of filling up space. Unlike *Pratap* publications, other newspapers in town bowed down to the government line and carried a vetted editorial that ironically defeated its very purpose. Vijay Chopra remembers:[334]

Virendra left the space empty, but Ramesh Chander wrote the editorials for *Punjab Kesari*. The clerks in the office would say don't put this and don't put that. Uneducated people were stopping the editorials, but we still published. *Pratap*, on the other hand, did not give in and stopped publishing editorials.

The loyal reader who picked up *Vir Pratap* to read Virendra's uncompromising words, however, wasn't satisfied. Circulation began to drop and revenues plunged – a downward graph that became increasingly difficult to arrest. As the financial situation imploded, the family huddled together – a situation where even the British had not succeeded, was unravelling in independent India. From where they were standing, it looked like it was time to close shop. The pull of the employees and their hopeful faces, along with thoughts of dependant families, was however stronger and so – once more – the family dug in deep. Virendra had never imagined that *Pratap* would be put to the test in free India.

It was not just censorship that was problematic for him – after decades, there was a return of an apprehension: That of arrest. *Punjab Kesari*'s Lala Jagat Narain was in custody and the family anticipated a similar outcome for Virendra. Lalit, who was amongst the handful to visit Narain in jail, was fulminating, and it was only a matter of time before he gave vent to his frustration and anger. In a public outburst at a meeting called by the local district commissioner, Lalit lashed out at the administration, calling the Emergency a 'dhikkar (shame)'. Feathers were ruffled and rumours of an arrest gained ground. It was after a phone call a few days later that the family understood why Lalit and Virendra were still not in custody. Notably, as during the British Raj, it was not Virendra who blinked. Punjab Chief Minister Zail Singh told him that he had personally stopped the arrests.

Twenty-one months later, when Indira called off the Emergency just as abruptly as she had imposed it, the body politic – after the blow it received – was beleaguered. Her decision was baffling and, while she was perennially conscious of being Nehru's daughter, what did Indira gain out of those tumultuous years? The ruling class, for one, wised up, and acknowledged the abiding relationship of the people of India with the electoral process and their vote. Shutting them down and depriving them of this fundamental process is a violation of democracy – the public bides its time, but it responds. As it did with Indira.

Since 1977, there has never been a disruption in the electoral process. However, the ruling class is also shrewd enough to circumvent it. Instead of targeting the nation as an entity, it now closes in on a few and then the message seeps through to the rest. In this manner, it has been able to capture all government institutions without overtly subverting democracy. This process, where votes count, remains sound but the establishment has found a subtle way of affecting the outcome.

Based on what material is available, it is clear that international reputation and opinion mattered to Indira, even when she publicly dismissed them, says Gyan Prakash.[335]

> The critiques penned by foreign critics, many of whom had been her father's admirers, hurt her. She wanted power, but not at any cost, or she would not have called for the election. There are conflicting indications as to

whether the IB [Intelligence Bureau] had predicted that she would win. But be that as it may, the decision to call for an election reflected a desire to win popular legitimacy. In this desire, something of the awareness of being her father's daughter seems to have played a role even if she was not her father.

What finally persuaded Mrs Gandhi to end the Emergency? Ramachandra Guha too delves into the lingering question. 'One cannot say for certain, but it does seem that she was stunned by the comments of those foreign observers impossible to dismiss as enemies of India.'[336]

Having said that, fingers also point to another, obvious inference. It is the Sanjay factor, some believe, says journalist Neerja Chowdhury, which was the real reason, as her younger son was becoming uncontrollable and a law unto himself.[337]

> For all practical purposes, he was running the government – and the party – for the nineteen months of the Emergency. And she had done nothing to stop him. She wanted her son to succeed her. But she wanted to curb his adventurism … Indira would have calculated that elections might steady Sanjay.

The impunity with which Indira was thrown out is a timeless lesson on how the country values its freedom. The Indian experience shows that quasi-authoritarian governments have a shelf life, however impossible it may seem in the moment.[338]

In the 130 years or so since the Mutiny – the last 90 years of the British Raj and the first 40 years of independence begin increasingly to appear as part of the same historical period – the idea of freedom has gone everywhere in India. Independence was worked for by people more or less at the top; the freedom it brought has worked its way down. People everywhere have ideas now of who they are and what they owe themselves.

Even if they take longer to recognize it sometimes.

Despite the seminal years of 1975–1977, did the Emergency make India any wiser? In 2021, the country was downgraded and classified as an 'electoral autocracy' by V-Dem, a Swedish organization that studies global democracies.[339] India also ranks 41 in the Democracy Index, which describes the world's largest democracy as 'flawed.'[340] Several other surveys share a similar tenor.

Sidharth Bhatia entered journalism when the Emergency was at its peak and looks back to a time of copies returned scalded with red marks from censors.[341]

The difference I find over the years is that journalists have become less sceptical. The new generation has very little sense of history but now a lot of senior people, who had that experience, have acquiesced to the new dispensation. They have compromised because of threats and fear, and they should have some knowledge of what has gone on before. Have we learned from the Emergency? We have. Have we put that into practice? Absolutely not. You can't seduce those who are willing to be seduced.

With the march of the global right wing, it is the hour of truth for the fourth pillar of democracy. In India, the slivering away of its free press to leave it exposed is in its second coming. Says Lalit:[342]

> When journalist Kuldeep Nayar was in jail during the Emergency, I went to meet his wife, Bharti, and she told me that I was the first person to come and sympathize with them. No one else had come; people were scared. People did not have the guts [then]; it is no different today.

Liberty and sovereignty are hard-won victories, and the cross of a Faustian bargain with freedom is borne – in no small measure – by an indifferent elite and a compromising middle class. There is no comparison with the current Indian middle class, admits Shourie. 'Today, they have only one objective and that is money. During the Emergency, there was still an afterglow of the Independence struggle and the public was committed to values.'

It is in India's all-encompassing nature to inevitably shake off the cobwebs or a personality cult, just as it did with Indira's government in 1977. Says Siddharth Bhatia:

> It is said Narendra Modi has modelled himself on Indira Gandhi because she was seen as a tough, no-nonsense person. If you notice, he has never actually criticized her and neither does the RSS – they had, of course, sent letters to her. The difference is that during the period there was never any threat to secularism, except for the

acts of Jagmohan and Sanjay Gandhi's involvement in Turkman Gate. Indira herself was never communal. Once Emergency was lifted, she took it all on her chin and was back in power in less than two years. Today, instead of questioning those in power, we now seem to be questioning democracy itself.

23

Before the Ink Dries: Elegies and Sunsets

Kabhi kisi ko mukammal jahan nahi milta (No one ever gets a universe that is absolute)
Kahin zameen, kahin aasman nahi milta (Somewhere you don't get the earth, somewhere the sky is missing)

It was not an easy decision. People may say what my grandfather started, I closed down – it was a moral dilemma, a dharam sankat. But knowing where journalism was going, and where it is going, in hindsight, it feels like the right decision. Journalism as we knew it is over. That journalism was passionate –rightly or wrongly – whether it was about Partition, Punjabi Suba or terrorism.[343]

On 31 March 2017, *Vir Pratap* published its final edition, ending a glorious – if, at times shaky – run that began 99 years earlier with *Pratap*'s launch. The mothership, which had formed one part of the bastion of the Urdu press in pre-Partition Punjab, had shut down in 1994 when a dwindling Urdu readership coupled with a rise in the circulation of Punjabi newspapers eroded its confidence. The publications did not merely give an account of a country through its uncertainties, pain and re-birth, but, along the way, also became the story itself – as did on many an occasion the three generations of men who ran the show. For *Pratap*, it was an overarching tale of transitioning from the loss of Partition to gaining a foothold in new beginnings.

The journey onwards was no less colourful, as though the chapters were writing themselves; often, in a hurry. Whether it was the Emergency in 1975 or the plunging darkness of terrorism that put *Pratap* on the hit list in the 1980s and 1990s, the ride was tumultuous and challenging but always righteous.

It was the early 1980s, Virendra was in Mauritius for an Arya Samaj gathering and Bhindranwale was on a rampage in Punjab. In his absence, the most senior editor, Des Raj Sharma, refused to write an editorial on him. I was never meant to be the editor – my academic background was different. That day I picked up the pen. And I put it down only after fifty years. At Delhi airport, on his return, Virendra met an acquaintance who told him, '*Kaka bada acha likhda hai* (The boy writes very well).' Bhindranwale was a sensitive topic and we had not informed my father [that we had written on him]!

Pratap was fortunate to enjoy the support of friends and acquaintances alike, but a journeyman must find his own path. The newspaper survived a partition and a bombing but could not outlive the calculating forces of a different nature – bowing down to the inevitability of commercialization. Even if the outcome was different, its brand of honest journalism would have been stonewalled by the current brazenness that questions even the country's intrepid passage to freedom.

> I decided to stop printing overnight. The pen at long last was out of ink. Manager Ramesh who had joined *Pratap* when he was still a young man agreed with me that it was time. I then called our employees one by one and set them free.

For some, it had been years for others, their life at Pratap Bhavan had flowed into decades. Journalism in its modern cut-throat avatar is highly impersonal. *Pratap*, on the other hand, was a teacher – pushing its employees so they could fly higher. Not everyone was willing to leave. For twenty years, Jagdish Kaur owned the front desk – the receptionist's chirpy, thin voice answering phone calls and welcoming visitors, without ever skipping a singsong note in her voice. That evening the phone too fell silent.

The kind of journalism that we started in 1919 was dead. My grandfather Mahashay Krishan was a crusader. Papers have survived but you can see – barring a few – they are compromising editorially and otherwise.

Pratap was launched in Lahore's Gawalmandi, in the year of the Jallianwala Bagh massacre; its press came to a stop at Nehru Garden Road in Jalandhar as India celebrated seventy years of Independence. The distance of 141 kilometres – less than three hours by road – had, by then, become insurmountable. 'Before independence, Lahore was home to several Hindu newspapers, all of whose offices I can claim to have visited. The five leading papers were *Pratap*, *Milap*, *Bande Mataram*, *Paras* and *Bharat Mata*. For some reason, all of them were based in the Gawalmandi and Nisbet Road area,' recollects eminent writer Abdul Hameed.[344]

I have seen the world change. The face of journalism has changed. In the past, it was based on ideology and ideals; now, it is entirely business. And I felt the economics was slipping out of hand. Big companies with crores were coming in and we just couldn't compete with them.

The family is practical and, ostensibly, tough. Life – personal and professional – leaves scars. Businessman, however, was not a tag anyone owned up to proudly or otherwise – reading business news in their own newspaper was only mildly simpler than number crunching. The new generation is doing its best to turn things around, but the lack of a corporate drive was at once the hour of acceptance and its nemesis.

Idealism that originally ignited the passion to practise journalism has significantly dimmed over the decades, says journalist Ruben Banerjee.[345]

> Newer generations of owners are at the helm of major media houses and many of them are moved by more mundane objectives such as profits and political clout rather than the earlier esoteric goals. Holding the government of the day accountable or making the world a better place to live in have largely receded to being distant thoughts for many of them.

Liberalization in the 1990s shook things up further. It pushed a capitalism-driven approach and, as big corporate houses took over newspapers on a business model, *Pratap* began to feel the pinch. Its uncompromising stance that journalists and editors must always be anti-establishment and hold the government of the day to account didn't help matters. The rot had begun to set in and an owner of a prominent media house infamously said, 'We are not in the newspaper business. If 90 per cent of your revenues come from advertising, you are in the advertising business.'[346] Despite its increasingly corporate leanings, the duty of democracy's fourth pillar is sacrosanct and steadfast. It is also one of sublime altruism – questioning those in power and serving society with honesty.

Journalism, for truth's sake, was receding like the low tide on a dark night. From the days when the manager of a newspaper was sidelined and an editor was the only authority, the shift was tectonic. Heavy investments in media houses gave corporates a direct entry into the hallowed newsrooms and editorial autonomy was no longer watertight. As the profit motive became paramount, the editor was devalued and no longer had the final word.

Gone were the days when men like Arun Shourie were supported by owners like Ramnath Goenka in the pursuit of speaking truth to power. When the Ambani-led Reliance Industries Limited took control of Network-18, CNN-IBN editor-in-chief Rajdeep Sardesai resigned. He wrote in his farewell letter, '... editorial independence and integrity have been articles of faith in 26 years in journalism, and maybe, I am too old now to change!'[347]

When asked to bend, Pratap proudly stood up even higher – whether it was the blank editorials during the Indira Gandhi–imposed Emergency or the crusade against Punjab Chief Minister Partap Singh Kairon for corruption charges. Kairon offered Virendra the post of a minister, which he refused and ultimately quit the Congress.

It paid the price for such honesty. Advertisements began to dry up. 'By extension, large advertising deals from the government means that dailies and media companies that do business with the state cannot resist the pressure of the ruling party while deciding their editorial stance and reportage,' says journalist Mitali Mukherjee.[348]

Editors like Virendra, who wrote fearlessly but from the heart, would have been anomalous in this altered reality that tilted against standalone vernacular newspapers. There was also generational conflict – Virendra and his contemporaries were more conservative and money was never a criterion for his generation. They were caught off-guard by this transformation to commerce, which in their eyes meant compromise. Government advertising to Pratap Bhavan was frequently interrupted because of the papers' independent stance.

While change is constant, coming up next was a bloodless bath on the fourth estate.

The first newspaper in Lahore was sold for one paise. Around the time of Independence and even in post-Partition Lahore, it was sold for four annas.

The advent of television news was a profound shock to the newspaper industry; its monopoly over the media was lost forever. Television news networks began to broadcast 24/7 with salaries far more generous than anything seen or heard in print media. Predictably, there was a churning and newspaper journalists – both prominent and reporters on the beat – looked for a piece of the television pie. Big newspapers still held on; they had monetary might behind them. Smaller ones, more and more of them, began to perish.

The landscape changed irrevocably, but the push and pull between television and print did settle down, and the relationship resembled almost a stately give and take. It was the fusion of digital and social media that skewed all calculations. News online was easily accessible and updates dropped faster than any television report. With cost-effective internet that was cheaper than a meal in a restaurant, an aspirational country logged on. The millennials went a step further – preferring to consume their news on Instagram and swearing by health reels on TikTok. The playground morphed into a play.

The pandemic accelerated this transition. In times of scare and superstition, digital news flourished. Newspaper subscriptions were cancelled in bulk for fear of catching the virus and the news diet overwhelmingly shifted online. The industry has still not recovered, pushing even corporate-run entities to re-evaluate. Will this media landscape survive the online onslaught in the coming years? The older generation stays accustomed to a newspaper's feel, but a cohort fixated on the digital has no similar respect or familiarity for this medium. Remarkably, regional news, despite the upheavals, maintains its renaissance phase.

> [The] media was different till 2014. Pre-Partition press was fired by a movement for Independence; everything else was insignificant. After Partition, initially, the media was supportive of the government as the country was rebuilt. And Nehru's personality was such that everyone had faith in him. That phase will never return.

The pandemic was also the coming out party of the Indian media as a profession that, by and large, abdicated its responsibility as the voice of the voiceless. Death and devastation did not move it – corpses floating in the Ganga and pyres lighting up the night sky were termed an 'international conspiracy'. Those who disputed claims and asked for accountability had to work faster than the flow of misinformation. Among them was Ruben Bannerjee, editor-in-chief of *Outlook* magazine in May 2021. Stating that the Government of India was missing, he took out a stark white cover resembling a 'Missing' poster. He says of the time:[349]

> My own experience tells me that batting for truth under [the] current circumstances could exact a high price. Of course, I regret having lost my job. But I am relieved, too. To be the editor and not be allowed to do cover stories on issues such as Manipur would have made me complicit in the many wrongs of today. In a way, my sacking saved me from what could have been a dilemma – to keep your job or be true to your profession.

Narratives that shape society are built by disseminating information with the aim of empowering communities, and the gap its absence creates is severe. And conspicuous. Overwhelming as it may sound, fortunately, it is not all bad. It is a space that regional reporters, fact-checkers and independent journalists on YouTube channels are trying to fill, replacing editors and conventional newsrooms. Even though – similar to online content on other platforms – it is a bottomless pit where fake news and propaganda thrive without any checks and balances, journalists like Ravish Kumar keep the torch burning. His cult following on YouTube indicates how sections of the public are sickened by the servility of a bulk of television channels.

The law in India is such that many YouTube channels are closed overnight with its help and no one knows what exact content the government has a problem with. Leaving this one apprehension aside, the challenge of YouTube's world is spectacular, says Ravish.

> In a way it is a cliffhanger. Sometimes, you are on top of a mountain, and, at other times, there is a depression in the ground under your feet, and you don't realize it. On YouTube, you are a player who is winning the hearts of the audience on the strength of his game alone in the field. Journalism is always better in a team but, for journalists like us who have no place in the current environment, there are no options left.

He adds with all other means of livelihood closed to him, he gets scared imagining his life without YouTube where he has been able to reach millions of new viewers.[350]

Others, not as experienced, are taking baby steps in the field. Villages like Tulsi in Chhattisgarh have transformed into YouTuber hubs, where people are quitting their day jobs to make videos and share their voices. Without finances for a proper set-up, as the light fades, they use motorcycle headlamps to shoot their reels. All is not lost. On social media, an ambitious India with 1.15 billion mobile phone connections[351] is also an 'influencers' market. The lure of the spotlight has many takers, but – similar to any other start-up – only a handful make it.

The viewer, meanwhile, is treading around minefields of fake news, propaganda and misinformation. With artificial intelligence also in the mix, some days truth is stranger than fiction. The genie is well and truly out of the bottle.

The question arises: What then is the media's role if it surrenders and changes the goalposts that are central to a democracy? In Rudyard Kipling's words, 'While Thrones and Powers confess,

That King over all the children of pride, Is the Press – the Press – the Press!'[352]

In India, the press, barring notable exceptions, has left the building.

Bhagat Singh, who wrote under a pseudonym for at least three newspapers, said, 'The real duty of the newspapers is to educate, to cleanse the minds of people, to save them from narrow sectarian divisiveness, and to eradicate communal feelings to promote the idea of common nationalism.'[353]

There is a deep chasm separating the principles of the Shaheed-e-Azam and the press at present. For a country that fought the British Raj as much through its resistance as its vibrant press – when newspapers defied colonial censorship and sedition laws – the demise of journalistic standards is glaring. In this environment, Mahashay Krishan's words are even more relevant, 'A journalist is not the same as an ordinary vendor. He not only sells news but he is also given the responsibility of raising his voice against oppression.'

Conversely, every evening television channels – at least the usual suspects – peddle polarizing narratives and misinformation with as much consistency as the weather report – a downsliding when editors abandon their journalistic oath. That a news channel hired an actor from a mythology drama to anchor prime-time news sums up what goes in the name of journalism in the country.[354] To quote a refrain that originated in a newsroom,

'If one person says it's raining and another says it's not raining, it is your job to look out the window and find out which is true.'

The windows of most Indian newsrooms are closed.

From journalism of ideology, we have reached paid news. The meaning of journalism has taken a 360-degree turn.

Television media's first major foray into tabloid journalism started with the murder of thirteen-year-old Arushi Talwar in May 2008, says journalist Nidhi Razdan.[355] Arushi was found dead in her apartment while the house help was discovered murdered on the roof.

> What followed was a media frenzy India had never seen, where forensic evidence was shot to pieces, and innuendo doubled up as evidence. Fast forward to October 2021 and the arrest of Aryan [Khan, son of actor Shah Rukh Khan]. They called him a druggie and a drug kingpin amongst other things. In the end, he was exonerated, and all charges were dropped. Not one anchor who vilified Aryan Khan has apologised. It was no different in the case of film star Sushant Singh Rajput.

Rhea Chakraborty, his girlfriend, was painted as a scheming drug queen who led him to his death. She too spent time in jail only to get bail after the Bombay High Court essentially said the charges against her did not stand. There was no apology to her either.

The toxicity on television has an online partner. Social media unleashed trends – paid, unpaid and fake – a spectacle that is as fierce, as it is misleading. Mumbai Police revealed that 80,000 fake social media accounts were active to mislead their investigation in the Sushant Singh Rajput case.[356] Another report by Microsoft Research India that outlined the role of politicians in keeping conspiracy theories alive pointed out how they[357] 'were instrumental in changing the course of the discourse by referring to the case as a murder, rather than suicide.'

Playing for profit is of the reason for this mindless genuflection. It has given rise to the phenomenon of fake news in India. Behind the scenes, but equally culpable, are the owners and editors of these organizations. The job of journalists is to be critical and hold power to account, and that doesn't mean holding only the Opposition to account. Mainstream media, particularly television, when it was asked to bend, didn't just crawl – it prostrated. Print media is not that different, says Nidhi Razdan. 'Firstly, don't allow the government to be a regulator of the media, that is a very bad idea.'[358]

The dumbing down of news is intense. Journalist Pamela Philipose sums up the fourth estate as:

… hyper-personalisation; loud, sensationalism; rupturing the private-public separation with voyeuristic intent; the thrill of the chase to the extent that it becomes blood sport; the gossipy edge stained by deep shades of misogyny; the close nexus with powerful interests looking to influence content; the daily churning out of heroes and villains; the intense competition for circulation with rivals; the constant feeding of the insatiable appetite of readers for more; and, yes, the dressing up of fake content to make it appear authentic.[359]

Misinformation is not just what is served as news day after day – it also comes in the form of manipulated TRPs. In 2020, Mumbai Police busted a scam in which money was paid by a prominent news channel to influence viewership.[360]

In the absence of any binding regulations, fact-checkers are putting systems in place to bring the truth before the public. It is a sad commentary on our times that we now rely on them to do a job that is ordinarily the responsibility of every stakeholder involved with the media. Misinformation is a systemic problem, admits journalist and fact-checker, and managing editor of Boom Live, Jency Jacob:[361]

> We have uncovered stories of online scams, identity theft, misinformation, how the internet plays a role in our daily lives, and how it affects everyone around. For elections, we gear up for a massive surge in political disinformation campaigns and hence strengthen our teams to ensure we debunk all those claims in a time-bound and impactful manner.

Religious fault lines are now an open wound, festering but not allowed by a section of the media to heal. This has made the job of fact-checkers an unenviable one. Also, who checks the fact-checkers?

There was a class of people, an educated class that once led the country. Go back to pre-Partition, Gandhi was a barrister. And so were Patel, Nehru and Ambedkar. They were all highly literate people and the country had confidence in them. Now, educated people are frowned upon and 'un-elitism' is a badge of honour. Even Bhagat Singh was a learned man.

In modern democracies, the independent media functions as a mirror that showcases the uncomfortable. Irrespective of the party in power, being anti-establishment is a badge of honour, for it shows a job well done. Yet, never more was the concept of a free press more in question. Journalist Siddique Kappan was arrested when he was on his way to cover the alleged gangrape of a Dalit girl in Uttar Pradesh's Hathras. He was charged under sedition, re-arrested by the Enforcement Directorate and released on bail 846 days later.[362] Some other journalists in jail still await their turn.

Press freedom also finds itself stonewalled by the frequent internet closures across parts of the country giving India the infamous crown of the internet shutdown capital of the world. While it tarnishes the image of India's digital revolution, the cost to individual freedom is far deeper.[363]

In a fractured democracy can the media's fall be arrested? Newspapers like *Pratap* which uncompromisingly covered the right fight were better off closing down. Emergency, official or unofficial, would have met with the same resistance.

The building does not matter. It is what is inside [that counts]. In 1962, after the war when China defeated India badly, PM Nehru sat the entire day in Parliament to hear abuses. He kept quiet and listened. The current Prime

Minister was missing from the entire Manipur debate. The leadership led by Nehru and Gandhi knew they had to leave a foundation for the future of India. They were wise. The deterioration started with Indira Gandhi.

The media's downfall corresponds with the fall of India's middle class. In the twentieth century, it spearheaded a fight for India's independence. Here and now, it hides itself in echo chambers. Missing an outrage that took it to the streets after the Nirbhaya rape case, the candles of the middle class now lie unused. The public has forgotten how to light them.

There are notable exceptions. Newspapers like the *Telegraph* from Kolkata and *Tribune* from Chandigarh – co-incidentally both published from states Bengal and Punjab, which felt the impact of Partition the most – as also *Indian Express*, barring the occasional blip, steadfastly uphold the pillars of journalism. It was with *Tribune* that Virendra hitched a ride across the border to Amritsar in August 1947, eventually moving to Jalandhar to open a new chapter in *Pratap*'s history.

Pratap started as an Urdu newspaper in 1919; the edition shut down in 1994. The language was not being taught in Punjab [anymore]. If a reader died, you didn't get another reader. If a sub-editor died, you didn't get another sub-editor and if a katib died you didn't get another katib either. Advertisements had also dried up because, in Punjab, Punjabi had taken over.

Most Hindu owners of Urdu newspapers migrated from Pakistan, although not many Urdu newspaper owners went to Pakistan during Partition – of about 450 Urdu newspapers before Independence, 350 chose to stay back in India.[364] Despite that, the language stands marginalized and read predominantly in Muslim households. In a polarized, misinformed environment, it has also been ghettoized by a section that considers the language itself to be anti-national. Says Professor Mrinal Chatterjee:

> There is a conscious effort in academia to equate Urdu with the Muslim identity, which is historically wrong. This is a dangerous trend because when you say a language is specific to a religion, you are degenerating it. The way many Hindus also think shows that the divide is widened. Whether it is being done by the extreme elements in both religions or to save the language is a different issue altogether. The fact is that it is being done and is very dangerous.

The freezing out of Urdu language plays to a gallery that is attempting to rewrite history pages, including the foundational journey of India's independence and its primary stakeholders. Poet and writer Gulzar, though, sees it differently – disagreeing that it is a dying language. Nor does its future worry him.[365]

> Urdu script may not be as prevalent or common today, because professionally it is not required but the script isn't the language itself. The language itself is still alive

as it always was. Urdu and Hindi are essentially the same language. It is the script that keeps varying.' Urdu was born in India; it is not foreign.

His words fall in with Gandhi's vision who coined the colloquial 'Hindustani, i.e., a correct mixture of Hindi and Urdu', which – according to him – was for Hindustan.[366] Notably, this, he believed, was in addition to vernacular languages and not as an imposition, especially in south India.

Says C.M. Naim, sounding markedly dejected:[367]

I am bemoaning the fact that Urdu was truly a shared heritage. A common heritage of Hindus and Muslims. Unfortunately, that has ended, pachatar saal mein [in 75 years] ... A community has disappeared and that is my lament. *Pratap* emerged because there was a large body of people, a whole community of non-Muslims, who wanted news brought to them in Urdu and wanted to express their own opinions in letters to the editor in Urdu. In 1947 who would have thought that *Pratap* would close? They were the backbone of the community ... Yehi maidan tha [This was the same field]. *Pratap* was printed in [the] thousands and circulated widely with agents and correspondents spread all over. There was a great discussion on what was published in the newspaper. Yeh zindagi joh thi [The life that was there before], it is not there anymore. That we have lost ... *Pratap* will not appear. The journalism and the prose of those times will not come back.

Yaad meri tumhe rahe na rahe, zikr mera koi kare na kare,
Marsiya mein hi apna likh jaoon, kaun jane koi likhe, na likhe.[368]

You may or may not remember me, someone may or may not mention me

I will write my own elegy, who knows if someone will write it or not.

Acknowledgements

'Who will want to read our story?'
'But not everyone has a story like ours to share.'
And so, a father and daughter with contrasting confidence sat down together to see where their family's past could lead them. Along the way, others joined as journeymen, dipping in and out, playing their part.

We owe our appreciation:

To Udayan Mitra, thank you for your patience and advice. To Paloma Dutta and the team at HarperCollins India for putting this book together.

To Saurav Das for the cover design.

An idea was born thanks to Swati Chopra.

From the other side of a timeless land divided, to Iqbal Qaiser for generously sharing his knowledge of a common past. His

Acknowledgements

help extended to sharing recent images of the house on Lahore's Nisbet Road and taking us on a parallel journey of nostalgia.

To Professor Chaman Lal, whose understanding of India's freedom movement, especially involving Bhagat Singh, is unparalleled.

To Rishi Majumder at the Indian History Collective who opened up his archives and friendship.

To Jyotsna Raman, for the book's first flush.

To young Ankush Pal, whose invaluable research and keen intellect gave us faith in Gen Z.

To Lalit Mohan for being a repository of family history. And for his historic interviews before time ran out.

To Niraja, the quiet force and our first line of checks and balances.

To Adi, the in-house critic.

To Rayna and Saira because everything is in a name.

And, last but not least, to the siblings and those chosen as family who are our wingmen.

Notes

Scan this QR code to access the detailed notes.

Index

Abdullah, Sheikh, 275
Advani, L.K., 315
Agarwal, Prabal Saran, 148, 196
Ahmed, Fakhruddin Ali, 308
Ahmed, Khan Bahadur Niyaz, 173
Ahmed, Razi, 245
Air India Boeing 'Kanishka', explosion of, 43
Ajit, 10
AK-47, 8, 29
Akali Dal, 31, 34, 249, 275
Akali Patrika, 10
Akalis, 13, 30, 33–34, 249, 275; leadership, 10–11, 30–32, 34–36; patriarch, 33; triumvirate, 21
Akal Takht, 14, 34
Akbar, Muhammad, 234

Alam, Sheikh Muhammad, 76, 133, 140
Alang, Krishan, 5
Ali, Asif, 108
Ali, Ehsaan, 127
Allahabadi, Akbar, 59
All-India Newspapers Editors Conference, 266–267, 269, 301
All-India Sikh Students Federation, 15
Allsebrook, John, Sir, 104
Ambani, 331
Ambedkar, 241, 340
American missionary society, 73
American press, 79
American War of Independence, 71
Amrita Bazar Patrika, 317, 319

Index

Amritsar, 13, 15, 23, 46, 78, 284, 288, 291–292, 294, 300; Jallianwala Bagh in 61; May 1984 curfew, 10

Amritsar: Mrs Gandhi's Last Battle, Tully and Jacob, 13

Anand, Jagjit Singh, 18, 47

Andamans Cellular Jail as 'Kala Pani', 55

Ansari, Mukhtar Ahmed, 71

anti-Sikh riots, 13

Armed Home Guard, 28

Arya Samaj, 57–58, 63–64, 180, 192, 245

Ashfaq, 200, 239

assassination attempts, 25, 150, 163; failures in, 149

assassins, 20

Assembly, bombing of, 71, 109, 111, 128, 137, 195–196; Irfan Habib on, 240

Atwal, A.S., shot to death, 38

Azad, Abul Kalam, 53

Azad, Chandrashekhar, 70–71, 80–81, 83, 99, 101, 116–117, 128–129, 148, 150, 152–153, 193–194, 199–200, 238–239; Agarwal on, 196; and bomb explosion again, 154; death of, 191, 197–198, 205, 223; to free Bhagat Singh and Dutt, 152–154; joining Krishan kirtan mandali, 86; leaving Lahore, 155–156; nickname 'Brahmachari', 195; Sukhdev Raj on, 197

Azimabadi, Bismil, 58, 192

Aziz, Khan Bahadur Abdul, 198–199

Babbar Khalsa, 22, 37, 43; taking responsibility for attacks, 22; terrorist, 37

Badal, Manpreet Singh, 31

Badal, Parkash Singh, 17–18, 30, 33

Badal, Sukhbir Singh, 31

Badaruddin, 298–299

Bahadur, Khan, 169, 176

Bali, Avinash Chander, 71–73, 75, 97, 121; arrest of, 91

Bande Mataram, Urdu daily, 59, 74, 227, 329

Banerjee, Ruben, 330, 333

Barkat, 230

Basanti Devi, 80

'Batukeshwar Dutt Zindabad', 111

Bengal partition, 136; George V reversal of, 124, *see also* Partition

Besant, Annie, 'Home Rule' agitation, 56

'Bhagat Singh Zindabad', 111

Bhagwati, Sachi, 151

Bharat Mata, 329

'Bharat Mata ki Jai', 105, 192

Bhargava, Gopichand, 76, 126–127, 251, 288, 296

Index

Bhartiya Nyaya Sanhita (BNS), 274
Bhatia, Siddharth, 323–324
Bhikshu, Chaman Lal, 108, 119–120, 166, 177, 238
Bhindranwale, Jarnail Singh, 6, 9, 13–18, 30–34, 37, 46, 327; cult of violence, 18; death of, 12; Sahni on, 42
Bhutani, Om Prakash, 283, 286
Bhutto, Zulfikar Ali, execution of, 234, 301
Bihari, Avadh, 125
Birla, K.K., 315
Bismil, Ramprasad, 58, 69–70, 136, 192, 200–201, 239
Biswas, Basant, 125
bomb: blasts, 6, 36; making, 136, 150, 159, 191; throwing, 107, 137
Border Security Force (BSF), 27
Borstal Jail, 127, 137, 139, 142, 145, 174, 179
Bose, Khudiram, 200
Bose, Rash Behari, 259; fleeing to Japan, 125; Nakamuraya curry of, 125
Bose, Subhas Chandra, 71, 78, 100–101, 121–122, 132–133, 140, 214–216, 220, 238, 241, 243; Indian National Army, 125; joining Nehrus, 143; and Virendra meeting, 121–122
Breen, Dan, 72
British club in Lahore, 161

British Raj, 54–55, 66, 77, 87, 106, 117, 124, 138, 170, 321, 323; capital from Calcutta to Delhi, 124
bulletproof jackets, 45
bus, 85; hijacking of, 20; killing of Hindu passengers, 20–21, 41

Canadian intelligence agencies, 43
capitalism, 111, 330
casteism, 242
censorship, xiv, 261, 271, 311, 313–315, 317, 319–320, 323
Central Assembly, smoke bomb at, 105–108
Central Investigation Department (CID), 74–75, 77, 89, 120, 150–151, 168, 171, 176, 181, 184, 196
Central Jail, 137, 145, 180, 188, 232; Lahore, 179, 186, 228; Mianwali, 113
Central Reserve Police Force (CRPF), 15, 27
Chakraborty, Rhea, 337
'Chambal ki Ghatti', 32
Chander, Ramesh, 9–10, 19, 27, 320, 328; killing of, 8–9
Chand, Krishan, 311
Chand, Mahashay Khushal (later Anand Swamiji) 352n89
Chand, Mahashay Rattan 'Ratto', 181, 188; arrest of, 180

Index

Chand, Master Amir, 125
Chandni Chowk, 125; raiding Gadodia Store, 199
Charan, Bhagwati, 72, 85–86, 121, 128–130, 143–148, 150–153, 159, 191, 209; bomb accident, 146–147; death of, 147, 150, 152
Charan, Dhanvantari, 72
Chatterjee, Mrinal, 59–60, 342
China war 1962, 340
Chopra, Kiran, 19, 24
Chopra, Vijay, 10, 16–17, 319; on his father's assassination, 16
Chowdhury, Neerja, 322
civil disobedience movement, 116, 136, 141, 204
civil liberties, 308; curtailing, 56
civil society, 225, 245–246
communalism, 242, 336
communism, 18, 47–48, 182, 187
conflict zones, 28, 40
conspiracy theories, 338
counterterrorism, 40
Cricket World Cup, West Indies in, 3
crowdfunding, 155, 194
Cry for Justice by Sinclair, 72
'Cult of the Bomb', Gandhi, 140
curfews, 10, 21, 27, 286, 288, 292
Curzon, Viceroy, 124

Daechsel, Markus, 61
Dal Khalsa, 19

Dang, Satyapal, 18, 177–178, 252, 257
Das, Deshbandhu Chittaranjan, 80, 122
Das, Jatindra Nath, 113–114, 116–118, 122–123, 126, 150, 175, 209; death of, 115, 118–119; funeral procession, 122; homage to at Delhi, 120–121; in hunger strike, 115, 126; Kiron warning death of, 118; as shaheed, 238
Das, Kiron, 116, 118–119, 121–122, 126, 137, 139, 163; arrest of, 127
Das, Rai Bahadur Bhagwan, 91, 169
Dawn, 302
Delhi Conspiracy Case, 125, 140
Delhi Electricity Supply Undertaking (DESU), during Emergency, 315–316
Delhi incident, 128
democracy, 40, 309–310, 312, 321, 324, 330, 335, 340; questioning, 325 *see also* dissent
Democracy Index, 323
de Montmorency, Sir Geoffrey Fitzhervey, 163, 168
Deoras, Balasaheb, 318
deras, 32
Dhanvantari, 127, 145, 154–155
Dhara, Amrit, 166

Index

Dhillon, Harbrinderjeet Singh (Harji), 6
"Dil se niklege n murh...", 234
dissent, 117, 135–136, 316
Dominion status, 100, 102
'Down with Imperialism', 104
Durga Devi (Durga Bhabhi), 85–87, 121, 145, 148–149, 151–154, 165, 201; to Azad, 152; 85, 149, 151; accompanying Bhagat Singh, 85; and Gandhi, 202–203; as Sharada in Bombay, 151
Dutt, Batukeshwar, 105–106, 108, 110–113, 123, 137, 141, 143–145, 152, 167; death of, 112; release of, 111; and smoke bomb, 103–104; truck permit for, 112
Dutt, Krishan Gopal, 254
Dyer, General, 224

East Bengal, 124
East Punjab, 287
economic grievances, 31
Editors Guild of India, 45
1857 war for independence, 134
elections, call for, 322, *see also* Emergency
'electoral autocracy' by V-Dem, 323
Emergency, 301, 307, 323, 331; Advani on, 315; called off, 321; excesses, 311, 314; Guha on, 322; Prakash on, 308, 310; proclamation, 308, 313
ethnic cleansing, 286–287
exhortation, 32
explosion, 4–5, 10, 45, 47, 104–105, 130–131, 136, 154
extremism, 7–8, 11–12, 17, 21, 23, 25, 40, 42, 99–101, 342

fact-checkers, 334, 339
farmers' agitation, 223
Fazl-i-Hussain, 249
Ferozedin, 287
Financial Express, with Tagore's "Where...", 312
Fischer, Louis, 117
Forman Christian College (FC College) in Lahore, 70
fourth estate, 310, 332, 338
Fraser, Andrew, assassination attempt on, 136
freedom fighters, 53, 55, 84–85, 87, 132, 136, 139, 142, 174, 192, 194, 238–239, 243; solitary confinement, 138
freedom movement/ freedom struggle, 60, 70–71, 84, 112–113, 128, 134, 140, 143, 163, 182, 200, 209–210, 223–225, 253
French Revolution, 71, 81
Furnace, British officer, 84

INDEX

Gandhi, M.K., 54, 56–57, 60, 71, 78, 99, 101,117, 178, 192, 202, 204, 214, 225–226, 274; Bose on, 216; crusade of non-violence, 71; Dandi March, 68; non-cooperation resolution, 102; non-violence, 140; RSS in death of, 241; train incident in South Africa, 136; to Viceroy Irwin, 205

Gandhi, Indira, xiv, 12, 17, 301, 308–310, 313, 315–318, 321–322, 324–325, 331, 341; assassination of, 13; as 'Iron Lady', 308; Rae Bareli election as null and void., 309; visit to Lahore, 252

Gandhi-Irwin pact, 202, 204

Gandhi, Sanjay, 13, 315–316, 325

Garewal, Naveen S., 36, 45–46

'Garibi Hatao', 308

George, H.M. King, 207

Geva, Rotem, 63

Ghadar Party, 125, 224, 245; uprising, 55

Ghosh, Rashbihari Sir (J), 259–260

Gill, K.P.S., 24, 30, 35, 37, 39–40, 42–43; "defeated rump", 40; as 'Super Cop', 44

Goenka, Ramnath, 316, 331

Golden Temple, 12, 15–16, 31, 33–34, 38, 45–46; marching to, 10–11; violences inside Harminder Sahib, 15

Gopal, Jai, 83

Gopal, Sarvepalli, 100

Gorky, Maxim, 72

Governor, conspiracy to kill, 162–172, 174, 180

Gujarat State Reserve Police, 27

Gujral, I.K., xiii, 24, 59, 203

Gulzar, 342

gurudwaras, desecration of, 19, *see also* Operation Blue Star

Hailey, Lord, 151

Hajari, Nisid, 286

Hameed, Abdul, 284

hangings, 96, 98, 112–113, 159–160, 162, 164, 192, 194, 214, 216–218, 225–226, 228–236, 239–240, 242, 244–245

Hansraj 'Wireless', 129–130

Haq, Ayesha 'Tammy', 298

Harbhajan, 286

Hardinge, Charles, Viceroy, 54, 124, 170; assassination attempt on, 125–126

Haryana, 8, 14, 17, 21, 198

hate campaign, 16

Hathras gangrape, 340

Hayat, Sikandar, Sir, 249, 264, 268

Heer, Shah, 285

heroism, 149, 172, 219, 222

Hilton, (J), 143

Himachal Pradesh, 17

Hindi language, ban on, 23

Index

Hind Samachar, 9–10
Hindu-Muslim: lines 352n89, (*see also* hate campaign; unity, 117
Hindus, 10–11, 13, 16–21, 23–24, 32, 34–35, 55, 58, 64, 75–76, 284, 342–343; attacks on, 16, 19–20; Punjabis, 17, 24; and Sikh divide, 13
Hindustani, 343
Hindustan Republican Army (HRA) (later as HSRA), 71, 192
Hindustan Republican Socialist Association (HRSA), 110, 114
Hindustan Socialist Republican Association, 103, 106
Hindustan Times, 316
'Home Rule' agitation, 56
human rights excesses, 40
hunger strike, 114–118, 122, 138, 143, 223, 238; Bhagat Singh, 175; Jatin Das, 175; Mukherjee on, 117

Iftikharuddin, Mian, 251–252
Ilahi, Ehsan, 91, 179–181, 187–189, 204–205, 230–232; to Russia, 182
Ilahi, Fazal, 180, 182, 186–187; arrest of, 182
Inderpal, 130, 132
Indian Express, 311–312, 316–317, 319, 341; blank page publication of, 312

Indian National Army, 125
Indian National Congress, 53–54, 204, 214
Indian Penal Code, 62, 274
Indian Republican Army, 160
Indo-Pak war, 301
Indo-Tibetan Border Police (ITBP), 27, 283
Intelligence Bureau (IB), 322
internet closures, 340
Ireland, 117, 122; freedom movement, 81
Irfan Habib, S., 150, 206, 222, 240, 242
Irwin, Viceroy Lord, 61, 103, 108, 126, 130, 136, 204, 215–217, 220; and Lady Irwin, 131–132; train bombing, 215
Islam, Nazrul, 118

Jacob, Jency, 57, 104, 139, 232, 339
Jacob, Satish, 13, 33
Jagmohan, 325
jail rules, 192, 229, 235
Jalandhar, 3, 6–9, 11, 23–25, 28, 65–66, 295, 297–299, 301, 312, 314, 316, 319
Jallianwala Bagh, xi, 61–62, 77, 224, 329
Jamat-IIslami protests, 294
Jan Sangh, 318
'Jatindra Nath Das Zindabad', 121
Jayakar, Pupul, 309

Jenkins, 89–95, 97, 184; permitting Virendra for exam, 185–187
Jinnah, Mohammad Ali, 223
journalism, xii, xiv–xv, 62, 263, 301, 323, 326, 328–331, 335–337, 341, 343; death of, 328; vernacular, 56, 74
journalists in jail, 340
JP movement, 309–310
'Jung Ka Rang', column by Krishan, 259

Kader, Abdul (J), 143
Kairon, Pratap Singh, 275, 281–282, 331
Kakori Conspiracy Case, 58, 69, 72, 136, 193
Kakori Train Robbery, 69
Kala Pani, 55, 180, *see also* Andhaman cellular jail
Kamala (pseudonym), 163–165, 168–169
kanyadaan, 64–65
Kapoor, Coomi, 311
Kappan, Siddique, arrest, 340
Kashmir policy, 275
Kasuri, Nawab Muhammad Ahmed Khan, 234
Kaur, Amarjit, 33
Kaur, Balraj, 48
Kaur, Jagdish, 47, 48, 328
Kaur, Ravinder, 287, 290

Kesari in Marathi, 59, 273
Khalid, Haroon, 245
Khalistan, 13, 18, 20, 34, 43–44; campaign for, 42
Khalistan Commando Force, 20
The Khalistan Conspiracy, 13
Khan, Abdul Ghaffar, 250
Khan, Abdul Jabbar, 250
Khan, Aryan, vilifying, 337
Khan, Ashfaqullah, 69–70
Khan, Maulana Zafar Ali, 76
Khanna, Durga Das, 71–73, 75, 77, 80, 82, 92, 160, 162, 165–168, 176–177, 180; arrest of, 171; sentenced to death, 360n172
Khan, Nazir, 176
Khan, Sikandar Hayat, Sir, 258–263, 266, 271–272
Khan, Zafar Ali, 76, 111
Kheruddin, 139
Khosla, Niranjan Prasad, 64
Kipling, Rudyard, 260, 335
Kishan, Hari, 166–167, 169, 176; execution of, 171; shooting de Montmorency, 169
Krishan, Mahashay, 53, 56, 59–60, 62–64, 72, 74–75, 98, 170, 172, 178, 181–184, 255, 258–260, 271, 273, 288–289, 336, 352n89; arrest of, 66; editorials, 288; jail stints, 61; 'Jung Ka Rang' daily column

by, 259; letter for Virendra's education, 183–186; released from Lahore Central jail, 62; trial of, 62
Kishan, Pandit, 142
Kishan, Ram, 127;
Kumar, Indresh, 5
Kumar, Ravish, 334

Lahore, 53–55, 59, 64–68, 70–71, 76–77, 84–88, 90, 118–120, 126–128, 140, 226–227, 235, 250–254, 257, 262, 265, 279–286, 288, 291–295, 299–301; culture of, 283; Mori Darwaza in 236; Khalid on 245; Nehru landed in, 253, 256; violence in 280
Lahore Central Jail, 57, 62, 113, 142, 169, 226, 231, 238, 245; phansi ghar, 231, 233–234
Lahore Conspiracy Case, 55, 73, 114–115, 137, 159, 195, 227, 231
Lahore Conspiracy Case Ordinance 361-64n188
Lahore Literary Festival, 245
Lahore Police, 87–88, 120
Lahore railway station, 86, 119, 136
Lahore's Punjab University, to attack annual convocation, 162–167
Lal, Chaman Diwan, 220, 241, 275
L.C.C Tribunal 361-62n188

letters, 4–5, 28–29, 181, 183–184, 198, 205, 213, 215, 239, 265, 324; of Bhagat Singh, 223, 361–364n188; for vehicle's withdrawal, 29
Liberalization, 330
liberty, 105, 189, 242, 274, 324
Light Machine Gun (LMG), 28, 48
'Long Live the Revolution', 57, 105
Longowal, Sant Harchand Singh, 18, 31–32, 46
Longowal, Tohra and Badal triumvirate, 21
Lucas, 73–74

Mahajan, Mehr Chand, 24
'Maha Punjab', 16
Mahratta in English, 273
Majithia, Dayal Singh, 280
Majithia, Sunder Singh, Sir, 249
Majumder, Rishi, 218
Malik, Ripudaman Singh, death of, 43
Malviya, Pandit Madan Mohan, 53, 71, 76
Manipur issues, 334, 341
marjeevedas (warriors willing to die), 31
Martial Law, 180
Martial Law Commission, 62
martyrdom, xiii, 122, 212, 219, 239–240
Maruti Gypsy, 29

Index

Marx, 182, 200
Marxists, 243
Masih, Kala, 234
Masih, Tara, 234
Maynard, John, Sir, 67
Mazumdar, Niharendu Dutt, 274
McSwiney, Terence, 122
Meerut Conspiracy Case, 86, 205, 220
Mehra, Sameer, 300
Mehrotra, B.N., 311
Mehta, Pran Nath, 207, 211–212
'Mera Rang De Basanti Chola', 139
Microsoft Research India, 338
Milap newspaper, 16, 59–61, 160, 288, 329, 352
militants or khadkoos (fighters), 23
misinformation, 333, 335–336, 339
Modi, Narendra, 324
Mohan, Chander, 29, 301; Lahore as birth place, 293
Mohan, Lalit (Virendra's son), 111, 149, 151, 198, 244, 280, 314, 320, 324
Mohan, Niraja, 6
Mohan, Sushila, 87, 145, 148, 152–154, 201
Mohani, Hasrat, 57
Mohar, Bhagwan Das, 82–83, 91–92
Mother, Gorky, 72

Mukherjee, Mitali, 331
Mukherjee, Mridula, 117–118, 216
Mukund, Bal, 125
Multan Jail, 180, 187–189, 226
Mumbai underworld, and bribe, 41
Muslim League, 54, 75, 249, 252, 255, 275, 282
Muslims, 32, 55, 57–58, 70, 75, 173, 187, 284, 287, 343, 352
My Fight for Irish Freedom by Breen, 72

Naim, C.M., 57, 60, 343
Naipaul, V.S., 223
Nand, Asa, 154, 248, 255
Narain, Lala Jagat, 9, 27, 320; assassination of, 9, 14, 24
Narang, Gokul Chand, 97
Narayan, Jayaprakash, 309
Narendra, Anil, 61, 64, 280, 292–293, 301
narratives, 33, 334, 336; extremist, 31; individual, 28; post-Partition, 32
National Herald, 312, 319
nationalism, 70, 73, 182, 241, 243, 265, 336
Naujawan Bharat Sabha, 72, 76, 182, 244
Nayar, Bharti, 324
Nayar, Kuldeep, 299, 313; in jail, 324
Naya Zamana newspaper, 18, 47

Nehru, Jawaharlal, Gopal, 100
Nehru, Jawaharlal, 66, 71, 100–102, 126, 133, 248, 253, 257, 262–264, 266–268, 271, 276; arrest of, 226; as Congress president, 133, 248–249; on his father, 101; in Lahore, 253; plan for election campaign, 251; and re-marriage, 253; unfurling flag of independence, 138–139; visit to Lahore, 256–257, 275
Nehru, Kamala, 199; death of, 249, 253
Nehru, Motilal, 71, 74, 76, 78, 99–102, 104, 107, 114, 143, 177
Nehru, R.K., 275
Network-18, Ambani taking over, 331
Neville, Anshuman, 291
newspapers: corporate houses taking over, 330; subscriptions, 333; vernacular, 273
Newspapers Editors Conference, 265
Nihang Sikh, 29
Niraja, 12, 27
Nirankaris, 30
Nirbhaya rape case, 341
Non-Cooperation Movement, 68, 159, 192
non-violence, 71, 81, 140, 214, 217, 219–220, 225
Noorani, A.G., 222–223, 227
North-West Frontier Province, 250

O'Dwyer, Michael, Sir, assassination of, 224
online content, 334
Operation Black Thunder, 15
Operation Blue Star, 12–13, 18, 33, 38, 43

Pakistan, 7–8, 32, 49, 112, 234, 281–282, 287, 292, 297–298, 342; birth of, 288; Lahore to, 292; Muzaffargarh constituency, 281; and Sikhs extremism, 8
Pal, Prakashwati, 201
pandemic, 333
Pandey, Gyanendra, 289, 299
Pannu, Jatinder, 47
'Panth khatre mein hai (The Panth is in danger)', 32–33
para-military forces, 28
Paras newspaper, 329
parcel bomb, at Pratap office, 4, 7, 47
Parmanand, Bhai, 248
Partition, xiii–xiv, 19, 281, 283, 287–291, 293, 296–297, 299–300, 326–328, 333, 341–342; survivors, 290; violence, 292

Index

passengers, 19–21, 135, 256; Hindu, 20; (of Kanishka. *See* Air India Boeing 'Kanishka', explosion of); massacre of, 20

Patel, Sardar, 76, 78, 103, 214–215; arrest of, 226

Patel, Vithalbhai, 76, 103–104

Patnaik, Biju, 227

patriotism, 73, 108, 215, 296

'Personal Security Guidelines', 26

Phalak, Lal Chand, 233

Philipose, Pamela, 338

Pillai, Kesava Shankar, 272

police officers, 36–37, 39–40, 42, 83, 89–92, 94, 97, 108, 119, 176, 186; abandoning weapons, 38; shot at, 80, 82, 84

political: disinformation campaigns, 339; prisoners, 114, 123, 137–138, 204–205, 216, 220, 238, 243

politics, 13, 27, 30–32, 43, 47, 132, 137, 219, 223, 244, 272; contemporary, 134; students in, 242

The Politics of Self-Expression, Daechsel, 61

Prakash, Gyan, 308, 310, 321

Prasad, Ravi Visvesvaraya Sharada, 318

'Pratap (Petitioner) vs Crown case', 274

Pratap, x: forfeiture of security case, 67; government order against, 262; in Lahore as evening newspaper, 54; launch of, xi, 327, 329; owners of, 18; pre-censorship on, 263; security detail, 28; shutting down Urdu newspaper, 341

Pratap Bhavan, 3, 29, 47, 65, 169, 313, 319, 328, 332; Chatterjee on bombing of, 60; explosion at, 8, 10, 16, 19, 22, 328

Pratap Urdu newspaper, 3

Press (Emergency Powers) Act (1931), 67, 274

press freedom, 272–273, 310, 340; clamping down, 313–316

Print media, categorization of, 317

prisoners, 95, 97, 111, 113–115, 138–140, 142, 145, 175, 180–181, 184–185, 187–188, 229–233, 235; to grind flour, 174; talks about release of, 206

Privy Council, 206, 228

Public Safety Bill, 102–103

Punjab: coping mechanism using Sikh dress, 24; politics, 31; splitting of, 17, 297; terrorism, 41

Punjab Congress, 249, 275

Punjab Government, 16, 27, 68, 119, 183, 262–264, 266–267

Punjabi newspapers, 7, 17, 327

'Punjabis', 24; expatriate, 55

Index

'Punjabi Subha', 16–17, 326
Punjab Kesari, 8–10, 16–18, 75, 320
Punjab Police, 28
Punjab Students' Union, 72, 76, 168; Conference, 75
Punjab: The Knights of Falsehood, Gill, 30, 42

quasi-authoritarian governments, 322
Quit India Movement, 226
Radhakrishnan, Sarvepalli, 167–169

Radha Soami sect, 32
Rai, Lala Lajpat, 59, 71, 74–78, 83, 91-92, 99, 127, 136, 195, 235, 239; death of, 79, 81, 99, 136–137; pyre of, 79; revenge for death of, 82
Rai, Shivnath, CID informer, 89, 95
rail roko agitations, 137
Railways, 134–135, 137; and Gandhi, 136; positions in, 136; symbolism of, 137; third-class passengers, 134–135; Wolmar on, 134
Raj, Sukhdev, 72, 85, 127, 145–146, 154, 197, 201–202, 297; and bomb explosion, 154–155
Rajguru, Shivaram, 57, 79, 82–86, 88, 205, 210–212, 221, 231, 233, 238, 245: cremation of, 123; execution of, 114, 228; as servant of Bhagat Singh, 86

Rajiv–Longowal Punjab Accord, 32
Raj Lakshmi, 64, 280
Rajput, Sushant Singh, 337
Ram, Chajju, Sir, 87
Ram, Chaudhary Chotu, 249
Ram, Dasaundhi, 177
Ram, Ganga, Sir, 67
Ram, Lala Achint, 257
Ramachandra, Comrade, 244
Ranbir of *Milap*, 160, 162, 166–168, 176–177, 180; arrest of, 171
random shootings, 19
Rashid, Salman, 290, 298–299
Rawalpindi jails, 226
Razdan, Nidhi, 337–338
rebellion, 55, 59, 132, 143
Red Fort Trials, 133
red-letter day, on 15 June 1991, 21
redressals, 40
red tape, 29
refugees, xii, 61, 65, 199, 210, 284, 287, 289, 291–292, 300
rehabilitation, sewing machine humour on, 28
religious fault lines, 339
Remembering Partition, Pandey, 289
revolution, 81, 105, 107–111, 133, 213, 221, 223, 236, 239–240, 242
revolutionaries, 54–58, 69–70, 106–108, 114–117, 119–120, 125, 128, 143–145, 147–148,

152–153, 160–163, 165, 192–194, 196, 200–201, 205–206, 216–217, 220–222, 224, 232–234; bodies handing over to families, 123; party, 92, 208, 212; peers as bomb-makers, 129
revolutionary movement, 73, 110, 144, 148, 159, 168, 191–192, 196, 200–201; failures in, 149
Reyat, Inderjit Singh, 43
Ribeiro, Julio, 24, 37–38, 41 assassination attempt at, 39
riots, 282, 285, 288, 295
Roadways bus, Haryana, 20; Punjab, 20
Rowlatt Acts, 56
Roy, Babu Kalinath, 62
RSS, 47, 318, 324
Russia, 72, 81, 182, 197, 205
Russian Revolution, 71, 81

Sacha Sauda, 32
Saggu, Balbir Singh, 46
Sahni, Ajai, 15, 40, 42
Salik, Abdul Majeed, 59
Salt Satyagraha, 141
Sandhu, G.B.S., 13
Sanyal, Sachindra Nath, 200
Sarabha, Kartar Singh, 55–56
Sarda Act, 65
Sardesai, Rajdeep, 331

'Sarfaroshi ki tamanna' Bismil Azimabadi, 142, 192
satyagrahis, 62, 68
Saunders, 85, 88–91, 93, 104, 149, 151; killing, 84–85, 88, 96–97, 104, 107, 128, 240
Savarkar, 242
Schuster, George, Sir., 104
Scott, James A., 78, 83, 93, 149; revenge assassination and, 82
secularism, 324
Sedition Law, 274
Sehgal, Mohinder Pratap, 299
Sen, Surya, 160
separatism, 36, 42–43, 47
Shadman Road roundabouts/ Fawara Chowk, 245
Shah Alami fire, 281
Shah Commission, 319
'shaheed', martyr, xii
Shaheede-Azam, 336
Shah, Khan Bahadur Syed Ahmad, 173, 176–177
Shahpur jail, as Punjab's Kala Pani, 226, *see also* Andamans Cellular Jail
Shah, Waris, 285
sharanarthi [refugee] journalists, 61
Sharma, Des Raj, 327
Sharma, Narinder, 318; meeting Bhindranwale, 46
Sharma, Thakur Dutt, 166

Index

Shastri, Lal Bahadur, 17
Shaurya Chakra, 47
Sheikh, Majid, 283, 285, 300
Shimla, 119, 296
Shiromani Gurdwara Parbandhak Committee (SGPC), 37
Shourie, Arun, 316–317, 324, 331
Sialkot, 61, 226, 228, 254
Sialkot Jail, 226, 281
Sikh constable, 28–29
Sikh diasporas, K-word, 43
Sikhs, 8, 11–13, 16–18, 21–22, 30–34, 37, 42–43, 55, 57–58, 75, 258; to extremism, 8; and Nirankari sect clash between, 12; politics, 30; psyche, 13, 35, 38
Sikri, Lala Jwala Das, 252
Simon Commission, 75–77, 82, 104
Simon, John, Sir, 75
Sinclair, Upton, 72
Sindhu, Virendar, 233
Singh, Ajit (uncle of Bhagat Singh), 245
Singh, Baba Kharak, 76
Singh, Baba Prithvi, 201
Singh, Beant, 35–37; assassination of, 36
Singh, Bhagat, 55, 71–74, 76–80, 82–88, 104–108, 111–118, 121–123, 139, 142–145, 149–154, 194–195, 200–201, 203, 205–207, 210–217, 219–225, 227–228, 230–234, 236–243, 245; accompanied by Durga Devi, 86; arrest, 146; Azad as mentor, 196; birth and life of, 245; and cinema, 195–196; court appearances, 142; cremation of, 123; death of, 204; definition of revolution, 109–110, 222; escaped from Lahore, 85; hanging of, 77, 228; on humanity, 218; hunger strike of, 114, 118, 238; letter to Punjab Governor 361-64n188; Nehru on, 214, 216, 239; Noorani on, 223; 'Philosophy of the Bomb', 140; Ramachandra on, 244; Shaheed-e Azam, 238; and Sindhu on hanging of, 233–235; smoke bombs, 103–104; with turban in white, 85; 'Why I Am an Atheist', 244
Singh, Buta, 11
Singh, Chander Pal, 221
Singh, Channan, 84
Singh, Chattar, 231; on hanging of revolutionaries, 232
Singh, Chaudhary Charan, 316
Singh, Balwinder, 47, 48
Singh, Darbara, 11, 14, 33
Singh, Dilawar, 37
Singh, Gurmeet, 32
Singh, Khushwant, 317
Singh, Kultar, 211

Singh, Mangal, 126
Singh, Master Tara, 282
Singh, Prithvi, 201–202
Singh, Rajendra, 69
Singh, Ramesh Inder, 17, 23
Singh, Ranjit, 47, 48
Singh, Roshan, 69
Singh, Sardar Bahadur Sukha, 91–92
Singh, Sardar Kishan (father of Bhagat Singh), 121, 235–236
Singh, Sushant Rajput Case, 337–338
Singh, Tripurdaman, 133, 272
Singh, Udham, 224–225; Gandhi on, 225
Singh, Zail, 11, 14; cabinet minister, 14; Chief Minister, 321; Home Minister, 31
Sinha, Vijay Kumar, 83, 143
social media, 337
solitary confinement, 138–139, 175
sovereignty, 100, 110, 138, 324
Special Press Advisor, 263
Srinivasan, 269
Statesman, 316, 319; 'Lord Irwin in Bomb Outrage.' headline, 131
sterilization drives, mass forced, 316
strife: communal, 19; sanguinary, 109, 221
Students' Union conference, 75
Subhan, Abdul, 301–302

Sukhdev. *See* Thapar, Sukhdev
Suri, Navin, 288
Sushila Didi. *See* Mohan, Sushila
Swaraj, 56, 273

Tagore, Rabindranath, 118, 243, 312
Talib, Rajendra Kumar ('Talib Sahib'), murder of 22–23
Talib, Rajiv, 19
Talwani, Saraswati (Shabto), 286–287
Talwar, Arushi, 337
Talwar, Bhagat Ram, British spy 'Silver', 169
Tandon, Purushottam Das, 199
Tape (J), 143
Tarn Taran, 21, 48; as Khalistan's capital, 44
Tata, J.R.D., 317
Telegraph newspaper, 341
temples desecration, 19
terrorism, xiii, 27, 29–30, 35, 37, 40, 42, 44, 47–48, 221–222, 326–327
terrorists, xiv, 17, 20–21, 23, 26, 34, 38, 40–41, 45, 47–49, 221–222; behind Khalsa College, 46; "martyred" militants, 17; released an edict, 23; weapons of, 48
Tewari, Manish 21, 347n29
Tewari, V.N., assassination of, 21
Thackeray, Bal, 317

Index

Thapar, Sukhdev, 79, 83, 147, 205, 210–212, 221, 228, 231, 233, 238, 245; cremation of, 123; execution, 114, 228
Tharoor, Shashi, 136
threats, 9, 11, 14, 23–24, 26–27, 117, 138, 323–324; daily occurrence, 28
Tilak, Bal Gangadhar, 273
Tilak, Lokmanya Bal Gangadhar, 'Swaraj is my birthright', 56
Tiwana, Khizar Hayat, Sir, 282
Tiwari, Chandrashekhar, 192
Tiwari, Kamal Nath, 143
Tohra, Gurcharan Singh, 18, 30
trains, attempting to blow up Viceroy, 130, 150; terrorist attack near Ludhiana, 21
train travel, 135
triad of Pratap, Milap and Tej, 61
Tribune, 36–37, 62, 67–68, 108, 227, 292, 341; from Chandigarh, 341; from Lahore, 67, 108
trinity of Badal, Longowal and Tohra, 31–32
Tripathy, Harsh Vardhan, 148
TRPs, manipulation, 339
Tully, Mark, 13, 33
Turmoil in Punjab, Inder Singh, 17
twenty-four-hour security, 27

ul Haq, Ehsan, 297
Unionist Party, 249, 258
untouchables, 117, 241
Upadhyay, 249–251
uprisings, 31, 101, 139
Urdu, 7, 23, 57–58, 74, 92, 261, 288, 343; equate with Muslim identity, 342; freezing out, 342; as inclusive language, 57
Urdu newspapers, 3, 56, 59–60, 160, 251, 312, 329, 341–342
Urdu press 56–58, 60, 327, 352n89,
Urdu-reading Hindus, 60

Vaillant, Auguste, 105
Vaishampayan, 152–153
Vajpayee, Atal Bihari, 293, 308, 318
'Vande Mataram', 105, 139
Veh Inquilabi Din, 59, 203, 315; Virendra in, 113
Verghese, B.G., 315
Verma, Virendra, 23
Vernacular Press Act, 273
Vidyarthi, Ganesh Chander (mentor of Azad), 128, 193
Vidyavati (mother of Bhagat Singh), 112
violence, 15, 18, 21, 30, 33, 101, 109, 202–203, 221–222, 280, 289
Virendra/Vir Ji, xi–xii, 4, 9, 54, 61, 64, 66, 140–141, 168;

annual examination, 183–187;
arrest of, 87, 126–127, 137,
171; and Bose, 121; car chase,
26; as chief editor, 4; in
Congress Seva Dal, 126; and
Das, 138; death of, 36, 198;
on death sentence to Bhagat
Singh, 220; to Delhi by rail,
120; detention, 228; driving
Jawaharlal Nehru, 256–257;
elected to Punjab Assembly
from the Muzaffargarh,
281; exams from jail, 247;
fifth imprisonment, 190;
fourth imprisonment, 174;
handcuffed, 89–90, 93, 97;
interrogation, 92; in jail, xii,
99, 182; joined FC College,
71; life, xii–xiii; to meet
Indira, 12; meeting Khanna,
160; meeting Longowal, 31;
Nehru's mail to, 248; and
police search, 172–173; and
Ranbir, 162; released on
bail, 98, 177; release of, 189;
in Saunders' murder case,
174, 184; to small cell, 95; in
students' politics, 89; visiting
Nehru, 249; working at
Pratap, 247
Virk, Sarbdeep Singh, 15, 18
Vir Pratap, Hindi daily, xiv–xv, 3,
5, 10, 301, 312–313, 315, 317,
319–320; final edition, 327

Vishwas, Basant, 125
'Vohra', 63
Vohra, Bhagwati Charan, death
of, 191
Vohra, Dev, 198
Vohra, Durga Devi, 201
Vohra, Hans Raj, 71–73, 75,
80–81, 92
Vohra, Radhakrishan, 63

war for independence, *see*
freedom movement/freedom
struggle
West Indies, 3
"WhatsApp university", 242
Williamson, Horace, 240
Wolmar, Christian, 134
women revolutionaries, 145, 200,
210; see also under *separate
entries*
World War I, 56, 259–260

Yashpal, 128–131, 145–148, 150,
152, 154, 215
youth, 30, 32, 61, 70, 80–81, 106,
111, 194, 203, 214, 217;
Alam to, 140; Chandra Bose
to, 140; Nehru to, 140; of
Punjab, 159
YouTube, 334–335; Tulsi in
Chhattisgarh as hub of, 335

About the Authors

A veteran journalist and columnist, **Chander Mohan** was the distinguished editor of the Hindi daily *Vir Pratap* for forty years. Born in Lahore in pre-Partition Punjab, he has been a leading voice in Hindi journalism in north India, writing searing and uncompromising editorials. From being a part of Rajiv Gandhi's press entourage to travelling to Lahore with Prime Minister Atal Bihari Vajpayee, he is privileged to have witnessed several eras of politics and media. Semi-retired, he pens 'Maryadain', a weekly column for a national newspaper, while managing several educational institutions in his hometown, Jalandhar. Journalism and education are his two passions, and he finds a way for both to complement each other.

As a journalist with nearly three decades of experience across TV, print and digital media, **Jyotsna Mohan** has always sought

About the Authors

to hold up a mirror to society. Her journey led her to pen her debut book, *Stoned, Shamed, Depressed,* an Amazon bestseller that dives deep into the secret lives of India's teens and reveals challenges that resonate with young people globally. A columnist for publications in India and abroad, her writings reflect societal issues and challenge the status quo, which she says is her family legacy! She brings this outlook to her online talk show, 'Table Talk with Jo'. Born in Jalandhar, Jyotsna now lives with her husband and two children in Abu Dhabi.

HarperCollins *Publishers* India

At HarperCollins India, we believe in telling the best stories and finding the widest readership for our books in every format possible. We started publishing in 1992; a great deal has changed since then, but what has remained constant is the passion with which our authors write their books, the love with which readers receive them, and the sheer joy and excitement that we as publishers feel in being a part of the publishing process.

Over the years, we've had the pleasure of publishing some of the finest writing from the subcontinent and around the world, including several award-winning titles and some of the biggest bestsellers in India's publishing history. But nothing has meant more to us than the fact that millions of people have read the books we published, and that somewhere, a book of ours might have made a difference.

As we look to the future, we go back to that one word— a word which has been a driving force for us all these years.

Read.